The Parents' Guide to Alternatives in Education

THE
PARENTS' GUIDE
TO ALTERNATIVES
IN EDUCATION

Ronald E. Koetzsch, Ph.D.

SHAMBHALA

Boston & London

1997

In loving memory of my mother,

Martha Emilia Koetzsch née Konuth-Bergner

Leipzig, Germany: December 6, 1906
Concord, Massachusetts: January 13, 1985

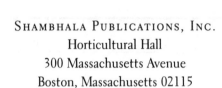

SHAMBHALA PUBLICATIONS, INC.
Horticultural Hall
300 Massachusetts Avenue
Boston, Massachusetts 02115
http://www.shambhala.com

9 8 7 6 5 4 3 2 1

FIRST EDITION
Printed in the United States of America
⊗ This edition is printed on acid-free paper that meets
the American National Standards Institute Z39.48 Standard.
Distributed in the United States by Random House, Inc.,
and in Canada by Random House of Canada Ltd

Library of Congress Cataloging-in-Publication Data
Koetzsch, Ronald E.
The parents' guide to alternatives in education /
Ronald E. Koetzsch.—1st ed.
p. cm.
Includes bibliographical references (p.   ) and index.
ISBN 1-57062-067-9 (alk. paper)
1. Alternative schools—United States. 2. Alternative education—
United States. 3. Private schools—United States. I. Title.
LC46.4.K64   1997   96-39064
371'.02'0973—dc20   CIP

Contents

⚘

Introduction

Nearly forty-five years ago, as a first-grader in Public School 207 in Brooklyn, New York, I was taught that when a teacher is talking the good student sits quietly, hands folded, looking forward, and listening intently. To this day, when I attend a lecture, I sit with hands folded and eyes forward and am loath, even when extremely uncomfortable, to get up to stretch my legs. If I need to go to the rest room, I hesitate and feel I should raise my hand and ask for permission "to leave the room."

When I was a seventh-grader in Cunningham Junior High School, my English teacher, Mr. Kent, taught us about the dangling participle. At six-three and two hundred pounds, Mr. Kent was a very impressive figure, and I have never forgotten his dictum that the use of a dangling participle was the sign of an inferior mind. Today, I still cringe when I hear or read a dangler—something like, "Despite having a flat tire, Mrs. Smith drove the car home," or "While he was in the bathroom shaving, Mr. White's dog bit the postman"—and I live in dread that I will unwittingly commit this offense against language, self, and culture.

Two years later, in James Madison High School, I discovered that the world is divided into people taking the college preparatory course, peo-

ple taking the business program, and those in the vocational program. I learned, too, or rather absorbed the idea, that students in the college preparatory course (of whom I happened to be one) are more valuable to the school and to society. After all, they are the ones who are expected to go to college, get good jobs, and run the country. I am still battling with this hierarchic and elitist view and the insidious assumption of self-superiority it bred.

There are many factors that help form a child into an adult human being. Genetic inheritance, early upbringing and training, family life, peer and friendship relationships, community life, physical and geographical environment, destiny, and the child's exercise of free choice all play a role. But a child's education is an immense, imponderable factor.

In the United States most children, from age five or six until at least age sixteen, spend most of their waking hours in school. This school experience helps or fails to help the child develop competency in reading, writing, spelling, and arithmetic. It teaches the child about the community, the nation, the world, nature, and the great personalities in literature and history. A child's formal education also helps form behavior, attitudes, social skills, and beliefs. As Wordsworth wrote, "The child is father of the man," and children are certainly shaped in large part by their schooling.

The public school system in the United States came into being around 150 years ago. By the end of the nineteenth century it dominated education in the nation. Since that time the majority of American parents have sent their children to public schools. Some more affluent parents have opted for expensive, exclusive private schools. Many Roman Catholics and members of conservative Protestant denominations have sent their children to parish schools. But most parents willingly and without hesitation have entrusted their children to the local kindergarten and elementary, middle, and high schools. At least until recently, public schools, for the most part, have been regarded with trust and respect, and have been perceived as providing a sound and valuable education.

But today the public school system does not enjoy the public's trust and confidence as it did even just twenty or thirty years ago. Many parents do not view the local public school as a good place for their children. They are concerned about such problems as overcrowded classrooms, apathetic teachers, poor training in basic academic skills, exposure to ideas and values that they as parents do not share, drugs, and violence. Nonetheless, most parents still do send their children to local public schools. Of the 40 million schoolchildren in the United States today, about 35 million are in public schools. But more than half the parents with children in a public school would place them in a private school if they could afford it. And more and more parents are educating their children outside the public school system.

Parents today can choose from a variety of educational alternatives that reflect the philosophical, religious, political, and social diversity of the nation. Many of these alternatives are rooted in the liberal or humanistic-progressive philosophical and educational tradition. From this point of view, mainstream public education is too authoritarian, teacher centered, textbook dependent, competitive, and narrowly focused on academic skills. Schools founded on the humanistic-progressive approach tend to be child centered and democratically run and to emphasize experiential learning, social skills, and the arts, as well as academic skills. In 1994, Macmillan published *The Almanac of Education Choice*. Most of the schools listed are part of the liberal alternative movement. Of this type alone, which includes free schools, holistic schools, progressive schools, and schools using the multiple intelligences approach, there are over six thousand listings.

Another kind of alternative school available today is based on a religious and culturally conservative tradition. From this perspective the public schools are too lax, too experimental, and permeated by what conservatives often refer to as "the religion of secular humanism." These alternative schools use traditional curricula and teaching methods and emphasize moral, religious, and spiritual values. There are thousands of these more conservative schools, which include Roman Catholic and mainline Protestant schools, Christian schools, Muslim schools, and the Mae Carden schools.

Some alternative educational approaches and schools cannot be easily placed on this left-right, liberal-conservative spectrum, but contain elements of both main approaches. The Waldorf schools, the Montessori schools, and the Friends schools are among these.

Some types of alternative education are available today within the public schools. Many public school systems offer special programs from kindergarten through high school. These programs often utilize some or many aspects of the "progressive," child-centered movement. In some places, parents can opt for a Montessori kindergarten, or an arts-based magnet school, or a school-within-a-school that features child-centered learning or bilingual education. Some of the public school options reflect traditional values, in education at least. In Washington State, for example, there are a number of "back-to-basics" schools called the John Marshall Fundamental schools.

Changes in public educational policy have made these public school alternatives accessible to many families. In the past, parents only had one option: to enroll a child in the local neighborhood public school. Now there is much more choice. In Cambridge, Massachusetts, for example, parents and children can choose any of the city's twenty-two schools, each with its distinctive approach. In Minnesota, a voucher system allows parents to send a child to a school outside their district, in fact to any public school in the state. This freedom of choice is available in more and more local school districts and in more and more states.

In the last several years a "charter school" program has been adopted by a number of states and is being considered by many more. Charter school legislation allows a group of parents, educators, or both, to propose a school that is an alternative to the public schools. The school must be nonsectarian and nonexclusive, and based on a coherent educational approach. If the state authorities approve the proposal and the group can attract a critical mass of students, the charter school receives state funding on the same per capita basis used for public schools. While the particulars of charter school legislation differ

from state to state, in effect, parents in states with charter school laws now have the right and opportunity to design and found their own publicly supported school.

Also, many individual public schools as well as public school systems are open to parental suggestions, wishes, and initiatives concerning the education that their children receive. In many places parents are actively involved in the decision-making processes about the education of their children. Professional educators are becoming increasingly open to parental input.

In addition to the options available in independent and public schools, there is the possibility of homeschooling. Twenty years ago, homeschooling, once the way most Americans were educated, was virtually unknown, and in most states was illegal. Today there are over a million American children being educated at home, and the number is rapidly growing. While each state has its own laws and requirements concerning homeschooling, it is now legal everywhere, and there are homeschooling associations and support groups in all states.

The net result is that today parents have a great range of options in choosing, and perhaps in creating, an education for their child. Parents can look to the many alternatives in the independent sector. They can homeschool. They can explore the growing number of alternatives within the public school system. They can lobby for changes in the local school system, organize a charter school or a small community school, or send their child down the block to the neighborhood public school, if in the end that proves the most attractive option. Parents whose work is not geographically fixed can look both near and far for the right school, public or private, and then if necessary relocate.

Choosing a school for a child is one of the most important decisions parents make. The school—its teachers, curriculum, educational philosophy, and values both explicit and implicit—will affect the child's day-to-day life. It will help shape the child's personality, view of life, behavior, and destiny as an adult. And it will also deeply affect the lives of the parents and the life of the family as a whole.

This book is designed to help parents make an informed, conscious choice about their child's education, a choice that is satisfying for them and for their child. It is, in effect, a consumer's guide to education.

Part One provides an overview of American education, both of its mainstream public sector and of the alternative movements. Chapter 1 looks at the origin and early development of the public school system in the United States. Chapter 2 treats the humanistic-progressive movement in American education, and chapter 3 describes the religious-traditionalist movement. Chapter 4 discusses the public school system today and the range of education alternatives now available.

Part Two deals with six important movements in present-day education. Five of these—whole language, cooperative learning, the social curriculum, multicultural education, and developmental education—grew out of elements present in progressive education. They may be understood as addenda to the long humanistic-progressive tradition in American education, and now are found in many schools, public and independent. The sixth movement, education for character, or "moral education," was once central to American education but today is absent in virtually all public schools. While it has been and continues to be an important element in religiously based schools, moral education is now being adopted by more and more nonreligious independent

schools. Parents need to understand these six movements and their role in American education today in order to make an informed decision about schooling for their child.

Part Three, "A Guide to Alternatives in Education," might also be called "The Educational Smorgasbord" since it looks at the many different types of programs and schools that are important viable alternatives to mainstream public education in the United States today. Each of the twenty-two chapters deals with a particular educational approach or type of school. Some of the approaches described, such as the Montessori and Reggio Emilia approaches, are primarily for preschool and kindergarten children. A few, such as Teenage Liberation and the International Baccalaureate, are relevant only to high-school students. Most are relevant for kindergarten through grade twelve.

The chapters of Part Three follow, albeit sometimes loosely, a pattern. Each presents in turn the history, the philosophy and principles, and the practical strategies of the educational approach in question. It then describes one and in some cases two actual schools that use the particular approach. Each chapter includes a list of resources for more information and a bibliography. Each stands more or less alone, so that if a reader is interested in a particular educational approach, he or she can focus on the single chapter that addresses it.

The chapters in Parts Two and Three are descriptive only. They do not try to evaluate the educational approaches or particular schools as good or bad, effective or ineffective. Educational methods and individual schools are neither good nor bad. Rather they meet the needs of and are appropriate for certain children or families, or they do not meet those needs and are not appropriate. The worldview, values, and expectations of the family largely determine the value of a particular educational method or school. Even when there seems to be a good match between family and school, things may go awry. Every school can boast of its successes with children, but every school and every approach has its failures as well.

Part Four offers some practical advice in choosing a school and in creating a school of one's own.

Many thanks to Samuel Bercholz and Peter Turner of Shambhala Publications for suggesting this book project. Thanks also go to the many people who gave me advice and help along the way, particularly Ronald Miller and Samuel Blumenfeld. They both were inexhaustible sources of information and insights, Ron about educational approaches of the humanistic-progressive movement and Sam about those of the religious-traditionalist movement. Sincere thanks also to the many teachers, children, administrators, and parents who graciously welcomed and helped me on my visits and answered my many questions.

I

AN OVERVIEW OF EDUCATION
IN THE UNITED STATES

1

Public Education

The Birth of a System

In colonial America, education was a private, usually family concern. Children were taught to read and write and reckon by their parents, older siblings, or other relations. Since most boys were destined to be farmers, tradesmen, or craftsmen and most girls were destined to be wives and homemakers, education for most children went little beyond the basic skills. Training for a particular profession was acquired informally at home or in an apprenticeship with a master in the community. In some of the colonies, such as Massachusetts—where from 1647, a law required that each town hire a schoolmaster and that all children learn to read and write—provision was made for publicly supported education at the elementary level. But even in Massachusetts, education remained a largely private and family-based activity.

During this early period of American history, only the relatively few young men who aspired to careers as lawyers, doctors, ministers, or teachers received a more advanced education. These studied at home with a tutor or in small private academies. They studied Greek and Latin and Hebrew, the quadrivium (mathematics, astronomy, music, and geometry) and the trivium (grammar, rhetoric, and logic). Their teachers were clergymen or professional schoolmasters with a largely ecclesiastical training.

It was not until the eighteenth century that the idea of public education as a universal, state-supported, state-controlled system became important. The first modern public school system, financed by the government and requiring attendance of all children, was established around 1770, not in North America, but in Prussia under King Frederick. Its avowed purpose was not only to educate and enlighten the populace but to produce obedient, patriotic citizens. Most of the teachers were military officers, who, because Prussia was between wars, were temporarily unemployed.

Thomas Jefferson was an early and passionate advocate of free, universal education, regarding it as the necessary basis of a successful democracy. He held that a public education system would educate all citizens so that they could make informed and wise decisions. Also, it would provide equal opportunity for children of poor and rich families.

The idea of universal, free, compulsory education gained wide support in the early nineteenth century. By 1820, there was a growing movement for public education centered in some states. The national populist political movement, founded and led by Andrew Jackson—elected president in 1828—supported public education as a way of reducing the privileges and advantages of the social, economic, and educational elite and of elevating the lower classes.

While there was support for public education in all parts of the country, Massachusetts emerged as the bellwether of the movement. In 1837, Horace Mann, a strong supporter of public education, was appointed secretary of the Board of Education of the Commonwealth. At that time, most Massachusetts towns and villages had "common" or public schools, supported in part by taxes and open to all children in the community. These were usually modest institutions, where children came—often sporadically—to learn reading, writing, and arithmetic for a few years.

Mann crusaded to improve these common schools by developing their curricula and increasing the length of the school year. He got the state to financially support local schools, called on local officials and on citizens to see public education as an important cause, and encouraged parents to send their children to common schools. Under Mann's direction, a "normal school," or school to train teachers, was founded in Lexington in 1840 to provide qualified teachers for the common schools of the state.

Mann argued that public schools would ensure that all people would acquire the basic skills for being a citizen and have an equal opportunity for social and economic advancement. He also held that such schools could help assimilate into American society the many immigrants who were then coming into the country.

In the twelve years of Mann's tenure, the common schools of Massachusetts expanded and improved, and public sentiment in favor of common schools grew. In the 1850s, legislation requiring attendance at school was passed. During this period many states followed the lead of Massachusetts, establishing common schools and teacher training colleges and making school attendance mandatory for all children. The establishment of a national public school system was underway.

One early and passionate advocate of free, universal education was Thomas Jefferson, who regarded it as the necessary basis of a successful democracy.

The founding of a universal, compulsory, and free system of education was founded on four assumptions:

- The state has the responsibility to educate all of its citizens.
- The state has the right to force all parents to send their children to school.
- The state has the right to force the entire community—including citizens without school-age children—to support by taxes the education of all children.
- The state has the right to determine the nature of the education it offers.

Many people welcomed the common public schools. Many did not. Some communities and parents resisted. In Massachusetts, for example, it wasn't until 1880—when children in Barnstable on Cape Cod were forcibly taken to school by state militiamen—that the public school system was completed in that state. Ironically, when the public school system was established in Massachusetts, the literacy rate was 95 percent; it has never been as high since.

By the 1880s, all of the states had adopted compulsory education laws and had set up public school systems. By the turn of the century, virtually all American children who were not attending private or religious schools were in public elementary schools. In many states public secondary education was also available, though not required. Secondary education was reserved for the small minority of students, mostly boys, who were to attend college and enter the professions.

Each state had its own laws about education and each city or town in a state had much autonomy in running its public schools. Nevertheless, the public schools across the nation shared many of the same characteristics. Children were taught basic academic skills under a fixed curriculum that emphasized the learning of reading, writing, spelling, and arithmetic and the acquisition of a certain body of knowledge about the world. They also studied literature, history, geography, and the natural sciences. The teacher was the focus of the learning process, lecturing and drilling the students. Students were expected to memorize their lessons and to recite them in class. They were given tests and received grades. Order and decorum were important. Children sat in rows of desks facing the teacher and the blackboard at the front of the room. They were expected to be quiet, to pay attention to the teachers, and to do what they were told. Discipline was strict and corporal punishment was used. The children lined up to march into and out of school. The beginning and end of the class day, and transitions from one activity to another, were marked by bells. Although schools were not allowed to teach religion, there were daily prayers and Bible readings. Reading textbooks, such as the "readers" of the McGuffey series, emphasized morality and virtuous living.

Two primary influences helped shape these public schools. One was the Protestant, largely Calvinist view of human nature that had dominated American culture up until that time. John Calvin (1509–1564), a French-Swiss theologian and religious reformer, emphasized the doctrine of original sin and of the natural depravity of the human being. By their nature, Calvin held, human beings are self-indulgent, lazy, prone to wrongdoing, and deserving of eternal damnation. Salvation can come only by the predetermined, arbitrary gift of divine grace to the undeserving sinner.

For Calvin, the truth about the world and human nature and destiny had been revealed in the Holy Scriptures. The human being does not have to discover truth, but rather to receive it as divine revelation and then obey the divine will.

Many of the groups that settled in the United States—the Puritans, the Dutch, the Scots—were Calvinists. Others, such as the German Lutherans and the English Episcopalians, had views similar to those of Calvin. The religious and private schools these various groups established were based on a negative view of human nature and on an understanding of truth as something to be received, accepted, and retained. Since children are by nature lazy and disorderly, they must be kept in order and compelled to learn—with threats, punishments, and rewards. Teachers were viewed as possessing and presenting the truth that students were to take in passively and memorize. When the public education system was established, the new common schools took over many of the assumptions and practices of the existing religious and private schools.

The other important influence on the public school was the concept of the factory system, then spreading into American life. The industrial revolution and the development of public educa-

By the turn of the nineteenth century, virtually all American children who were not attending private or religious schools were in public elementary schools.

tion occurred at around the same time in the United States. Handcrafting of products was being replaced by mass production. Large numbers of workers labored in factories and mills. These workers were carefully organized so that the factory would operate efficiently. Many worked on assembly lines, performing the same task over and over. They were strictly disciplined. Their work began and ended at a specific time usually marked by a bell or horn. While at work they had to pay undivided attention to their task. They could leave their station only at breaks and lunchtime, or with special permission.

The public schools incorporated many of the characteristics of the early mills and factories. The regimentation, discipline, and piecework was applied both to teachers and to children. The school day was strictly regulated by the clock. The school buildings themselves were built like little factories—square, made of red brick, with separate rooms for each group of students. Like the factory, the public school was a world unto itself, often surrounded by a fence and separated from the community and life outside.

By the end of the nineteenth century the American public school system was established as the dominant element in American education. It was huge, comprised of hundreds of separate local school systems, thousands of schools, hundreds of thousands of teachers and administrators, and millions of children. It was bureaucratic, possessing layer upon layer of officials at the local, district, and state level. The pedagogy was authoritarian, teacher centered, competitive, individualistic, focused on orderliness and efficiency, and dedicated to children acquiring specific intellectual knowledge and specific academic skills. Memorization,

Even as the public school system was forming, however, alternative educational initiatives were arising.

rote learning, tests, grades, and rewards and punishments were key parts of school life. Public schools aimed to educate children but also aimed to make them obedient, hard-working, good citizens.

The huge, publicly financed education system gave rise to a large number of businesses, institutions, and organizations, including textbook publishers; manufacturers of school supplies, who produced everything from chalk to notebooks to school desks; construction companies, which built and renovated the schools; service companies, which provided maintenance and other services; private and state colleges and universities, which trained and certified teachers; and teachers' unions.

Even as the public school system was forming, however, alternative educational initiatives were arising. Some of these were based on a more optimistic view of human nature and of the child's desire and ability to learn, and on democratic, egalitarian principles. Some were based on a desire to keep religious and moral education and the transmission of a particular religious and cultural heritage as the core of the educational enterprise.

Today public education is still the dominant force in American education. Of the roughly 40 million children in school about 35 million are in public schools. While the public school system is still for the most part bureaucratic, hierarchic, authoritarian, and conservative, a great deal of experimentation, reform, and restructuring has gone on and continues to go on within it. The number and variety of educational alternatives outside the public school system have greatly increased and continue to do so. Thus, within and outside the mainstream public school system today there are many alternatives.

2

Dissenting Voice Number One
The Humanistic-Progressive Tradition

❦

Even before the Calvinistic-factory model of education became, through the establishment of the public school system, the official way of mainstream education in the United States, there were dissenting voices. Various educational reformers, belonging to what can be called the humanistic or Romantic intellectual tradition, had long been speaking out in favor of an approach to education that had a different philosophy, aim, and practice.

The seminal figure in the development of the humanistic education tradition was Jean-Jacques Rousseau (1712–1778). Rousseau was a philosopher and political theorist, a leading figure in the French Enlightenment, and one of the shapers of the Romantic movement in philosophy. Rousseau held that the human being is by nature good. Human corruption and evil are the result of corrupting external influences in the family and in society; they are not necessary manifestations of human nature. Rousseau rejected the Calvinist view of the human being—and of the child—as naturally predisposed to sin, indolence, and self-indulgence. In his novels, *Emile* and *Eloise,* he proposed that children, if left to themselves, will grow into loving and free beings of nature, and out of their natural curiosity will learn what they need to know. Human nature is

good and the child inherently curious. Properly protected and nurtured but otherwise left to their own devices, children will largely educate themselves and become good, useful, and happy people.

Rousseau emphasized that the emotional and artistic dimensions of human nature are as important as the intellectual dimensions. Education is not just filling the child with information; it also involves drawing out the affective, artistic, moral, and social capabilities latent in the child and helping the child develop his or her innate creativity and goodness.

Later reformers in this tradition developed Rousseau's core ideas and put them into practice. Swiss native Heinrich Pestalozzi (1746–1827) worked with orphans in the aftermath of the Napoleonic Wars. Pestalozzi also maintained that human beings are inherently good and are able to take responsibility for their own intellectual and moral development. He rejected coercion, corporal punishment, and rote memorization in education and emphasized the need for a stable, nurturing, love-filled, homelike atmosphere and the importance of the gentle encouragement of the child's moral intuition. For Pestalozzi, education should include manual labor; physical exercise; the learning of practical skills; drawing, singing, and handcrafts; field trips; and the collecting of natural objects. He felt that allowances should be made for individual differences among children and that children should be grouped by level of development rather than by chronological age. Pestalozzi held that there is a natural development that takes place in the growing child. He advised letting the intellectual ability of the child develop according to its natural pattern, which begins in observation, concrete experiences, and self-directed activity, and which moves toward the comprehension and the formation of abstract ideas.

Pestalozzi's work was spread to the United States by his disciple Josef Neef, who arrived in 1808. Neef traveled around the country, principally in Pennsylvania, Kentucky, and Indiana, helping to establish schools using Pestalozzi's ideas. Education, he said, is not just the transmission of information to the student. Rather, it is the gradual unfolding of the abilities and personality of the child. In this process the teacher is a guide and friend.

At about the time Neef was active in this country, the Transcendentalist movement was beginning. Transcendentalism was European Romanticism transplanted to the United States and expressed in the American idiom. The leading Transcendental thinkers—Ralph Waldo Emerson, Henry David Thoreau, George Ripley, Bronson Alcott—all advocated an approach to education based on the inherent goodness and potential of the human being. They celebrated experience, activity, and exploration as essential to education. They emphasized the development of a critical and open mind and the gaining of practical skills. Thoreau (as a young man), Bronson Alcott, and

The leading Transcendental thinkers all advocated an approach to education based on the inherent goodness and potential of the human being.

Bronson's daughter Louisa May Alcott founded schools based on these principles.

An important educational reformer of the late 19th century was New Hampshire-born Francis Parker (1837–1902). Parker went to Germany as a young man and studied the work of educational reformers there. In Quincy and Boston, Massachusetts, and later in Chicago, he instituted various school reforms. Parker asserted the absolute worth and dignity of the individual and the human being's capacity for development. He emphasized the active role of the child in education and said that schools should appeal to the real interests of children, encourage self-expression, feature noncoercive individual instruction, and incorporate the arts and crafts and learning through experience. He advised that children learn the alphabet by reading simple words (rather than by rote memorization), math by manipulating objects (rather than by looking at numbers on a chalkboard), and geography by taking field trips (rather than by reading a textbook). Parker rejected grades, rewards, rankings, and corporal punishment as motivators in education. He emphasized that schools should help the development of all aspects of the child—the physical, artistic, social, and moral dimensions as well as the intellectual dimension.

Thus prior to the establishment of the public school system and throughout the period during which it was growing, humanistic educators were expressing alternative ideas and establishing alternative schools. They were, however, at best a marginal factor in the United States until the appearance of John Dewey. Dewey (1859–1952) was a philosopher and social thinker, as well as an educational theorist. He was instrumental in developing both the school of philosophy known as pragmatism and the intellectual and social movement of "secular humanism." Dewey was clearly the outstanding theorist and proponent of the humanistic approach to education in the twentieth century, an approach that came to be labeled "progressive education."

Born in Burlington, Vermont, of an old farming family, Dewey was educated at the University of Vermont. From 1894 to 1904, Dewey was head of the Department of Psychology and Pedagogy at the University of Chicago and established an experimental "laboratory" school there. In 1904 he went to Columbia University in New York City, where he was a professor of philosophy. For decades Dewey was a dominant figure in the American intellectual landscape. He died in 1952 at the age of ninety-three.

Although raised as a Christian, Dewey was a materialist, humanist, evolutionist, secularist, and pragmatist. In Dewey's view, the only reality is what we experience through our senses in nature and in our everyday life. There is no transcendent or supernatural domain. There is no revealed, ultimate truth. Ideas and thought must deal with actual sensory stimuli and situations, not with abstractions and concepts. An idea is true insofar as it helps us to understand things in the world or to realize a desire.

The human being, for Dewey, is a biological organism that, through evolution, has emerged from lower forms of life. The individual is determined by heredity and environment but has intelligence and the potential for limitless growth. Further evolution of the human race and the refinement, maturing, and perfecting of the individual and of the society are the unequivocal good toward which humanity should strive. Also, for Dewey there are no absolute moral norms. Time, place, and the particular persons involved

in a situation determine what is ethical. Dewey believed that our moral judgment evolves as our experience and judgment develop.

Dewey's vision of the nature and aims of education is based on this world view. The purpose of education, he held, is not to fill the child's mind with theories and abstract knowledge. Nor is it to introduce the child to the collective wisdom of the culture. Rather education should help the child to develop a lively interest in the world, to learn to think critically, to become an active member of the community, and to live successfully and happily in modern, democratic, industrial society. To that end, education should nurture in the child an openness to experience, a desire to learn in every situation, and an impulse to continue to learn and develop throughout life. Dewey also believed that by creating informed, active, productive citizens, schools could help bring about moral, social, and political reform.

For Dewey, the system of education prevalent in the public schools of the early twentieth century was too adult centered, formal, authoritarian, theoretical, abstract, and socially and politically conservative. Drawing on the work of earlier reformers and his own experiences in education, Dewey advocated an approach to education that differed radically from mainstream public and private education of his time.

Dewey proposed an education that

> assumes children are curious, want to learn, and need primarily to be encouraged and directed in their learning;
> provides children with an exciting school environment, in effect a "child's museum" with both natural and manufactured objects to handle, observe, and wonder about;
> has a curriculum based on the interests of

the children and on the realities of the environment in which the children live;

uses the teacher as a facilitator and guide in learning;

teaches reading, writing, and arithmetic and other academic skills, but not to the exclusion of life skills;

emphasizes experiential learning (i.e., learning by doing in concrete, meaningful situations);

provides many, varied opportunities for artistic expression;

teaches crafts and practical skills;

prepares children for life in a democratic society by having a democratic classroom in which group decision making and problem solving play an important role;

has the children study a few things deeply rather than many things superficially;

provides opportunities for children to go into and to learn from the community; and

meets all the needs of the child—physical, emotional, social, and intellectual.

Dewey soon began to have a great impact on the American educational landscape. His books and articles were widely read, and many of the teachers and administrators whom he helped train at Columbia University's Teachers College assumed positions of power and influence in schools around the nation. Public and private schools alike adopted progressive ideas and methods, and many new private schools were founded expressly as progressive schools.

In elementary schools, where Dewey's ideas prevailed, work on basic academic skills, rote memorization, and mastery of subject content were de-emphasized. Play, artistic and craft activities, special projects, and field trips into the community became more important.

Deweyan progressive ideas also influenced high school education in the United States. Through the early part of the twentieth century high schools offered a demanding liberal arts curriculum. They aimed to prepare a relatively small percentage of the students for further academic study in college. In 1894, a commission on secondary education staffed by leading educators recommended that high schools offer a rigorous, broad training in the liberal arts, which included classical languages and literature, English and world literature, history, mathematics, and the sciences.

After the First World War, many states extended compulsory education to sixteen years of age, making some high school education obligatory for all children. During this period there was a national debate on whether students should be tracked into separate academic and vocational courses. Dewey held that all students should have a basic academic education. Ironically, Dewey's longtime promotion of the experiential and practical elements of education probably helped the cause of those favoring vocational and business programs. These advocates of multiprogram education prevailed, and from the early 1920s "comprehensive" public high schools began to be established. These schools offered the traditional rigorous academic program for the elite students. But to less motivated or gifted students (often judged so by the newly introduced Intelligence Quotient tests) the schools offered less demanding alternatives—watered-down "general" academic programs, vocational training, and business programs. In these the aim was not to graduate a literate, liberally educated person, but rather to prepare students for life and work through courses on "life enhancement" "social adjustment," "leisure activities," and work skills.

From the late 1940s until the mid-1960s, progressive educational ideas were out of favor in the United States. They were seen as too lax, romantic, and permissive, especially for a country engaged in a worldwide life-and-death struggle with the communist enemy. When the Soviet Union launched the first *Sputnik* in 1958 and thus seemed about to win the space race, the United States became obsessed with academic rigor, especially in mathematics and the sciences. Education was seen as essential to national survival. "Progressive" became almost a dirty word in American education, and progressive elements disappeared from most public and private schools. Only a few small, independent schools retained a clear and explicit progressive orientation.

Humanistic-progressive education in the United States did not by any means die, however. In 1961, the book *Summerhill* appeared in America. In it, A. S. Neill described life in a school that he founded in Leiston, Suffolk, England, in the 1920s. Summerhill, which is still in operation, is child centered, democratic, permissive, and based on the idea that children will grow and learn if left to their own devices. In the laissez-faire world of Summerhill, students are largely free to do what they please. They do not have to go to class or to study if they do not want to. The school is governed by an all-school meeting run on democratic principles in which every person, including children in the lower grades, has an equal vote.

Neill's ideas about education received widespread attention during the 1960s and early 1970s when many American traditions and institutions were being called into question. They helped stimulate a fresh critique of the mainstream educational system from the humanistic-

Alternative schools, inspired by neoprogressive thinkers, sprang up—in inner-city ghettos, in the suburbs and rural areas—frequently within intentional communities.

progressive perspective. For example, Jonathan Kozol, author of *Death at an Early Age* (1967), pointed out that most African-American and other minority children were receiving inferior educations and were thus being kept on the periphery of society. Paul Goodman, author of *Growing Up Absurd* (1960), decried the authoritarian nature of the system and its negative influence on young people. John Holt, in a series of books about education, celebrated homeschooling and lifelong self-directed learning and criticized schools as a place where true learning is in fact discouraged.

Alternative schools, inspired by these and other neoprogressive thinkers, sprang up—in inner-city ghettos, in the suburbs and rural areas—frequently within intentional communities. These were small schools, founded and run by teachers and parents; they were child centered, libertarian, and permissive to varying degrees; and they were relatively unstructured. Children were given a voice in what and how they learned. In the early 1970s, there were probably about one thousand such alternative schools around the country.

Most of these radical, neoprogressive schools did not last long; in fact, the average life span was about eighteen months. But during the 1970s, the humanistic-progressive ideas and practices they embodied found their way into many of the nation's public school systems, as well as into many well-established independent schools. Once again, experiential education; interest-based curricula; child-centered learning; the ideal of the teacher as guide and facilitator rather than authority figure and source of information; in-depth, long-term projects; and a de-emphasis on tests, grades, and competition became popular educational concepts. But these innovations were seldom, if ever, referred to by their proponents as "progressive." There was still a widespread public antipathy toward "progressive education."

During this renaissance of humanistic-progressive education several new elements were introduced and gained acceptance. Some were practices that had been present earlier but in seed form only, and now appeared in developed form. Some were older practices, slightly adapted and with a new name. These progressive addenda include the following:

- Whole language: An approach to reading and writing in which children from the outset deal with language and its meaning in real situations. They learn to read by reading real books, magazines, and stories, not readers. They learn to write by writing letters, stories, even their own "books." Free expression of thoughts and feelings is emphasized. Spelling, punctuation, grammar, and organization are taught but as secondary concerns.
- Cooperative learning: Noncompetitive learning in small groups, with students taking responsibility for each other's learning.
- Multicultural education: The study of the history and culture of minority groups. The culture and values of male-dominated, Caucasian, Anglo-Saxon Protestant America is de-emphasized.
- Social curriculum: Programs in behavior and social interaction, emphasizing democratic and consensual decision-making and conflict-resolution techniques.
- Developmental education: An approach based on the idea that children move

Since the late 1980s, there has been a widespread trend toward specific content-rich curricula and emphasis on the basic skills of reading, writing, and arithmetic.

through definite developmental stages, and not necessarily at the same rates. Younger children are allowed much freedom to explore and play and are not pressed into academic activities. Class groupings are multiage.
- Open classroom: The organization of the classroom into several separate areas or learning centers. Children are free to work at the center and activity they choose, and to move from one to another. Children spend little or no time sitting in rows listening to the teacher.
- Multiple assessment: The evaluation of students not only by pen-and-pencil tests but by a variety of their projects, including artwork, compositions, presentations, and videos.

By the early 1980s, progressive and neoprogressive ideas and practices had taken root in most public school districts. While the influence was greatest at the elementary level, it was also present at the junior and senior high levels. About one-quarter of the nation's school districts established some kind of alternative secondary school program—a school-within-a-school, or a "school without walls," for example. Also, many private schools were founded on progressive lines, and many traditional private schools adopted progressive methods.

In 1983, a commission sponsored by the Reagan administration published a report about education called "A Nation at Risk." It asserted that public education was in a lamentable state. Thousands of students were graduating from high school every year unable to read or write and unqualified to become productive members of society. Test scores of students in other industrialized countries and in some second world countries were higher than those of American students. Thus the nation was at risk in the competitive world economy. The United States would not be able to compete successfully with Germany, Japan, and the other nations whose educational systems were more efficient and effective.

The 1983 "Crisis Report," as it came to be known, plus the general conservatism of the late 1980s, led to a backlash against the progressive programs in the schools. Many programs were reduced or eliminated. There has since been a widespread trend toward increased academic rigor, specific content-rich curricula, and empha-sis on the basic skills of reading, writing, and arithmetic. The federal government's "Goals 2000" report, calling for national curricula standards, manifests this trend.

But progressive education is still an important factor in American education. Progressive ideas and practices are present in the private and public educational sectors, often in a slightly adapted form and with a new label. There are still many avowedly progressive private schools. Progressive elements are important in many of the proposals for the reform and restructuring of the public education system. And most of the alternative programs still existing in the public schools are essentially progressive in nature.

3

Dissenting Voice Number Two
The Religious-Traditionalist Movement

❧

The educational reformers of the humanistic-progressive movement have not been the only dissenters in American education. From the early years of the common school movement, members of various religious groups have shunned public education and educated their children in their own schools. The religious school movement is today more important than ever. The majority of students not in mainstream public schools are in religious schools or in quasi-religious schools. Of the 5 million children being educated outside the public school system, about half are in Roman Catholic schools. And there are far more children in Lutheran parochial schools (about 400,000) than there are in all the progressive private schools.

The majority of students not in mainstream public schools are in religious schools or in quasi-religious schools.

❧

Most of the schools that predated the public schools in the United States were set up to educate the children of a particular religious community. Roman Catholics, Jews, Friends, Lutherans, Presbyterians, and other groups each had their own schools. When the public school system was established, some groups, such as the Friends and the more liberal Lutherans and Presbyterians, readily sent their children to public schools and gradually closed their own.

Some groups, however, chose to maintain their own system of education. Conservative Lutherans and Presbyterians rejected the public schools.

From about 1880, the Roman Catholic Church encouraged each local parish to establish its own parochial school to educate its children. Many of the parishes that founded schools were ethnic parishes, comprised entirely of recent immigrants from Italy, Poland, Ireland, Germany, or other European countries. Often the language of the "old country" was the language used in the school. The Seventh-Day Adventists, a sect that emerged in the last decades of the nineteenth century—just when the public school system was being established—also chose to found their own schools.

For these groups, a primary aim of education was to develop devout, moral, and loyal members of the faith community. The public schools were perceived as nonreligious, basically secular institutions that would corrupt their children. In a public school at that time, the Bible might be read. There might even be prayers and some moral education. But this did not constitute a true education in the faith. The Catholics viewed the public schools as "Congregationalist and

Unitarian parochial schools," controlled by the dominant Protestant culture and liable to lure Catholic children away from the Church.

In the religious school movement, parents and educators were primarily concerned about the secular nature of public education, that is, the absence of real moral and religious teaching. They were less concerned about the basic academic curriculum, teaching methods, and classroom organization. In large measure, most shared the Calvinistic view of human nature, truth, and authority that lay behind the original paradigm of public education: Children are not by nature eager or able to learn on their own. They need a structure and external motivation. There is a distinct body of knowledge that children should master. Thus the religious schools tended to be teacher centered and authoritarian, to rely heavily on textbooks, and to emphasize memorization of material.

As the public school system was developing in the late 19th century, some religious groups closed their schools, some continued to operate their schools, and some began to found their own schools. In the first half of the twentieth century, the number of religious schools and the number of children they were educating gradually increased. The Roman Catholic system in particular grew large, with thousands of schools and millions of children. It became in effect a shadow system to the public system, in some urban areas being extremely large. This increase in religious schools was primarily a result of population growth within the various groups, not of defections from the public schools. The public system still thrived, with almost all Protestants and Jews, and even a majority of Catholics, sending their children to public schools.

In recent decades, the religious school movement as a whole has enjoyed increased vitality,

for several reasons. First, all religious elements have been eliminated from the public schools. In 1961, the United States Supreme Court ruled that prayer in the public schools violated the separation of church and state established in the Constitution. This began a radical change in all public school systems. Until that time, nondenominational religious activity was present in most public schools. Prayer, Bible readings, and moral education based on biblical teachings were part of daily school life. Henceforth, public schools had to be explicitly and consciously nonreligious. The reading of the Bible as literature, the mention and discussion of religious issues, the teaching of moral principles, and any religious activity was legally proscribed. The public schools became totally secular institutions.

At the same time, humanistic and progressive ideas and practices were again finding their way into the public schools in a variety of forms and under a variety of names. For many people these neoprogressive elements seemed too permissive, too lax, too indulgent. They did not seem to lead to self-discipline or the real academic competence. They also embodied values and beliefs with which many religious persons would not be comfortable. Dewey, the chief prophet of progressive education, was also a leading figure in secular humanism.

Meanwhile, a religious revival began—which has continued to this day—mostly of conservative Christianity. Evangelical and fundamentalist groups gained many converts, mainly in the Bible Belt that stretches across the South, the Southwest, and into southern California, but also in every part of the country.

Thus in the last decades, the public schools and a significant proportion of the American people have been moving in opposite directions. The population as a whole has been becoming more religious and more conservative, a trend reflected in political life. Meanwhile, the schools have become more secular and, despite the calls after the 1983 "Nation at Risk" report for academic rigor and higher standards, they have become more liberal and progressive—at least in the eyes of conservative observers. Hence, more and more people have found the public schools less and less attractive.

The results are patent and unmistakable. In two decades, fundamentalists and other conservative Christians have created a nationwide network of over 15,000 schools with over 1 million children. In the early years of this Christian school movement, many schools (most but not all in the South) were founded to avoid forced racial integration, but today virtually all Christian schools are open to children of all races. There are many integrated and many African-American and Hispanic Christian schools. Another 1 million children from Christian families are being schooled at home using specially designed Christian curricula.

Mainstream Protestant church schools also continue to thrive. They educate children of their congregations, as well as many children of unchurched parents who want a structured, traditionally oriented education with a moral and religious element. Roman Catholic schools, after hard times in the 1960s and 1970s, are enjoying a renaissance. In many inner cities, Catholic schools are the school of choice for minority parents who want their children to have a rigorous and disciplined school experience. Schools meant to educate children of a certain religious community, such as Jewish day schools, Muslim schools, and Mennonite schools, are increasing as well.

In many inner cities, Catholic schools are the school of choice for minority parents who want their children to have a rigorous and disciplined school experience.

The religious-traditionalist movement also includes schools that do not have an explicit religious orientation. These have been founded by parents and educators concerned about the decline of moral values and academic standards in the public schools. For example, today there are about eighty schools founded on the educational theories of Mae Carden (1896–1977). Miss Carden developed a phonics-based reading method and a rigorous, content-rich curriculum for grades one through eight. In Carden schools, children study artistic and musical appreciation, comply with a strict dress and behavior code, and are exposed to moral and (nondenominational) religious teachings.

The Core Knowledge schools provide another example of traditionalist education without an explicit religious orientation. The Core Knowledge curriculum was developed by E. D. Hirsch, author of _Cultural Literacy: What Every American Needs to Know_, published in 1987. In 1990 Hirsch set up the Core Knowledge Foundation, which advocates a rigorous, comprehensive curriculum from kindergarten through the eighth grade. Already over 150 schools in the country have adopted the program, the great majority of them public schools. Many of the public Core Knowledge schools have been successful "magnet schools," attracting Caucasian students into inner-city school systems.

The religious-traditionalist movement is thus a very potent force in American education. It provides an alternative for parents who are attracted neither to the mainstream public schools nor to the schools and programs based on humanistic-progressive ideas.

4

The Public School Mainstream Today
and the Range of Alternatives

❦

American education is dominated by what may be called mainstream public education. The public school system is huge, consisting of some 88,000 schools (66,000 elementary, 22,000 high schools) and about 2.5 million teachers teaching about 35 million students. Efforts to improve, reform, and restructure public education are widespread, varied, and ongoing. There is great diversity in the public school system. Nevertheless, most public schools today conform to a particular pattern to which much of the following description would pertain.

The school building is large, rectilinear, and made of brick or reinforced concrete. It has fluorescent lighting and, if relatively recent, has a central ventilating system and windows that either do not open or open very little. While some school buildings are attractive and well maintained, many are stark, unattractive, and run-down. This disparity reflects the fact that some school districts spend $3,000 per student per year while others spend as much as $12,000.

The student population is large. In 1959, Harvard President James Conant delivered a report advocating that, for the purposes of efficiency and quality, small schools should be absorbed by large ones. Since then, schools across the country have been consolidated, resulting in the closing of small, local schools and an increase in the size of the average school. The traditional one- or two-room schoolhouse is virtually unknown except in Amish and Mennonite communities. The typical elementary school today has between 250 and 300 children. Middle schools are usually larger, and comprehensive and regional high schools range between 1,000 and 4,000 students. Because of their size, most schools are impersonal; students do not get to know all or even most of the other students and thus remain anonymous to much of the school community.

Classes consist of between twenty and thirty children of roughly the same age. The classroom is a large room equipped with chairs and desks for the students and a larger chair and desk for the teacher. In an elementary school classroom there may be movable tables and chairs, as well as some open areas. In a middle or high school the students' desks and chairs more or less fill the room and are often arranged in rows oriented to the front, facing the teacher's side of the room.

The pedagogy is teacher centered. The teacher does most of the talking in the classroom, presenting and explaining material, asking questions, and soliciting answers. Sometimes the teacher reads from a textbook. There is little or no time for discussion of the material. One class-

17

room study indicates that only 2 percent of classroom time is spent in participatory discussion.

The student is expected to sit quietly and to listen attentively to the teacher and to take notes as necessary. He or she is not to speak or move out of the seat without the teacher's permission. The teacher may spend a good amount of time and energy maintaining order in the classroom.

Much or most of what the children learn is decided by a fixed, predetermined curriculum. For each subject—spelling, reading, arithmetic, social studies, science—there is a textbook and a student workbook. Sometimes the children read the textbook in class or fill out workbook sheets or answer questions on a photocopied sheet.

The various subjects are taught separately, in isolation from one another. The day is divided into segments and in each period a particular subject is studied. In an elementary school the children usually do most or all subjects with one teacher in one room. In middle and high school they change teacher, subject, and room every forty minutes or so.

In some subjects, children are grouped according to ability. In the elementary grades there will be, within a class, several reading groups, ranging from remedial to advanced. Each group has its own materials and period of instruction from the teacher. In a middle or high school, this "tracking" extends to other subjects and will determine which students are in a particular class. Thus there will be an advanced or honors math class composed of the brightest students and a general class, composed of less talented students. The emphasis is on acquiring basic academic skills, such as reading, writing, and arithmetic, and on mastering the content in various subject areas such as social studies, English, and science. Art, music, crafts, and physical education receive relatively little attention. In a typical middle school a student has one forty-minute music class a week.

In some schools academic standards are low. Students who do not master the work in a grade level may nevertheless be promoted to the next grade. In a high school many students may be marking time until graduation.

In the learning of academic skills, the principle "the earlier the better" pertains. Thus, a kindergarten child may have daily reading instruction and a first grader a computer class each week.

Learning is primarily individual. Each child is expected to independently learn, master, and demonstrate the skills taught and the knowledge acquired.

The teaching of history, literature, and geography largely reflects the dominant Caucasian American culture. There are "multicultural" units and maybe even a "multicultural" teacher, but the prevalent ethos is still that of a dominant white culture. Female and minority students may experience subtle and perhaps unintended but real discrimination. Teachers may call on them less frequently or have lower academic expectations of them.

The main tool for assessing students' progress is the pencil-and-paper test, in which students fill in a blank or choose a correct answer from several offered. For each subject students receive a number or letter grade, and their grades are sent home to parents periodically on report cards. In middle and high schools students may receive a class rank based on their grades.

Children take standardized national or statewide tests, sometimes several during a year. There is a lot of anxiety among teachers and administrators about the performance of their students as compared with that of children in other schools and other states. Often much classroom time is spent in preparing children for the tests.

Starting from the fourth or fifth grade, there

are units on sex education (taught from a biological and health perspective), on drug use and abuse, and on HIV-AIDS awareness. There may also be units about gay and lesbian issues that stress the importance of tolerating different lifestyles.

There are no courses on religion or on religiously based morality. Teachers, wanting to maintain value neutrality, consciously avoid mentioning religion or spiritual values and their relevance to daily life. If the Bible or another religious text is studied—a rare occurrence—it is presented as a work of literature.

The theory of evolution is taught to explain the creation of the world and the existence of the human race. The human race is presented as the end product of a mechanistic process of evolution and as having primates as ancestors.

The teachers' primary qualifications to teach rest on their having taken the necessary number of education courses and on their being certified by the state as a teacher. Students and parents are unlikely to know anything about the personal beliefs of the teachers, their religious or philosophical orientation, moral standards, or their lifestyle. Students have little or no contact with their teachers outside the school.

As an institution, the school is at the bottom of an immense bureaucratic pyramid. While on some matters (such as teaching style and disciplinary procedures) the principal and teachers have autonomy, many important matters are out of their hands. Decisions about curriculum, funding, hiring, and the use of standardized tests are made at a higher level in the bureaucracy. The curriculum, materials, teaching methods, and even the particular textbooks have been determined by a person or persons far away from the teacher and children. There are more administrators, supervisors, inspectors, and other bu-

reaucrats in the New York City public school system than there are in all of France, and in New York State there are more than in all of Europe. New York State, not atypically, spends seventy-five cents of each dollar budgeted for education on supporting this bureaucracy. Twenty-five cents is spent on the local school and for what goes on in the classroom.

The school is to a large degree a world unto itself, separated from the child's home and from the surrounding community. Parental involvement in the school is often limited and organized in very specific channels, such as parent-teacher conferences or parent organization meetings. Parents' questions, suggestions, and complaints about school life may not be particularly welcome. The children go on occasional field trips to museums or parks, but within the school environment they have little contact with community members.

Dress, language, behavior, interests, conversation, and other aspects of life in the school largely reflect the dominant media culture. Sexual sophistication and innuendo, probably picked up from television programs, may be in evidence even among kindergarten children.

Peer pressure to conform to patterns of dress and behavior is very strong. Teasing, bullying, intimidation, and physical assault are not uncommon occurrences in elementary and middle schools as well as in high schools. Hundreds of thousands of incidents of violence carried out by students against other students and against teachers are recorded every year.

Drug and alcohol use and sexual promiscuity may be part of the school culture. This is more likely in high schools but is also possible in middle and even in elementary schools, and pertains to rural and suburban as well as urban areas.

Certainly not all public schools conform to all

elements of this description. But the description—particularly regarding curriculum, pedagogy, and school and class organization—more or less fits the majority. The problematic elements—large class size, low academic standards, violence, influence of the drug culture—are present more in some schools than others. Social and economic conditions contribute to these problems, but schools in poor or inner-city areas are not the only ones affected. Schools in rural areas and in affluent suburban areas are not at all immune.

The public schools have a difficult, perhaps impossible job—to educate every child who walks through the door. Many schools succeed or come very close to succeeding in this task, thanks to dedicated and talented teachers and administrators and the support of the community. But many are having problems in fulfilling that charge, at least in a way that satisfies many parents. The parents of about 1 million American children choose home-schooling rather than the public school system. The parents of another 4 million children have chosen to pay twice for their child's education—once through property and other taxes and once through private school tuition. Many parents have their children in public schools only because they cannot afford a private school.

There are many alternatives to mainstream public education, outside the public school system but within it as well. There are a large number of independent schools based on the ideas and practices of the humanistic-progressive tradition. These schools feature child-centered learning, experiential education, informal classroom environments, strong arts programs, and cooperative learning, and the like.

The parents of 4 million children have chosen to pay twice for their child's education—once through property and other taxes and once through private school tuition.

———⚓———

Among them are Montessori schools, many of the Friends' schools, the holistic schools, "free" schools, Foxfire schools, and multiple intelligences schools. Each of these types of schools, while it possesses basic elements of the humanistic-progressive orientation, also has its own particular ideas and methods. And each individual school of each type is unique. A Montessori school will be similar to, but also in many respects, unlike other Montessori schools.

Within the public educational system as well, there are many schools which are based on humanistic-progressive ideas or which include such programs. Some are "magnet" schools established to effect racial integration. Some are "site-based management schools" at which teachers and parents have been given control of the school and have chosen to institute an innovative program. Some are the result of top-down efforts at reform by the educational establishment. In any case, there are now in the public school system, Montessori preschool programs, Foxfire programs, multiple intelligences schools, and bilingual multicultural schools, and many other progressively oriented schools and programs. Many public schools are members of the Coalition of Essential Schools, which promotes progressive education along with site-based management, school-size reduction, and community involvement.

There are also the thousands of independent schools of the broad religious-traditionalist movement. These include the Roman Catholic, Protestant, Christian, and more conservative Jewish day schools. They include schools that have no religious affiliation but emphasize rigorous academics, moral education, and a traditional curriculum—among them the Carden schools, Core

Knowledge schools, and private high schools using the International Baccalaureate program.

The public schools cannot appropriate the religious elements that characterize the religious-traditional movement, but many have adopted the conservative approach to learning, the broad curriculum, and the academic rigor that characterize the religious-traditional approach to education. For example, a large number of public elementary schools have adopted the Core Knowledge curriculum and almost a hundred public high schools now offer the challenging International Baccalaureate.

There are also schools and educational approaches that do not fit neatly into either the humanistic-progressive or religious-traditionalist approaches. Waldorf education, for example, which originated in Germany, is based on a developmental view of the child, emphasizes the arts, and stresses hands-on experiential education. But Waldorf education is teacher centered, has a specific comprehensive curriculum, includes a structured classroom environment, and has a definite, if implicit, spiritual orientation.

Thus in the United States today, families dissatisfied with mainstream public education have a variety of alternatives from which to choose. There are elementary schools with just thirty children, high schools with eighty. There are schools in yurts, on farms, in homes, in church basements, and in pastel-colored domed buildings. There are schools where children lounge in jeans in living-room settings and there are schools where children wear uniforms and stand when the teacher enters the room. There are schools where children sit quietly and straight, with eyes on the teacher, and schools where children move freely around and may choose to participate or not in the class. There are schools without textbooks, curricula, tests, or grades. There are schools where the children decide what they will study, and even whether they study or not. There are schools where children in kindergarten start learning the names of the presidents, the names of trees, and other information that comprises our basic cultural heritage. There are schools where the dominant Caucasian culture is studied as one of many. And there are close to a million home schools where parents educate their children or children and young people educate themselves.

Mainstream public schools still dominate education in the United States, but the many school alternatives reflect the full philosophical, religious, political diversity of the nation. Every family can find an educational approach that is appropriate both for its children and for the family as a whole.

Part Two of this guide will look at several of the important trends in education that have shaped many innovative schools in the public and independent sector. Part Three will present twenty-two distinct types of alternative schooling that are commonly available in the United States today.

II

SOME CURRENT TRENDS IN
AMERICAN EDUCATION

The following six chapters deal with important elements in American education today. While they have been developed fairly recently, five of these elements—whole language, cooperative learning, the social curriculum, multicultural education, and developmental education—are based on the philosophical and practical assumptions of progressive education. They can be understood as addenda to the classic progressive educational approach. In a typical progressive school or program today, most or all are likely being used. Some have become widely enough accepted that they may even be found in more conservative, even religiously oriented schools. For example, many Protestant schools and some fundamentalist Christian schools use elements of whole language. Thus all parents negotiating the complex world of contemporary education need to understand these approaches. The sixth movement— education for character—is largely a phenomenon in conservatively oriented schools but is also attracting attention in the mainstream independent school world.

5

Whole Language

Whole language is an approach to reading and writing that was developed in Australia and New Zealand in the 1970s and introduced in the United States in the early 1980s. Whole language is now used in virtually all public and independent schools that have a progressive inclination. It is so widely accepted that many schools that are not progressive use it, usually in combination with other reading approaches.

The traditional method of teaching reading in the United States is the phonics method. According to educational historian Samuel Blumenfeld, "Phonics goes back to the ancient Greeks. It basically is the way people have learned to read throughout Western history."

With the phonics approach, the child learns to identify the letters of the alphabet and to associate the appropriate sound with each. Then the child learns the sounds of the letters in combination and the various rules that apply. The two-vowel rule, for example, states that a vowel becomes a long vowel if it is followed by a consonant and an "e" that ends the word, as in "bake," "cake," and "pike." Once the child has learned the sounds of the letters and of the combinations, the rules of phonics and the exceptions, he or she can sound out almost any word. During this learning process, the child is given simple stories and reading selections. Traditionally, these stories have been classics of children's literature or didactic, informative stories written and gathered in a reader for children of a certain age group and reading ability. Vocabulary sections in the readers list new words used and give their meanings. Special vocabulary books build up the child's store of words.

At the same time, the child is learning to write the letters, combine them into words, and combine the words into sentences. In the traditional process, the child learns to write the letters after particular models. Usually the child practices forming the letters until handwriting becomes legible and attractive. The child will perhaps copy sentences that the teacher has written on the blackboard. Also, the child learns the parts of speech, grammatical rules, and proper usage and studies the correct spelling of words. In time, although perhaps not until the fourth or fifth grade, the child begins to write compositions and simple stories, usually on a topic given by the teacher. The child learns that in a paragraph the first sentence states the main point of the paragraph, the body of the paragraph develops this point, and the final sentence reiterates.

This approach was virtually universal in the United States until the early twentieth century.

In the first decades of the century, psychologists, among them William Thorndike at Columbia University, developed what is called the "look-say" or "sight-recognition" approach to reading instruction. With this method, the child is taught to identify words as a unit, rather than to sound them out. The teacher, for example, holds up a card with the word DOG on it and says "dog." Children repeat the word and learn to associate it with the particular group of letters. In the first grade they learn short, simple words, and as they pass through the grades they add longer, more difficult words to their vocabularies. They learn to recognize words as whole words and, helped by context, illustrations, and word configuration, learn to guess how to pronounce new words. Phonetic principles usually are not taught in the early grades so children do not learn how to sound out words when they first learn to read. For each grade level there is a basal reader with specially written stories using only words that the children have already learned to identify. The "Dick and Jane" series was one series of graded readers developed for the sight-recognition method. They relate the not-so-exciting adventures of Dick and Jane and their dog Spot.

The sight-recognition method was adopted by many, perhaps most, schools in the country, supplanting or supplementing the phonetic approach. For decades, American children learned to read and say "Run, Spot, run." For the most part, spelling books, vocabulary books, grammar books, and penmanship training remained part of language education during this period. In the late 1950s, publishers tried to make the stories in the basal readers more varied and interesting, but otherwise the system was relatively unchanged.

The whole language approach assumes that children are natural learners— that they love to learn and can motivate and direct themselves.

Whole language is an approach to reading and writing and to learning in general. It is basically an application of progressive educational principles to language learning. Whole language is holistic, child centered, and experiential, emphasizing learning by doing. It aims to nurture and develop the creativity of the child. Whole language assumes that children are natural learners; that they love to learn and can motivate and direct themselves; and that if they can direct their learning they will be more committed to it.

The phonetic method is an analytical approach to reading, moving from mastery of the parts to mastery of the process itself. In contrast, whole language is based on the principle that learning should begin with the whole and then proceed to the part. Thus from the outset, the teacher reads real stories to and with the children. Children learn to identify whole words and to see how they are combined to make sentences. Real, intact books that have literary merit and are appropriate to the age of the children are used. Basal readers with stories written to teach certain words, excerpts from books, and abridged versions of books are generally not used. Lessons in reading are not a distinct, isolated event, but take place within the context of the reading of a poem or story or other piece of literature. Phonetic instruction can be a part of the whole language approach as a supplementary technique.

In the early grades, teachers usually choose books for the children. Older children generally are free to choose books for their own reading. The teacher may make suggestions (and many do), but ultimately older children choose what they read and take responsibility for reading it. That children read is more important than what they read. Teachers in the younger grades keep a "reading journal" for each child. Older children keep their own reading journal, recording what they have read and their response to it. Vocabulary building comes through the actual process of reading as children come across words they do not know and have to find out their meanings. Usually there are no vocabulary lists or exercises.

In the whole language approach, writing is also understood as best learned by actual doing and so-called process writing is taught. In process writing children learn that the creation of a written document is a process. One goes through several stages before producing a final product. The first stage is brainstorming, in which children allow their ideas to emerge spontaneously and in unedited form. Then they group and connect the brainstormed material. This usually involves making a "web," with lines connecting the main and subsidiary ideas. They write a first draft, get comments from other students and from the teacher, and then write a second draft. This incorporates spelling, grammatical, and punctuation corrections as well as suggestions about organization and content. They get more feedback and then make a final copy.

As soon as they are able to form letters, children are encouraged to write, to create real documents that have a purpose, that have something to communicate. Thus children write the kind of things they are reading: news articles, stories, poems, letters, commentaries, persuasive pieces, stories that will published and distributed, letters to real people, shopping lists they will take with them to the store, and other items of personal importance. The class does real things with words.

In the whole language approach, grammar, spelling, and punctuation are usually not studied as separate subjects. Rather, they are dealt with as they come up in the process of writing. Chil-

dren are encouraged to use words even if they are not sure of the correct spelling and to write out a sentence even if they are unsure of the grammar and punctuation. "Invented spellings," and sentences that are "approximately correct" are tolerated and sometimes not immediately corrected. The communication of overall meaning is considered more important than the fine points. The theory is that too many corrections may create anxiety in the student and hamper creativity.

Writing, like reading, is a social activity. In the writing process students confer on, evaluate, and edit each other's work. Children learn through experience that social interaction and the exchange of ideas are a stimulus to thinking and to learning.

In writing as in reading, children make choices and assume responsibility. Sometimes the teacher assigns a topic, but usually, especially in the middle and upper grades, children decide what they want to write about. They also choose the students with whom they will work. They are largely responsible for setting their own goals and assessing their own progress, though teachers periodically meet and confer with students to help them assess their progress toward their goals. There are no tests and no grades. The work leads to finished products such as a book published by the class or an exhibition displayed in the school or elsewhere.

Also, with the whole language approach there are no ability-based groupings, no dividing of the class into advanced, average, and slow readers, for example. Each discussion or writing group is heterogeneous. The more advanced children work together with and help the slower ones. The day has a predictable pattern and there are big blocks of time set aside for reading, writing, and reflection.

The Marion Cross School

Norwich, Vermont

The Marion Cross School is a K–6 elementary school. The school has had the same principal, Milton Frye, for over twenty years, and has an experienced and dedicated faculty. It is widely known as a successful school. For years, Marion Cross has been using the whole language approach.

Terri Ashley teaches a first-grade class of about eighteen children. The classroom is well stocked with classic children's books, and the children are encouraged to read them. Each day they have thirty minutes of silent reading time. They also have time to form small reading groups and read aloud to each other. Several times a week they read to the teacher or to a parent volunteer in books chosen by the teacher. In this "reading conference" the child receives individual reading instruction. Ashley keeps a journal of the books each child has read and includes the child's comments. With the aid of charts, the children learn and sing songs, memorize poems, and recite them together. Ashley also uses "big books" that are large enough so that the whole class can see the pictures and read the text together. The children write stories and accounts of their experiences and read these aloud to each other in small groups. Sometimes they act out a story and thereby discover the need for editing and rewriting. They write and publish their own books.

While using a whole language approach, Ashley also uses traditional methods. She teaches the children phonetics as a way to decode words, and as part of an individualized reading program she has some students use spelling books or basal readers.

In Cam Cross's third-grade class, the dominant approach also is whole language. On a typi- cal day the students will be exposed to and will use language in a variety of ways. For example, they may imagine that they are soldiers at Fort No. 4—a restored pre–Revolutionary period fort they have visited—and write a letter home to their families. Or they may write a description of a local cemetery and its two-hundred-year-old headstones in their journals. Every day the students read silently in books of their own choosing, and when Cross or a teaching assistant comes by, they read aloud. Students work on short stories that will be collected and published together. Cross reads aloud to the children each day for thirty minutes, usually from a novel such as *Watership Down*. After the reading the children discuss what has been read in small groups.

Cross comments that "whole language involves the use of language in all its forms and fosters and nurtures a variety of skills. I don't see whole language and the traditional approach as mutually exclusive polarities. I teach the children phonetics. I encourage them to use the Scott-Foresman Spelling Book series. And I use the SRA (Science Research Associates) Reading Program which consists of reading booklets color-coded according to difficulty with questions about content, spelling, and grammar." In Cross's class some of the smaller reading groups are formed according to ability. "I have children who are reading at a first-grade level and others who are reading at a tenth-grade level. You just can't mix them together all the time," he says.

This eclectic approach is very common. All of the schools I visited that were using the whole language approach were also using phonetics. The director of one such school, a conservative, religiously oriented school, observed:

> We use whole language and the process writing approach, and they are very effec-

tive. But we also use phonetics and the traditional methods of teaching reading and writing. Children learn from drill, memorization, and recitation, just as they learn from reading real books and writing stories. And about 30 percent really rely on the step-by-step analytical approach, phonetic drills, and lots of repetition. Not all children learn by osmosis, which to some degree is what whole language assumes.

Also, even with our older children we control what books the children read. They have freedom to choose, but from a list of books that we consider well written, informative, and wholesome. Many of the books written for children and promoted by the publishing industry today are problematic in terms of their subject matter and the message they convey.

Elements of whole language have found their way into most American schools, public and private, progressive and conservative. In the early years, whole language zealots totally rejected phonetics, spelling books, vocabulary lists, and other traditional tools of teaching reading and writing. At one time in some school districts in California it was virtually forbidden for a teacher to give a spelling test. Today the "both/and" rather than the "either/or" attitude seems to pertain to most schools systems.

For More Information

Whole Language Umbrella is an organization that promotes and distributes information on whole language. Its location changes according to the home base of the current director. To find out its current location, contact:

> Jerome Harste
> 100 Heritage
> Bloomington, IN 47408
> Tel.: (812) 336-6925
> Fax: (812) 856-8287

> The Center for Teaching and Learning
> 3605 Cross Point Road
> Edgecomb, ME 04556
> Tel.: (207) 882-9706

The Center for Teaching and Learning is a demonstration school with an internship program, utilizing whole language and related approaches to learning.

For Further Reading

Most of the following books about whole language are meant for teachers and administrators but are also helpful to parents.

Ashton-Warner, Sylvia. *Teacher.* New York: Simon and Schuster, 1963. Ashton-Warner describes how she discovered "organic" reading and tells how to teach it.

Atwell, Nancie. *In the Middle: Writing, Reading, and Learning with Adolescents.* Portsmouth, N.H.: Heinemann, 1987.

Blumenfeld, Samuel. *The Whole Language/O.B.E. Fraud.* Boise, Idaho: Paradigm Company, 1995. A history of the way reading has been taught in public schools in the United States, and a critique of current methods, written by a leading conservative historian of education. A dissenting view about the value of whole language.

Calkins, Lucy M. *The Art of Teaching Writing.* Portsmouth, N.H.: Heinemann, 1986.

Crafton, Linda. *Whole Language: Getting Started, Moving Forward.* Katonah, N.Y.: Richard C. Owen Publishers, 1991. Primarily a guidebook for teachers, this book also is helpful for parents interested in the concept of whole langauge and how it is applied in practice. Contains many excellent bibliographies of books for children according to topic.

Goodman, Kenneth. *What's Whole in Whole Language.* Portsmouth, N.H.: Heinemann, 1986. An explanation of the special characteristics of whole language as compared with other methods of teaching reading and writing.

Harste, Jerome, Kathy G. Short, and Carolyn Burke. *Creating Classrooms for Authors.* Portsmouth, N.H.: Heinemann, 1988.

6

Cooperative Learning

Since its inception, American public education has been based primarily on an individualistic and competitive model of learning. In the original factory paradigm of the school, the child is a pieceworker, working largely alone to master skills and to acquire knowledge, and competing with other workers for the limited supply of rewards.

Most children today in most American schools still learn primarily as individuals. If they need help they ask the teacher. When called on to answer a question, when taking a test or writing a paper, the students are on their own. It is generally against the rules for students to help each other. Performance in class and on tests establishes a clear hierarchy, with the brightest at the top with their A's and the sluggards at the bottom with their C's, D's, and F's. When one student gives a wrong answer or fails a test the position of the others is improved.

To a person educated in traditional American public schools, it is hard to imagine another approach to learning. But there are other models. I discovered this years ago in Japan when I began teaching English in a girls' college. In the first week of classes I asked one of the students, "What is the plural of the English word *life?*" She looked thunderstruck and glanced pleadingly to left and right. Immediately, the entire class formed a de jure research group. After much whispering, consultation, and turning of heads the class arrived at a consensus answer. This was communicated to the young lady who smiled confidently and replied, *"Lives."* At first I was disturbed by this academic collectivism, but as it seemed perfectly normal for the Japanese, I came to accept it. The Japanese have a highly communal sense of identity and generally work and solve problems well in a group.

A cooperative approach to learning is not unknown in American educational history. In the one-room schoolhouses that existed in colonial times and occasionally were found until the 1960s (they still are common in Mennonite and Amish communities), older children taught younger children as a matter of course. In the early 1800s, the "Lancastrian" system, in which older and brighter students worked as teaching "prefects," teaching younger and slower students, was adopted for a time by some school systems. And various schools in the humanistic-progressive tradition have stressed cooperation rather than competition and have eschewed tests, grades, and other competition-inducing elements.

In the last decade or two, cooperative learning

31

has become a distinct proselytizing movement in American education. There are organizations that advocate and promote cooperative learning; institutes that offer staff training and development; scores of books and articles on the subject; cooperative learning curricula that are grade and subject specific; and cooperative learning lesson plans and teachers' guides. Cooperative learning is increasingly important in both public and private schools, particularly those with a progressive orientation.

Two leading theorists of cooperative learning are Roger Johnson and David Johnson, both professors at the University of Minnesota. As brothers growing up on an Indiana farm, they competed fiercely with each other in matters large and small, but as adults they have cooperated in their academic and professional work. In their book *Learning Together and Alone*, the Johnsons describe three patterns of classroom life—the competitive, the individualistic, and the cooperative. They argue that the cooperative is the most effective paradigm for learning and should dominate in American schools.

According to the Johnsons, in the competitive pattern all students are in a win-lose struggle to see who is the best. A few will win, most will lose. The student learns "I can succeed only if others fail" and works to excel above his or her classmates. If the student thinks there is no chance of winning, he or she may give up. Competitive learning is based on several assumptions: that competition is inherent in human nature; that it motivates students to work hard and brings out the best capabilities in each; that it is fun; that it builds character; and that it prepares students for life in the real world, that is, a place of economic, social, and personal competition.

In cooperative learning the student learns "I can succeed only if others succeed."

In the individualistic pattern students work independently to achieve certain preset learning goals. They work at their own pace and in their own space, use their own set of materials, and seek to master specific skills and knowledge. If they need help they receive it on an individual basis from a teacher who circulates among the individually occupied students. Their success or failure is not connected to that of other students. If they complete the work satisfactorily and master the prescribed material or skill they will get an A. It is possible for every student to get an A. The student learns "I can succeed regardless of the success or failure of others." This approach was quite popular from the late 1960s through the early 1980s. It was seen as an antidote to the stresses of competitive learning and as a way to apply behavioral psychology to learning. Today, individual learning is common in the many small "teacherless" Christian schools where children work at individual cubicles and make their way through graded sequential workbooks for the various subjects. Many homeschoolers use individual learning as well.

In cooperative learning, students are divided into small groups that, in terms of ability, are heterogeneous. Each group member is charged to learn the material or master the skill; to see that everyone in the group also masters the material; and ultimately to see that everyone in the class has mastered it. The student learns "I can succeed only if others succeed." In the group, students work together, help and encourage each other, and make sure the slower students keep up.

There are many classroom patterns that seem to be, but are not true examples, of cooperative learning. Students may sit together while each does his or her own work; one student in a group may do all the work; and students may do their own assignments and then confer and help each other; but none of these is true cooperative learning.

Cooperative learning, according to the Johnsons, does involve physical proximity, discussion, sharing, and helping, but it involves other key factors as well. They see five elements as essential:

- Positive interdependence: a clear perception by all members of the group that the success of each individual is dependent on the success of all
- Individual accountability: each person being responsible for a fair share of the work
- Promotive interaction: mutual help, encouragement, sharing
- Group skills: the teaching, modeling, practice, and use in group situations of decision-making, communication, leadership, trust-building, and conflict-resolution skills
- Group processing: self-objectification by the group, including discussion of whether and how it has achieved its goals; which behaviors have been useful and productive and which have not

Cooperative learning can be used in mastering certain information, learning particular skills, and in doing research projects. For example, the topic for a particular session in grammar may be the dangling participle. The teacher introduces and explains the topic and then divides the class into groups, each with the grammar books and workbooks it needs. The teacher explains that the aim of the lesson is that each student learn what a dangling participle is, be able to identify one, and know how to correct the offending sentence. The

students go into their groups and study the material. They work together to understand and master the concepts. Those who grasp the concepts first help and encourage those who are slower. The teacher monitors the groups and, as necessary, intervenes and offers help. At the end of the class, each group checks to make sure that each member has acquired the desired skills. The teacher might randomly quiz students verbally or give a formal, written quiz. Each student gets a grade based on his or her own performance and then a bonus based on the performance of others in the group.

In the case of a research project about the Civil War, for example, the teacher might again divide the class into groups. Each group chooses a specific research theme. One group might study the causes of the war, another the day-to-day life of the soldiers, another the war's impact on American society, another the course of the war and its major battles. Within each group the task is then divided among the members. In the first group, one student might look into the role of slavery, another into economic factors, another into broader cultural factors as causes of the war. Students work on their own to gather material and then present it to the group. The group organizes a presentation of its findings to the rest of the class. After several weeks, each group makes its presentation. At the end of the project, each group reflects on its own work and the teacher assesses the work of the various groups.

This type of cooperative learning is called "formal cooperative learning." There is also "informal cooperative learning." Informal cooperative learning is best used when the teacher is presenting a great deal of content-rich material. It gives the students an opportunity to form small groups, briefly discuss what has been presented, and raise questions and correct misunderstandings that have arisen. For example, if the teacher is lecturing on the periodic chart of the elements, he or she might every twenty minutes or so pause and ask the class to form small groups to review the important points made in the previous twenty minutes. For five minutes, students in groups of four or five may discuss, for example, the similarities of the group of elements that includes fluorine and bromine. After five minutes the teacher asks one group to briefly present the gist of its discussion and solicits questions from all groups. Then the teacher continues for another half hour before pausing again. Interspersing a lecture with such short group sessions keeps students focused and alert, makes the learning more personal and immediate, and helps students retain and transfer the information to other settings.

Cooperative learning also can involve the use of "base groups." These are "mini-homerooms," groups of between four and ten students who meet on a daily basis. The students discuss how their work is going, exchange support, encouragement, and assistance in completing assignments, and perhaps discuss personal matters. In one school I visited each class was divided into base groups of about ten students, and the school day began with a twenty-minute meeting of the group. These groups seemed to provide an intimate, relaxed, and supportive environment for the children.

Research indicates that cooperative learning has many benefits. Students in cooperative learning situations are more motivated, learn more, and retain more than students in competitive school environments. They have more self-esteem, develop more positive interpersonal relationships, are healthier emotionally and psycho-

Research indicates that students in cooperative learning situations have more self-esteem and develop more positive interpersonal relationships.

logically, and are much more likely to remain in school. Also, cooperative learning fosters the so-called higher-order skills, such as problem setting, problem solving, investigation, inference making, and analysis, capacities distinct from the so-called lower-order skills such as memorization and recall. Since the students have to actively restructure the material, exchange points of view, receive new information, and refine their thinking, they gain a deep understanding of what they study.

Also, students involved in cooperative learning learn social skills that will help them in their later personal and professional life. As the Johnsons point out, while competition is a fact of human existence, cooperation is also an intrinsic part of every domain of human life—the home, office, and factory. All education is in essence a cooperative enterprise, in which the students and teachers agree—usually tacitly—to fulfill certain roles so that learning will take place.

One argument for the wider use of cooperative learning in American education is that the ability to cooperate and do group work is increasingly important in the business world. Recently, I took part as an instructor in a one-day team-building workshop in Hanover, New Hampshire, for managers and sales personnel from a major computer corporation. After a morning of trust-building and communication-skills exercises, the group was divided into five-person teams for an orienteering exercise. Each team member attended a mini-class on an aspect of orienteering. One person learned how to use a compass, another how to read a contour map, another how to gauge distances walking through the woods. Afterward, each shared what he or she had learned with the rest of the team. Then the team set off on a challenging orienteering course laid out in dense woods on the side of a mountain. Using their newly learned skills, the team had to locate five check points. It was a classic exercise in cooperative learning.

At the end of the day one of the managers said to me:

> Today in business the world is so demanding and complex, the resources stretched so thin, the competition is so strong, that it's impossible to be the "Lone Ranger" anymore. You can't do all that needs to be done on a job by yourself. You need to work together, to cooperate, to encourage and help each other. You need the synergy, the creation of a whole that is greater than the sum of the parts. Otherwise, you're not going to make it. That's why this cooperative work is so important. We've got to learn to work together.

Though zealous advocates of cooperative learning, the Johnson brothers do allow that competitive and individual learning also have a place in education. They remark that competitive learning creates anxiety and can actually lessen a student's learning ability. But it can be useful in certain situations. Competitive learning, they hold, should be used as a change of pace in a basically cooperative learning environment, but only after an atmosphere of trust and good feeling has been established in the class. For example, the teacher can pose questions about drill material—such as the multiplication table or historical dates—and individuals or groups can compete to be the first to answer. This competition should be carried out in a spirit of fun and friendliness. It should provide an opportunity for students to learn how to win and lose gracefully. According to the Johnsons, competitive work

should occupy about 10 percent of class time. The reality today is that between 80 and 93 percent of all learning that goes on in public schools is based on the model of the teacher presenting material to a group of competing and isolated individual students.

The Johnsons maintain that individualistic learning also should have a role in education, albeit a minor one. It is appropriate for simple, straightforward material and for material needed as a basis for future learning. Individualistic, isolated learning teaches self-pacing, self-responsibility, and self-evaluation. The Johnsons say that 20 percent of learning should be individualistic.

Cooperative learning is an important element in progressive and liberal schools and programs. It is much less important in religious and traditionally inclined schools, where it is more likely to be found in noncompetitive games on the playground than in the classroom. To most traditionally minded educators and parents, cooperative learning smacks too much of collectivism and socialism. They are likely to see it as something that undermines individual effort and a sense of personal responsibility. The director of a conservative, religiously oriented independent elementary school said to me:

> Cooperative learning is very big in the public schools in our area. Some parents come to me saying that their child is gifted and a fast learner and is being held back by always having to learn in a group with less able students. Others come saying that their child is being taught math by other students, not by the teacher, and is just not getting it. We have the children work together on plays and other projects but we teach them that learning in class is basically their own responsibility and based on their own effort.

FOR MORE INFORMATION

The International Association for the Study
   of Cooperative Education
Box 1582
Santa Cruz, CA 95061-1582
Tel.: (408) 426-7926
Fax: (408) 426-3360

This is a nonprofit organization dedicated to the
study and practice of cooperative education. It offers
individual/household and institutional memberships.
Member benefits include a subscription to *Cooperative Learning: The Magazine for Cooperation in Education.*

FOR FURTHER READING

Children's Creative Response to Conflict Staff. *The
Friendly Classroom for a Small Planet.* Philadelphia:
New Society Publishers, 1988. A practical manual for
creating an environment of cooperation in the classroom.

Dishon, O'Leary. A *Guidebook for Cooperative Learning: A Technique for Creating More Effective
Schools.* Holmes Beach, Fla.: Learning Publications, 1994. Meant for teachers and administrators, it also is useful for parents wanting to
understand the implications of cooperative
learning.

Johnson, David W., and Roger T. Johnson. *Learning
Together and Alone: Cooperative, Competitive, and
Individualistic Learning.* Needham Heights, Mass.:
Allyn and Bacon, 1994. One of the standard works
on cooperative learning, it provides both a theoretical explanation and a practical guide. It includes an excellent glossary of terms related to
cooperative learning.

Schoel, Jim, et al. *Islands of Healing.* New York: Project Adventure Company, 1988. Describes a variety
of group-initiative and problem-solving activities
that utilize the therapeutic potential of cooperative activity.

Sobel, Jeffrey. *Everybody Wins.* New York: Walker
Publications, 1984. A collection of cooperative
games, many designed for very young children.

7

The Social Curriculum

At one time, children in America were likely to arrive in school with basic good manners, the ability to control themselves, and a sense of how to resolve conflicts without resorting to verbal or physical violence. Parents took the time and energy to teach children how to behave, how to treat other people, and how to settle a disagreement. Today the situation is very different. Many children come to school well trained and able to behave in a socially acceptable way. But many children come without even knowing how to say "good morning," "please," or "thank you," without knowing how to share, and ready to start a fight at any moment. I don't know what it is, parents in part, television and movies in part. But it is not a matter of class. I get children from well-to-do families as well as children from families on welfare who are out of control.

This is the lament of one public elementary school teacher. It reflects a problem that pertains to many schools across the country and has led to the development and widespread use of the "social curriculum." The social curriculum is a series of teacher-directed classroom lessons and exercises through which children learn manners and commonly accepted standards of behavior that apply both in school and in other social situations. They learn how to control their emotions and behavior so that they can act in a socially constructive, accepted way. They also learn strategies and procedures for resolving conflict situations. Proponents of the social curriculum say that it helps children develop valuable life skills. They also hold that it creates the safe and orderly environment in the classroom that allows other learning to go on.

Many individual teachers and schools have developed a social curriculum for their own use. Elaborate and well-developed social curricula are also available from various publishers and educational foundations. One of these is "The Responsive Classroom" program developed by the Northeast Foundation for Children (NFC) in Greenfield, Massachusetts. The foundation is a teacher education and outreach organization that includes a consulting teachers division, a publishing division, and a laboratory/demonstration school. NFC presents the Responsive Classroom program in staff development workshops around the country. Many

> *The social curriculum is a series of teacher-directed classroom lessons and exercises through which children learn manners and commonly accepted standards of behavior.*

schools, including public schools in Washington, D.C., and in West Haven, Connecticut, use the program. Follow-up studies indicate that among children exposed to this social curriculum, social skills and conflict-resolution abilities increase and problem behavior decreases.

The Greenfield Center School

GREENFIELD, MASSACHUSETTS

The Greenfield Center School is NFC's laboratory/demonstration school and is a leading example of a school based on a developmental understanding of the child (see chapter 9). It is also a school where much time and trouble are taken to ensure that children learn to behave in a socially positive and constructive way. The Responsive Classroom social curriculum is an important part of school life. Its goals are to create an orderly classroom climate that is conducive to learning and to give children attitudes, social skills, and habits that will serve them well throughout their lives—social manners, self-control, self-esteem, cooperation, empathy, and the ability to resolve conflicts.

In the school office a saying from a Chinese philosopher is prominently displayed:

> I am kind to those who are kind
> And also to those who are unkind.
> Thus, there is an increase in kindness.

It is 8:15 AM on Wednesday and the children in the Prime Blues class are arriving one by one. As they enter the room, teacher Chris Pinney greets each by name. "Good morning, Raymond," she says. "Good morning, Ms. Pinney," comes the reply.

The children settle down, some on the car-

peted floor, some at tables, and, individually or in groups, begin working with math games and math puzzles. They chat quietly, and, except to get another game or puzzle, stay in their places.

After about twenty-five minutes, Pinney stands in the middle of the room and raises her right hand. In a few moments all the children have stopped their work, have become quiet, and are looking attentively at the teacher. "It's time for morning meeting," she says in a voice that is both soft and low. "So put your things away, please, and gather in the meeting area." The children quickly put puzzles, games, and workbooks in their appointed places and gather in a slightly irregular circle on the floor of the meeting area. As the children arrive Pinney sings a little song that begins: "I see Jackson, he's all ready. . . ." Above the meeting area is a poster that reads:

Rules for Morning Meeting
1. Just bring yourself—not anything else.
2. Stay in your own space.
3. Raise your hand to talk.
4. Keep your hand down when someone else is talking.
5. Look at the person talking and keep your body still.

A child who has been designated as the "Greeting Starter" rolls a ball across the carpet to another child saying, "Good morning, Miriam." "Good morning, Darius," Miriam replies, then rolls the ball on to another child, saying "Good morning, ———."

"Let's do boy-girl, boy-girl," a child suggests.

"Well, how many want to have it that the boys roll to a girl and vice versa?" asks Pinney. "And how many want to roll to anyone?"

The "roll-to-anyone" party wins and the morning round of greetings continues until everyone, including the visitor, has been greeted by name.

Pinney makes a few announcements about the schedule for the day, reminding the children that during "choice time" they can do the activity they want, but that there is a limit to the number of children who can be in each of the various areas: for example, reading or math games.

Several children then present objects they have brought from home. A girl named Sylvie shows the model horse her father gave her when she was sick. A boy interrupts her presentation and the teacher says softly, "Malcolm, you know you shouldn't interrupt. Go to time-out." Without a word, the boy leaves the circle and sits alone some distance away. The meeting ends with a song, and the children go to their activity of choice. Pinney explains:

> We spend the first six weeks of the school year teaching the children the procedures and rules of the classroom and what is acceptable and what is not acceptable behavior. I remind the children as necessary of what is acceptable and reinforce good behavior.
>
> We go over all the different areas of the room, what each one is for, what the materials are, how they should be used. We don't assume any knowledge or any established behavior patterns in the children. Everything is explained and the appropriate behavior modeled. We go through all the rules and the reasons for the rules. I stress the central rule of the school, which is "Treat others like you want to be treated." We go through the consequences for breaking a rule. If you interrupt, you go to time-out until you know you can come back without interrupting again.
>
> At the same time we go over basic manners and rules of interaction. Some chil-

dren come to school without basic social skills. They have to be taught how to say "good morning" and "thank you."

To some degree this is just classroom management, necessary to create a classroom environment where the children feel comfortable and safe and can learn. But it is more than that. It is teaching the children social skills, how to get along with other people and how to treat others with respect and compassion.

In the classroom of the Upper Primes, a second-grade class made up of children who are "developmental seven-year-olds," there is a wall poster titled "Solving Problems." It reads:

> If there is a problem, stop and talk.
>
> 1. Sit facing each other, with empty hands, apart from the others.
> 2. Take turns explaining your view of the situation.
> 3. Offer reasonable and related decisions until both people agree.
> 4. If you can't agree try again at the end of the day.
> 5. If you still can't agree bring it to a problem-solving meeting.

One of several staff members in the room explains:

> Early in the year we introduce the children to ways of resolving conflict. We do role-playing of situations that often arise in the classroom: one child being teased or bullied by another; two children wanting to use the same resource material at the same time; one child claiming that the other has taken something without permission.

There is a clear procedure for two children to follow when there is such a problem. We demonstrate and practice the procedure so that each child understands it and has experience with it. Then when a real problem arises we let the children work it out between themselves as much as possible. Children need practice in solving conflicts just as they need practice in doing their arithmetic.

If the children directly involved can't find a solution then it goes to a class problem-solving meeting, which has a very specific structure and agenda.

In her book *Teaching Children to Care: Classroom Management in the Responsive Classroom*, Ruth Charney, a teacher at the Greenfield Center School, describes the procedure for a class problem-solving meeting. The rules for such a meeting include:

All will attempt to solve the problem.
There will not be any put-down—physical or verbal.
All will listen to the person speaking and not interrupt.

The steps of the meeting are:

Introduce the problem and review the rules of the meeting.
Gather information about what people have observed and feel, not what their moral judgments are.
Begin discussion with the question, for example, "What do you need in order to stop picking on people?"
Propose solutions, using brainstorming to come up with various possible approaches to the problem.

Choose a solution that is workable, realistic, and within the school rules.
Choose a consequence if the solution is not abided by.
Close the meeting.

The problem-solving class meeting can be called to deal with a specific problem between two or more students, or it can deal with a problem involving the whole class, such as teasing, petty thievery, clique formation, chaos during transition times, or bullying.

The purpose of the meeting is not to attach blame to one party or another or to give the teacher a pulpit for expressing moral judgments. Rather, it gives the children a chance to develop listening and problem-solving skills, to express their thoughts and feelings openly and honestly, to think about moral and ethical issues, and to learn cooperation and respect for others.

Charney suggests other techniques for improving the behavior of individual students and of the class as a group. One of these is "clear positives." Rather than instituting negative rules—"Don't run in the halls," "Don't bully"—she lets the children decide on what positive behaviors they would like to cultivate. Rules emerge such as "We will all try to be orderly during changes from one activity to another," and "I will be more respectful and friendly to the girls in the class." These clear positives can be expressed in an oral or written contract.

The Responsive Classroom is just one of many social curricula in use across the country. Another is the "Social Competency Curriculum" distributed by "Reach Out to Schools," an organization in Wellesley, Massachusetts. Each week of the school year, a particular and difficult issue or situation that children are liable to confront is presented. For example, in one exercise the students are asked to imagine that they have seen another student do something wrong. They must then decide if they will remain silent or tell the teacher, that is, become a tattletale. The children role-play the situation, brainstorm for solutions to the dilemma, and discuss how they would behave. The teacher, who has received special training from Reach Out to Schools, primarily plays the role of facilitator.

"Children need practice in solving conflicts just as they need practice in doing their arithmetic."—social curriculum teacher

The Solomon Schechter Lower School, a Jewish day school in Newton, Massachusetts (see chapter 23), uses the "Social Competency" program. Principal Lucy Tannen remarks, "The program is excellent. It takes only about thirty minutes a week. But it gives the children a chance to experience, think about, and to discuss personal and social issues and situations that can be challenging and difficult."

Another typical social program is "Project Charlie," used in the New Haven public school system. It was developed by a Yale psychologist and introduced in 1990 by school officials dismayed by the high incidence of violence, dropping out, drug use, and pregnancy among the city's schoolchildren. The program teaches children how to reduce stress in their lives; to talk about, analyze, and control their feelings and impulses so that they are not controlled by them; and to foresee the consequences of different behaviors. They learn to control themselves in a conflict situation and to resolve conflicts without resorting to verbal or physical violence.

The children are taught specific techniques and strategies. When I visited the Lincoln-Bassett School (see chapter 13) I spent some time with a kindergarten class. At one point, the teacher asked the children what they do if they

start to get angry. Immediately, a thicket of hands flew up. "Count to ten very slowly," "Take ten deep breaths and blow out hard," "Run around the block," "Beat on a pillow," came the answers. Children learn that when there is a conflict, it is more constructive to start sentences with the word "I" rather than "You." "I" sentences—"I am very angry," for example—help a child know what he or she is thinking and feeling. "You" sentences—"You shouldn't have taken my pencil"—tend to be accusatory and to create more tension.

Project Charlie also teaches children to read the nonverbal physical messages others send. For example, the children are shown a picture of three girls laughing at another standing by herself. They are asked to describe how the lone girl, shoulders and head dropping and eyes filled with tears, feels.

The Project Charlie program gives children practical personal and social skills. It increases their emotional self-awareness and control, what is sometimes called "emotional intelligence," and their ability to act in a constructive, socially acceptable way. Involving about nineteen thousand students in the New Haven system, it has significantly reduced problem and violent behaviors in school and pregnancy among school-age girls.

Another important organization in the social curriculum movement is "Educators for Social Responsibility" (ESR), a private, nonprofit organization based in Cambridge, Massachusetts. ESR's main concerns are that teachers in many junior and senior public high schools spend most of their time maintaining classroom order and very little time teaching, that students do not respect their teachers, and that physical and verbal violence among students is part of school life, with the result that in many schools students are neither safe nor able to learn.

ESR's "Peaceable Classroom and School Program" is meant primarily for very difficult school situations. Teachers and administrators are trained to communicate in an open and caring way, to empathize with other people's points of view, to accept ethnic and cultural differences, to cooperate, and to settle conflicts on a "win-win" basis. Teachers and administrators receive special training to help students develop these same skills and capacities. The program has been widely and successfully used in the public schools of New York City and elsewhere.

Thus schools have many social curriculum programs to choose from. By and large, progressive and liberal educators have taken the lead in developing and disseminating these programs, especially those that feature conflict resolution techniques and exercises to increase self-control, self-esteem, and social sensitivity. Such programs are being used today in many progressively oriented public and private schools.

Religious and traditionalist educators have been less quick to adopt the school curriculum. For them it involves the appropriation by the school of a part of education that traditionally has been the domain of the family and the religious community. Conservative educators certainly require mannerly behavior, self-control, and a considerate, respectful attitude in the classroom. But they tend to assume that out-of-school training in the home and in the church, augmented by the skillful use of authority by the teacher, is sufficient to ensure an orderly, civilized school environment. Role-playing, special instruction in emotional and behavioral self-control, and conflict resolution exercises are not seen as legitimate parts of school life. Some religious schools, particularly those of more liberal groups

such as the Friends and non-Orthodox Jews, do have social curriculum programs. And conservative schools, dealing with more and more children who do not have stable home environments, may in time have to adopt some elements of the social curriculum.

Resources

For More Information

Northeast Foundation for Children
71 Montague City Road
Greenfield, MA 01301
Tel.: (800) 360-6332

Northeast Foundation for Children is an organization dedicated to the improvement of classroom teaching through professional development programs, summer workshops, long-term collaborations, and internships. It publishes a newsletter called _The Responsive Classroom_ and sells books and classroom materials relating to classroom management, conflict resolution, and developmental education.

Educators for Social Responsibility (ESR)
23 Garden Street
Cambridge, MA 02138
Tel.: (800) 370-2515
Fax: (617) 864-5164

ESR offers books, videos, curricula, and teacher and administrator trainings on conflict resolution, violence prevention, character education, diversity education, and social responsibility.

National Association for Mediation in Education
(NAME)
1726 M Street, NW, Suite 500
Washington, DC 20036-4502
Tel.: (202) 466-4764
Fax: (202) 466-4769

Founded out of a concern about the epidemic of violent and disruptive behavior in the nation's schools, NAME is a part of the National Institute for Dispute Resolution. It seeks to promote conflict resolution programs in schools and colleges. NAME offers various conflict resolution curricula, as well as videos, tapes, books, and articles about conflict resolution. It publishes a newsletter, *The Fourth R*, holds national conferences, and promotes networking at the national, state, and local level for educators and others interested in conflict resolution.

For Further Reading

Charney, Ruth S. *Teaching Children to Care: Management in the Responsive Classroom.* Greenfield, Mass.: Northeast Foundation for Children, 1995. A practical guide to creating an orderly, peaceful classroom in which children respect and care about each other and the teacher.

Faber, Adele, and Elaine Mazlish. *How to Talk So Kids Will Listen and Listen So Kids Will Talk.* New York: Avon Books, 1982. A step-by-step guide to meaningful communication with children that is based on mutual respect and encourages cooperation of children at home and at school.

Kreidler, William J. *Creative Conflict Resolution: Over Two Hundred Activities for Keeping Peace in the Classroom.* Glenview, Ill.: Scott Foresman and Co., 1984. Provides conflict resolution exercises that work in school as well as at home and in other situations.

————. *Conflict Resolution in the Middle School: A Curriculum and Teaching Guide.* Cambridge, Mass.: Educators for Social Responsibility, 1994. Helpful hints on how to work with a rambunctious age group.

Nelsen, Jane. *Positive Discipline.* New York: Ballantine, 1987. A practical, step-by-step guide for teachers and parents for establishing a discipline based on encouragement, kindness, and mutual respect.

Paley, Vivian Gussey. *You Can't Say You Can't Play.* Cambridge, Mass.: Harvard University Press, 1993. A kindergarten teacher's approach to eliminating "rejection" from the classroom.

Wichert, Susanne. *Keeping the Peace: Practicing Conflict Resolution with Preschoolers.* Philadelphia: New Society Publishers, 1990. A guide to teaching the essential skills of conflict resolution—careful listening, clear communication, empathy, understanding of consequences, and negotiation—to young children.

8

Multicultural Education

The majority of Americans are Caucasian, middle-class, speak English as their native language, and are descended from people who came to this country from western or eastern Europe of their free will. They belong to what can be called the dominant culture of the United States.

But many Americans do not belong to this group. They are not Caucasian; they are poor; they speak Spanish or another language as their native tongue; they or their ancestors came from Africa, or Asia, or South America. The ancestors of some (e.g., African-Americans) did not come voluntarily; those of others (i.e., Native Americans) were here long before the first European settlers arrived.

From its beginning, the public educational system was based on, taught, and promoted the Caucasian, mostly Protestant, largely male-oriented dominant culture. The study of history, literature, and science focused on the deeds and accomplishments of, as the barbed epithet goes, "dead white men." The teacher-centered, textbook-based, individualistic, and competitive model of education was founded on western European educational and cultural traditions. The beliefs and values inherent in the system were those of the mainstream culture. Thus early on, some outsider groups—such as Roman Catholics

and conservative German Lutherans—shunned the public schools and started their own.

With the birth of the civil rights movement in the late 1950s, the monoculturalism of public education in the United States was challenged. African-Americans and other minorities, such as Hispanics and Native Americans, began to assert the right of their children to receive a public school education that dealt with their own culture, history, heroes, literature, and traditions. They also asserted that Caucasian children as well should study minority cultures and history. Through this, children of the dominant culture would gain a more accurate and balanced view of American history and civilization and, as a result, would develop tolerant and respectful rather than condescending and discriminatory attitudes toward minorities.

Around the same time, the feminist movement challenged the dominance of men in American culture and the focus in school curricula on the accomplishments of men. And the gay and lesbian communities began to seek recognition, respect, and acceptance in mainstream society.

Since then "multiculturalism" has become a major element in American education. Almost all public and private schools, including those predominantly or exclusively Caucasian, have curricula that are to some degree multicultural. Virtually all American schoolchildren spend some time studying the role and the experience of African-Americans, Native Americans, and Hispanics in American history. They read poetry and fiction by minority and woman writers. They learn about contemporary culture in Africa and Mexico. Thus even in an all-white school in rural Vermont, students study the life of Martin Luther King and read poems by the freed-slave poet Phillis Wheatley. Children in an elementary school in a Boston suburb celebrate the Mexican "Halloween" to get an appreciation for Hispanic culture. Many high schools offer courses in women's literature, and in a regional high school in western Massachusetts, multiculturalism includes observance of a "Gay and Lesbian History Week."

These multicultural curricula and activities serve some of the intended purposes of multiculturalism. Minorities learn about and develop pride in their own history and in their past and present culture. Caucasian students acquire knowledge of and an appreciation for minority cultures. But for some proponents of multiculturalism this is not enough. They want to achieve more radical goals by more radical means. They want a basic transformation of society that will give minorities full participation in American life. To this end they propose a much more thoroughgoing multicultural education. They argue as follows:

The minorities in the United States do not enjoy the same resources and privileges as most Americans. They are economically, socially, and politically disadvantaged. One main reason is that African-Americans, Hispanics, Native Americans, "poor whites," and—to some degree—girls do not do well in American schools.

Advocates of multicultural education hold that minorities fail in school because of the system, not because of any inherent weakness of their own.

Almost half of all minority students drop out before they graduate from high school. Many of those who do graduate barely manage to do so. Only a small percentage go on to college and find lucrative jobs. As adults, most are unemployed or employed at low-paying jobs and remain part of the large and growing American underclass. The unspoken assumption of the dominant culture has been that this failure is due to the inherent inferiority of the minority groups. The children are not smart enough, it is felt, and not motivated enough to do well in school and go on to do well in life.

Advocates of multicultural education, such as Sonia Nieto, author of *Affirming Diversity: The Sociopolitical Context of Multicultural Education*, hold that minorities fail in school because of the system, not because of any inherent weaknesses of their own. She, with others, asserts that nearly every aspect of the mainstream public school system puts minority children at a disadvantage. These include:

- the large, impersonal public school bureaucracy that disenfranchises and alienates parents and local communities
- school buildings that are depressing, large, and usually run-down prisonlike fortresses
- tracking programs that classify minority children by scores on standardized tests or by subjective evaluations as slow learners, and that put them, often for their whole school careers, in remedial programs
- a "chalk-and-talk" style of pedagogy that makes students passive recipients of information, emphasizes rote learning, and produces promising candidates for the social and economic underclass

- a language for instruction and examination that for many children is not their native language, and that for others is a type of English different from what they speak at home
- a learning approach that is predominantly individualistic and competitive and hence largely an expression of Caucasian, male culture
- Caucasian teachers who, consciously or unconsciously, act in a discriminatory way; who, for example, look at and call on Caucasian students more than minority students; who have lower expectations for students of color; or who assume girls to be less gifted in science and math than boys
- a curriculum that, although it may contain a course or two on African-American history or Hispanic culture, is still based on Caucasian European and American culture and on what dead, Caucasian men have done, written, and said

According to this point of view, schools must be completely reorganized and redesigned so that minority children have an equal opportunity to become full participants in American society. Schools must meet the needs of minority students and help them succeed. The aim of education is to prepare all students equally for full participation in a pluralistic society.

Escuela Fratney (The Fratney School)
Milwaukee, Wisconsin

Escuela Fratney is a school that is thoroughly multicultural. It is located in an integrated, poor, working-class neighborhood in Milwaukee. Some years ago, the century-old building that Escuela Fratney now occupies housed a traditional public school that was to be closed. Local parents, activist teachers, and community leaders convinced city officials to let them use the building for a school that would meet the needs of the community's children. Escuela Fratney was born. Today it is an ethnically diverse school with about three hundred children in thirteen classes from kindergarten through the fifth grade.

Escuela Fratney is a site-based school. It is run by a management council consisting of the principal, nine teachers, five parents, one community representative, and one school staff representative. The council solicits suggestions and ideas about school matters from the entire community and reaches decisions by consensus. Fratney is funded by the city of Milwaukee as a public school but is virtually autonomous.

The whole language approach is used. Children learn to read using real books that are interesting and relevant to their lives. They learn to write using "process writing," which emphasizes free expression of thoughts and feelings. The school is bilingual. Students use English and Spanish equally, spending two weeks using one language in class and then two weeks using the other.

The curriculum focuses on four themes relevant to the children's lives: "We Respect the World and Ourselves," "We Can Make a Difference," "We Share Messages and We Communicate," and "We Share the Stories of the World." In working with these themes, children do research on their neighborhood and local community, write about their own lives and experiences, study and become involved in social and environmental issues, study the written and oral literature of many different countries, practice conflict resolution, and engage in other projects. Cooperative learning, which girls and children of color generally find more agreeable than competitive learning, is emphasized.

There is no tracking or ability grouping. All students do the same work. Slower students receive extra instruction to help them keep up. The only standardized tests used are those mandated by the state. The children are assessed by various types of products: artwork, compositions, class presentations. Pen-and-pencil tests do not play a major role.

The teaching staff is heterogeneous and bilingual and includes many teachers from the surrounding community. Teachers guide and facilitate the children's learning. They try to encourage all students equally and to avoid language and behaviors that support racial and gender stereotypes.

According to Bob Peterson, one of the founding teachers at Escuela Fratney, "There has been no study of the children after they leave Fratney, but the anecdotal evidence is that they are doing very well, even in the local junior highs which are quite traditional public schools."

Multicultural education as embodied at Fratney is basically progressive education tailored for a largely minority and bilingual community and student body. It includes all the classical progressive elements plus neoprogressive addenda such as whole language, cooperative learning, and multiple assessment. In addition, it is bilingual and multicultural and actively tries to overcome racist and sexist attitudes and practices.

The Atrium School
WATERTOWN, MASSACHUSETTS

Advocates of multicultural education assert that it is for all children, not just for minority children. Caucasian children also suffer from the test-driven, teacher-centered education that dominates in the public schools. Caucasian girls are impeded by the sexism of teachers and of male students. For their own good, Caucasian boys and girls need to acquire an understanding and appreciation of minority cultures. They need to be able to communicate and to work with persons of other cultures; otherwise they will be disadvantaged in their professional and social lives. About 25 percent of all Americans are members of a minority group, and that percentage is growing. Moreover, the world economy is increasingly integrated. Caucasian Americans must be able to work with all kinds of people in this country and abroad.

Some predominantly Caucasian independent schools have taken multicultural education seriously. The Atrium School near Boston is one of these. It is a progressive school that serves an affluent, largely Caucasian area that includes Cambridge, Brookline, Watertown, and other neighboring communities.

The school curriculum is a rich multicultural one. Students study minority cultures in North America and cultures in other parts of the world. But the school is also strongly committed to creating a culturally diverse learning community and to teaching children how to get along with people who are different from themselves. In class, teachers create opportunities for each child's culture to be presented and appreciated. Children become aware of injustice in society and learn how it can be changed. They see that their own behavior, such as excluding certain children from games, can involve discrimination and injustice.

The founding philosophy of The Atrium School mandated that the school include children and families of many different backgrounds and continue to accept children by lottery. In

1988, the school established a "Diversity Committee." Active recruitment of minority students and financial assistance for needy families led to an increase in the percentage of children of color from 6 percent in 1991 to 17 percent in 1994.

Also, in the 1993-1994 school year the faculty, staff, trustees, and parents engaged in a one-year antiracism training program with two consultants. The participants examined their culture, their school, and their personal lives to understand the pervasiveness of racist and discriminatory attitudes, and developed curricular strategies to combat these attitudes in children.

Many Caucasian parents around the country are carrying on their own private multicultural educational programs. These are parents who could live in an all-Caucasian area, or who could send their children to a private school. Instead, however, they choose to live in an integrated area, sometimes in the inner city. And they choose to send their children to the local, public school, usually a school in which most of the children belong to minority groups. Sometimes the school is a magnet school, offering an arts-based program, an emergent curriculum, or other special program. But often it is just a typical public school with workbooks, ditto sheets, and the other paraphernalia of mainstream public education. In Burlington, Vermont, I met a Caucasian woman who, while she could afford to live in an affluent area, has chosen to live in a poor section of the city and to send her child to the neighborhood school. "We don't have to be here," she told me, "but this is the real world. I am doing my son a favor."

Resources

FOR MORE INFORMATION

National Coalition of Advocates for Students (NCAS)
100 Boylston Street, Suite 737
Boston, MA 02116-4610
Tel.: (617) 357-8507

This is an umbrella organization that has member organizations all over the country (its information packet includes a list of member organizations). NCAS advocates for African-American, Hispanic, Asian, Native American, and other minority children and families. It publishes a wide variety of periodicals and books and sponsors various projects. NCAS is also active with immigrant groups and in the movement for HIV/AIDS awareness and education. NCAS has a National Center for Immigrant Students, which publishes a newsletter called *New Voices*.

Escuela Fratney
3255 North Fratney Street
Milwaukee, WI 53212
Tel.: (414) 264-4840

The Fratney School is perhaps the pioneer and leading school in the application of multicultural principles in elementary education. Some of its teachers, with others from the Milwaukee area, publish the periodical *Rethinking Schools*. Its statement of purpose reads: "*Rethinking Schools* is a nonprofit, independent newspaper advocating reform of elementary and secondary public schools. Our emphasis is on urban schools and on issues of equity and social justice. We stress a grassroots perspective combining theory and practice and linking classroom issues to broader policy concerns. We are an activist publication and encourage teachers, parents, and students to become involved in building quality public schools for all children." To obtain a copy of this periodical, contact *Rethinking Schools*, 1001 East Keefe Avenue, Milwaukee, WI 53212, (414) 964-9646 (phone); (414) 964-7220 (fax).

Comer, James P., and Alvin Poussaint. *Raising Black Children*. New York: NAL-Dutton, 1992. This book deals with the special emotional, educational, and social problems facing African-American children and is helpful both for African-American parents and for teachers wanting to understand their students better.

Konner, Melvin. *Childhood: A Multicultural View*. New York: Little, Brown & Company, 1993. This book shows how children of various cultures experience the different stages of growing up and focuses on how parents and communities in different societies shape children in different ways.

National Coalition of Advocates for Students. *The Good Common School: Making the Vision Work for All Children*. Boston: National Coalition of Advocates for Students, 1991. This book presents a program to reform schools to make them more responsive to the needs of all children, and is a guide to advocacy-driven school reform.

———. *Barriers to Excellence: Our Children at Risk*. Boston: NCAS, 1991. This report, commissioned by NCAS, looks at the status of poor, minority, handicapped, and other at-risk children in the nation's schools. It recommends changes in local, state, and federal policy that will help keep these children from being left behind in the rush toward educational excellence.

Nieto, Sonia. *Affirming Diversity: The Sociopolitical Context of Multicultural Education*. New York: Longman, 1992. A major work setting forth the theory, practice, and justification of multicultural education.

Perry, Theresa, and James Fraser (eds.). *Freedom's Plow: Teaching in the Multicultural Classroom*. New York: Routledge, 1993. A collection of essays celebrating the cultural diversity of the United States and calling for a reflection of that diversity in the nation's classrooms.

9

Developmental Education

One belief that permeates mainstream American education is "younger is better," that is, the earlier a child learns how to read, write, do math, and use a computer the better. Thus preschoolers are drilled in phonics and kindergartners are introduced to computer keyboards. Parents mention with pride that their seven-year-old is reading at a fifth-grade level.

This emphasis on early and accelerated learning rests on the assumption that the process of learning, once begun, will continue at a constant rate. Hence the child who starts earliest will learn the most and will be the ultimate winner in the race to get into Harvard. There is also the implicit belief that the child is a miniature adult who can learn and do what an adult can learn and do.

The developmental approach in education is based on another understanding of the child and of learning. It holds that the child is not just a small version of an adult human being. Rather, the child is a unique being unfolding and developing according to a specific pattern and timetable. Just as a plant seed develops in stages from seed to seedling to young plant to mature flowering organism, a human being goes through discrete stages in developing from infant to toddler

The developmental approach holds that the child is a unique being unfolding and developing according to a specific pattern and timetable.

to school-age child to adolescent to adult. At each stage there are particular things that can and should be learned. And at each stage there are others for which the child is not yet ready. Forcing children to learn skills or activities for which they are unprepared can be harmful.

Arnold Gesell (1880–1961), an American psychologist and pediatrician, was a pioneer in studying the development of the infant and young child. Observing and filming infants and children in a controlled, laboratory environment and then following their later development, Gesell gathered an immense amount of data about how children grow and change.

Gesell concluded that there is an inherent pattern of development in children in each of four areas: motor skills; adaptive behavior; language skills; and personal and social skills. Gesell held that children must reach a certain level of maturation and must have developed the skills of one stage before they can move on to the next. He also pointed out that children mature at different rates. Chronological age and developmental age correlate, but only roughly.

Gesell formulated broad characterizations of children at the different developmental ages. For example, the average four-and-a-half-year-old has a short attention span, is inconsistent with his or her behavior, is prone to confrontations, and is concerned with the question What is real? The typical seven-year-old is quiet, thoughtful, moody, sometimes depressed, and a good listener who will take time with his or her work. And the typical nine-year-old has become an individual, is competitive and truthful, and can take personal responsibility.

While most children reach each stage of development at the normative age, some reach it earlier and some later. Developmentally, children can be either older or younger than they are chronologically. Rapid or slow maturation does not correlate to intelligence or academic ability. A child whose social skills are less developed than those of his or her peers may in fact be the brightest among them. Albert Einstein, for example, did not begin to speak until he was almost four.

The French-Swiss psychologist Jean Piaget (1896–1980) is another major figure in twentieth-century developmental psychology. Piaget's extensive research led him to believe that the mind of the child evolves through a series of clearly defined stages.

Piaget asserted that each infant develops according to an inherent, fixed, genetically determined pattern. There are four main stages. During the first two years of life the child is a being of sense and motion. During this "sensorimotor stage," infants explore and develop their innate reflex actions and their ability to move in and to explore their immediate environment. They become aware of themselves as a separate physical entity and learn that objects around them have a separate and permanent existence.

Between the ages of three and six children begin to think symbolically. They learn that

words can represent objects in the physical world and that these can be manipulated in speech just as the objects themselves can be manipulated in space. During this "pre-operational" stage, children are egocentric and live in the moment in the immediate visible environment. Their thought processes are intuitive rather than logical. They learn through actively exploring and discovering the world, and through play.

Between the ages of seven and eleven children are in what Piaget calls the period of "concrete operations." Now they begin to think in a logical manner. They can classify objects according to similarities and differences and begin to understand time and number. Socially, children are able to cooperate with others.

The period of "formal operations" begins around the age of twelve and extends into adulthood. The adolescent becomes capable of manipulating abstract ideas and of reasoning deductively—applying general truths to specific cases. Thinking becomes orderly and logical, and the young person can formulate and test hypotheses about why and how things happen in the world. Thus the developing child is constantly creating and re-creating his or her own model of reality and achieves mental growth by integrating simpler concepts into higher-level concepts at each stage.

Both Gesell's and Piaget's ideas have important implications for education. If, for example, as Gesell holds, social age, intellectual age, and chronological age do not correlate, children should not be put in classes only according to their age. A much more flexible approach, which groups children according to developmental stages and has children of several different birth years in the same group, is indicated. And if, as Piaget asserts, there is an organically determined timetable for the development of thought processes, what is taught must correlate to the developmental stage of the child. Repetition and reinforcement *can* make children learn a skill or grasp, at least in some respects, a concept for which they are not ready. But such forced teaching may harm the child's overall development and ability to learn.

Current research into the development of the brain seems to corroborate the ideas of these early developmental psychologists. Jane Healy, author of *Endangered Minds: Why Our Children Can't Think and What We Can Do about It*, has looked at the implications of recent brain research for education. She maintains that there is a specific age at which the typical child is ready—in terms of neurological and physical development—to learn to read, to do arithmetic on an abstract rather than a manipulative basis, and to do other intellectual tasks. However, the developing brain of a child is a malleable and highly adaptive organ. Thus children can learn to do certain things before they are optimally ready to do them. They can read at three, do mental math at four, and operate a computer at five. But in fact the young child has to jury-rig the neural connections to do this. The parts of the brain meant for these tasks are not yet operable. And when the child's brain is actually ready, the appropriate brain centers will not receive the stimulation they needed, and problems may result.

Healy observes that many children and adolescents today have lost the ability to concentrate, to think clearly, and to deal with concepts. She faults two factors. One is the electronic media, especially television and video games. Because of the speed and randomness of the sensory and cognitive stimulation they give, these in effect scramble the neural patterns of the growing

> *Advocates of developmental education believe that if types of learning are introduced before the child is ready for them, healthy and well-rounded development will be impeded.*

child's brain. The other factor is children's experience of premature, intense academics. According to Healy, the epidemic of learning disabilities, dyslexia, and attention deficit disorders is due largely to "superbaby" and other early childhood accelerated learning programs.

In mainstream public and private education the impulse for early learning and early mastery of skills has dominated and still dominates American education. Most parents do not question this impulse unless a child reacts negatively to academic pressure in the early grades. In fact, "school phobia" is an increasingly common phenomenon among America's young children.

But the developmental understanding of the child has not been without influence in the educational world. Piaget's work, highly regarded in academic circles, has influenced many educators, particularly those with a humanistic-progressive approach. In the 1920s and 1930s progressive schools began adopting developmental principles. Because of their desire to put the child at the center of the educational process, progressive educators did and still do readily accept the developmental approach. Thus many progressively oriented schools today utilize developmental principles, particularly in their younger grades. In addition, two of the important alternative school systems—Montessori (see chapter 25) and Waldorf (see chapter 32)—are based on developmental approaches. Maria Montessori and Rudolf Steiner (the founder of Waldorf Education) were both active before Gesell and Piaget—Montessori in fact influenced Piaget's work. Each used a developmental understanding of the child as the basis of their educational theory and practice.

The Greenfield Center School

The Greenfield Center School is a laboratory/demonstration school that is part of the Northeast Foundation for Children (see chapter 7). The school's outreach literature explicitly acknowledges that the curriculum and pedagogy are based on a developmental understanding of the child.

The school was started in 1982 by a small group of public school teachers who were frustrated with what they had experienced in the public schools. They did not believe, as one later expressed it, "that five-year-olds should be exposed to the abstract reality of letters in order to learn how to read, that six-year-olds should have to fill out an arithmetic workbook, or that ten-year-olds, who live primarily in their immediate time and place, should have to study the United States government."

The school founders organized the school and its curriculum around the ideas of Gesell, Piaget, and other developmental thinkers. The teachers acknowledged that while these theorists differ in particulars, they share several underlying principles:

1. Children mature through certain predictable stages.
2. Growth is a function of structure—the child's genetic and biological structure, and that of the environment.
3. Children go through these stages in the same order but not at the same speed.
4. There is little relationship between development and intelligence.
5. Growth occurs in spurts. There is no straight line of development. There are alternating periods of equilibrium and disequilibrium.

This developmental approach manifests in the school in many ways. Children are grouped according to their developmental age rather than their chronological age or their academic skills. The child's levels of physical, social, language, and behavioral development are all taken into consideration. Thus the classes are mixed in terms of chronological age. A "lower prime" class has children who are from seven to nine years old. An "upper prime" class has children between eight and eleven.

For each class, the layout of the classroom, the curriculum, the teaching methods used, the expectations of the teacher, the activities, and the educational materials are appropriate to the developmental stage of the children. Thus, in the lower prime class, for example, children learn to read and write but through the practical use of language, and each child learns at his or her own pace. Children learn math by using manipulatives (objects such as shells or stones that are handled), games, puzzles and blocks, and through play activities such as cooking and shopping. Time is set aside for exploring the environment, for experimenting, doing puzzles, and solving problems. Children build large structures of wooden blocks and then take them down block by block. Much of the learning is individual. There are no handwriting drills, workbook exercises, or textbook exercises for the younger children. As teacher Susan O'Reilly McRae explains:

> The curriculum reflects the stages of development and the natural interests of the children. Five-year-olds are eager to explore and learn about the home environment through concrete experiences. The

six-year-old is more able to go out into the larger community to explore stores, farms, and the features of the natural environment. The seven-year-old is able to look at the broader systems in the community, how they provide the necessities of life, water, food, etc. By the time they are ten or eleven and in grade four the children are drawn to faraway places and times long ago. In grades five and six they want to know about practical occupations, what people do, what they themselves can do, and about human history. So, for example, we study and visit the textile mills in Lawrence, Massachusetts. In grades seven and eight the children want a global view, a broad perspective, so we use the study of the rain forest of South America as a take-off point.

One upper prime class was studying water when I visited the school. Some children were constructing a water reservoir on a sand table. Others were trying to figure out, using the bills from the town water office, how many gallons the school uses daily. Others were exploring the school plumbing system. They wound up in the school office, taking turns going down through a trap door into a crawl space to inspect the school's pipes. Other children were doing research on water striders, whirligig beetles, and other aquatic insects.

The Greenfield Center School has many elements of a typical progressive school. The classrooms are open, that is, the children sit in clusters rather than in straight rows and are free to move around and to leave the room; most of the learning is experiential and student directed rather than abstract and coming from the teacher; the teacher functions primarily as a guide and facilitator for learning; and the curriculum is theme based rather than comprehensive. But underlying all these elements is the recognition that children at each developmental stage have specific needs in terms of learning and environment; that the school should meet these needs; and that the school should allow its children to develop at their own pace without being rushed.

The Greenfield Center School is a laboratory school. Teachers there are constantly engaged in research, observing the children, testing their theories against the realities of the classroom, and refining theory and practice. The school is also a demonstration school. Visitors and observers are welcome. The school's parent organization, the Northeast Foundation for Children, trains teachers to implement the ideas and practices used at the school. It offers one-day and one-week workshops, visits, and internships at the Greenfield Center School, as well as long-term collaborations with schools and school districts. Currently, the Washington, D.C., Early Childhood Program, the Baltimore, Maryland, Early Childhood Program, and the public schools of West Haven, Connecticut, are among the Foundation's clients.

Resources

FOR MORE INFORMATION

> Northeast Foundation for Children
> 71 Montague City Road
> Greenfield, MA 01301
> Tel.: (800) 360-6332

The Foundation promotes a developmental approach to education. It has a Resource Materials Division, which provides resources to help teachers develop their professional skills. These include a semiannual newsletter, books, audiotapes, and videotapes.

Society for Developmental Education
Route 202, Box 577
Peterboro, NH 03458
Tel.: (603) 924-9621

The Society—whose motto is "Childhood should be a journey, not a race"—promotes developmental education and the multi-age classroom. It offers workshops and customized training programs, which, while meant primarily for teachers, can be useful for parents as well. The Society sponsors an annual national conference on "Multi-Age Continuous Progress Practices." Its Crystal Springs Books catalogue makes available books, videos, and educational materials, also meant primarily for professional educators, but also perhaps of interest to parents. Information about memberships in the National Alliance of Multi-Age Educators is available through the Society. The Society's basic information packet, available on request, includes an extensive bibliography on developmental education.

Gesell Foundation
310 Prospect Street
New Haven, CT 06511
Tel.: (203) 777-3481
Fax: (203) 776-5001

Based on the work of Arnold Gesell, this foundation has been promoting developmental education since 1918. It conducts "developmental observation assessment workshops" to help teachers, counselors, administrators, and other professionals involved with children to understand and meet developmental needs. It sells books for parents and teachers interested in learning about the typical behavior of children from birth to sixteen years of age. It also provides psychological and developmental evaluations of individual children.

The Bank Street College of Education
610 West 12 Street
New York, NY 10025
Tel.: (212) 875-4400

This is a teacher education and staff development center using a developmental approach similar to that of the Greenfield Center School.

Pathfinder
11011 Tyler Foote Road
Nevada City, CA 95959-9309
Tel.: (916) 292-1000; (800) 200-1107

Pathfinder is an organization working with children and families. Its directors are Sambhava and Josette Luvmour. The Luvmours have developed an innovative developmental approach to child rearing and education called "Natural Learning Rhythms." The Luvmours have used insights about human development from Piaget, Gesell, Steiner, and other developmental thinkers to formulate their own expression of the developmental stages in the child and adolescent. They have focused on what the child needs at each stage of development, not only from teachers but from parents, as well as from the larger environment. The Luvmours emphasize the importance of the family as a healthy, communicating unit in the healthy development of the child and adolescent.

For Further Reading

Elkind, David. *The Hurried Child.* New York: Alfred A. Knopf, 1984. Citing evidence of short- and long-term ill effects, Elkind, a professor of child development at Tufts University, argues against early and accelerated academics and argues in favor of letting children grow up slowly.

Gesell, Arnold. *The First Five Years of Life: The Child from Five to Ten.* New York: Harper and Row, 1993. Gesell, who observed thousands of children at all ages in clinical studies, describes the characteristics of the various stages of development of the infant and the young child.

Healy, Jane. *Endangered Minds: Why Our Children Can't Think and What We Can Do about It.* New York: Simon and Schuster, 1990. An excellent survey of recent brain research, which also makes practical suggestions for bringing up and for educating children. Healy presents convincing arguments against premature intellectual education and against excessive exposure to television and other electronic media.

Luvmour, Sambhava, and Josette Luvmour. *Natural Learning Rhythms: How and When Children Learn.*

Berkeley: Celestial Arts, 1993. An exposition of the developmental stages of children and how their needs at each stage can be met.

Northeast Foundation for Children Staff. _A Notebook for Teachers: Making Changes in the Elementary Curriculum._ Greenfield, Mass.: Northeast Foundation for Children, 1993. A practical guidebook for teachers, but also helpful for parents. It discusses the developmental stages of children and what at each stage they should be doing and learning. Lots of helpful pictures and charts.

Pearce, Joseph Chilton. _Magical Child._ New York: Dutton, 1976. Pearce brings together brain research, education, and his own spiritually informed understanding of the nature and destiny of the human being. He argues strongly not to rush children into adulthood. His _Magical Child Matures_ (New York: Dutton, 1984) is a sequel.

Piaget, Jean. _The Grasp of Consciousness._ Cambridge, Mass.: Harvard University Press, 1975. One of the many books in which Piaget describes the development of the infant and young child. Not easy reading, and the neophyte might do well with a secondary source.

Pulaski, Mary. _Understanding Piaget._ New York: Harper and Row, 1971. An accessible introduction to Piaget's views on child development.

Wood, Chip. _Yardsticks: Children in the Classroom, Ages 4–12._ Greenfield, Mass.: Northeast Foundation for Children, 1994. A guide to what children should be doing and learning in the classroom in each grade level. Based on a developmental understanding of the child.

10

Education for Character

———ꞷ———

A primary goal of education in the United States, from its beginnings in colonial times through the early decades of this century, was the moral training of children. Thomas Jefferson said that the main task of public education was "the cultivation of virtue." Early public schools aimed to teach moral principles and to promote moral behavior. Truthfulness, honesty, self-discipline, self-control, loyalty, courage, perseverance, compassion, and consideration were explicitly and implicitly taught and promoted. In private and religious schools before and after the establishment of the public school system, moral education played an important role. And for much of its history, the public school system also included rudimentary, nondenominational moral instruction. The McGuffey readers, used by generations of public school children, were designed to promote moral and socially responsible behavior.

In recent decades, moral education, particularly in the public system, has fallen on hard times. Moral relativism and cultural pluralism have combined to drive the teaching of moral principles and behavior out of the schools. Critics of moral education contend that teaching a particular moral code or

Critics claim that a value-neutral approach to morality in the school has contributed to the moral decline of American young people.

———ꞷ———

value system violates the relativity of morals and values. What is right for one person may not be right for another. Educational theorists warn against the dangers of a particular religious or ideological group establishing a "moralistic hegemony" and then presenting its code of morality as standard and universal.

Thus in recent decades the belief-neutral and values-neutral principle reigning in public education has been applied to questions of morality and behavior. Public schools do not teach that there are absolute standards of right and wrong, although there are some universal ground rules. Children are discouraged from lying, cheating, stealing, or behaving in a disruptive manner. Many schools teach children basic manners, strategies for controlling their emotions and behavior, and principles of conflict resolution. Many schools also help children to clarify their own moral principles and values. But rather than indoctrinate children with standards of right and wrong behavior, teachers affirm a student's self-chosen values in an open and nonjudgmental environment. The "different strokes for different folks" principle dominates. Children are encouraged to exchange opinions, explore their feelings, and determine what behaviors they are comfortable with. They are taught to recognize and to tolerate all values and moral frameworks.

While such an approach may be interesting and helpful to the student, it is not moral education. Moral education seeks to help the child develop a clear inner sense of what is right and what is wrong—a conscience—as well as the habit of behaving according to that inner moral sense.

Some educators and parents are not happy with the way most public schools handle the issue of morality. Mary Beth Klee, director of Crossroads Academy in Lyme, New Hampshire (see chapter 14), comments, "Comfort—one's own—has become the barometer of moral behavior. Tolerance for all patterns of behavior is advanced as a high value."

Critics such as Klee claim that this value-neutral approach to morality in the school has contributed to the moral decline of American young people. Forty years ago, rape, robbery, assault, drug abuse, and pregnancy were rare among young people. Now they are endemic. Every month, 525,000 attacks, robberies, and shakedowns occur in the nation's public schools. About 135,000 students carry guns to school. Two of every five fourteen-year-old girls will be pregnant by the time they are nineteen. Many young people seem to have lost a sense of morality. They feel free to have sex, get drunk, or commit a violent crime just because they have the desire to do so. The "just do it!" attitude, critics say, has permeated the younger generation.

Certainly various factors are operative here: broader social changes, the breakdown of the family, and the violence and antisocial behavior portrayed daily in the media. But, critics say, the absence of moral education in the public schools and the dominance there of an attitude of moral relativism have contributed to the present crisis.

Schools can and should teach moral principles and promote moral behavior.

This view is increasingly widely held and is one reason for the steady growth of religious schools in the country. Educators in religious schools say that the desire for moral education is a major reason that parents, both religious and nonreligious, send their children to religious schools.

Klee, a strong advocate of moral education, comments:

> There are indeed universal moral values that are not particular to a given religion or group. Not all values are equal. Honesty, responsibility, courage, diligence, generosity, self-discipline, and self-control help people lead fruitful lives and help society function well. Duplicity, irresponsibility, cowardice, sloth, self-indulgence, and selfishness lower the quality of our individual and collective lives. Tolerance of the unacceptable is not a virtue.
>
> We are not a religious or sectarian school, but at Crossroads moral education is a very important part of the program. "Smart is not enough!" We use literature as a primary means for developing character and teaching moral principles. Plato said that schools should provide students examples of good and heroic behavior in myths, epics, and tales. These exemplars will inspire young people to love the good, to do what is right and noble. In his 1993 book, *Why Johnny Can't Tell Right from Wrong: Moral Illiteracy and the Case for Character*, William Kirkpatrick makes a similar point. He observes that children act out in real life the dramas that are being played out in their imaginations. And what children see on television, in the movies, and in their video games is for the most

part violent, self-indulgent, and immoral. Kirkpatrick says that schools and parents need to consciously cultivate character through literature.

At Crossroads, we choose the books for the children, whether they are in the first grade or the eighth, very carefully. The children read the classics of children's literature and books that offer inspiring examples of behavior. We avoid literature and picture books that ask children to be grown-ups. There is a growing tendency in children's literature to expose very young children to very large moral and social problems. The intention, I believe, is to sensitize the children to injustice. But in fact the opposite often is the result. Such literature can engender despair and ultimately cynicism in the child. I refuse to ask our six-year-olds to deal with the bombing of Hiroshima—even if there is a striking picture-book presentation of that event designed especially for kindergartners.

Each month each class at Crossroads focuses on a particular virtue, such as honesty, compassion, courage, loyalty, or perseverance. Every class day begins with a moment of silence and the reading and discussion of a story which illustrates the virtue that is being highlighted. If you visit the second grade today, for example, they will be learning about perseverance. The teacher will read a picture-book story about a Cambodian girl who, despite being deaf, becomes a famous temple dancer, dancing out the tales of the gods.

"We work with the parents on this also," continues Klee. "We encourage them to reduce and monitor the children's time with television and video games. We encourage them to read appropriate books to and with the children. We are a private school," she adds,

> but public schools can and should do similar things to develop a strong moral sense in their students. Plato said that educators should help children to fall in love with the Good. Moral education is not finger wagging, pontificating, or reprimanding. It is calling children to the Good in an attractive way. And yes, you may do some finger wagging at some point, but for the most part schools that are proactive on virtue do not have to be reactive on conflict resolution.

This emphasis on moral education at Crossroads is evident at other schools stressing traditional curricula and values. It is a major element in Carden education (see chapter 11), for example. Mae Carden held that one of the main aims of education is the development of character—which includes honesty, stamina, enthusiasm for life, consideration for others, and determination. In Carden schools, exemplary and inspiring literature is used to help develop moral attitudes and behavior in children. These schools also provide clear and specific guidelines for behavior and for the observance of good manners. At Carden Memorial in Salt Lake City, for example, one of the guiding principles is that "manners are not optional."

The Hyde School
BATH, MAINE

The Hyde School is an independent, coeducational high school (grades eight to twelve) in which moral education, there termed "education for character," is the overriding concern. Hyde School was founded in 1966 by Joseph Gauld on the principle that character is the most important element in education and in life, and that if good character is developed everything else—including fulfillment of academic potential—will follow.

Hyde School has about 230 students, almost all of them boarding students, and is situated on a beautiful parklike former estate. The quiet, genteel setting belies the rigorous and demanding way of life that the students must adhere to.

All students get up at 6:00 AM. There is a daily room inspection, and each student has a job to do on campus every day. Students must carry a full academic load and play on an interscholastic athletic team each term. They must participate in a community service activity such as working in a day-care center or nursing home. There are periodic wilderness challenge trips. As part of the process of personal challenge, each year each student must audition in the performing arts before the entire school. For many this means singing a song, solo and a cappella.

A student guilty of a serious ethical violation, such as the use of an illegal substance, lying, cheating, or stealing, may be put on "two-four." For twenty-four hours the student is asked to reflect on what must change in his or her attitude and conduct. He or she gets up at 5:30 AM for a special physical workout and may spend the day doing work on the school grounds. The student eats alone and may talk only to other students in the dean's area.

The attitudinal and behavioral standards at Hyde School are clear and unequivocal: no lying, no stealing, no cheating, no drugs, no alcohol, no oral sex or sexual intercourse. Students take responsibility for their own behavior, and school life is based on a strict honor code that pertains

both in and out of the classroom. Students are expected to turn themselves in if they break a rule. If a student (Student A) knows that someone else (Student B) has broken a school rule, Student A must confront Student B and urge him or her to confess the infraction. If Student B does not do so, Student A must report the violation.

Admission to the school is not easy. It is based entirely on an interview of the prospective student and parents by an experienced teacher or administrator. Students are asked questions that require them to consider larger themes: Who am I? Where am I going with my life? How do I get there? The student is admitted only if he or she shows a strong commitment to a fundamental change in attitude and behavior.

Life for Hyde School parents is challenging as well. Parents cannot just leave their child at the school, go home, and hope that the school will fix what they have helped make askew. Parents must commit themselves to and participate in the Hyde School program. They must promise to examine their own feelings and purpose in life and do so in the context of their moral and spiritual values.

"We have discovered that the participation of the parents is absolutely necessary," says Assistant Headmaster Paul Hurd. "In some schools, particularly in the public schools, parent activity is marginalized. Here we bring parents in as learners and teachers as much as we can. If we can get the parents fully engaged, we can help almost any young person head in a positive, productive direction."

Parents must come to the school at least three times a year—regardless of how far away they live—for two Parents' Weekends and one Family Learning Center weekend. At these times parents spend time with their children, alone and in small and large groups, examining family relationships and working to improve them. Families may also experience the Hyde ropes course together, with the child holding the safety rope for parent and vice versa.

Parents also attend a monthly regional meeting to share their parenting experiences with other Hyde parents in their area. They try to understand how their family operates and how to improve family life. In their personal life and in the family life at home, parents are expected to apply the principles on which Hyde is founded and to work on their own character development.

The "character components" for which a Hyde student strives are displayed on the school emblem above the stage in the performing arts center and in many other places in the school:

Curiosity: I am a learner.
Courage: I learn the most about myself through challenges.
Concern: I need a supportive and challenging community in which to develop my character.
Leadership: I lead through asking the best of myself and of others.
Integrity: I am gifted with a unique potential, and conscience is my guide in continually uncovering this potential.

Also at the core of the Hyde approach are five principles:

Destiny: Each of us is gifted with a unique potential.
Humility: We believe in a power and a purpose beyond ourselves.
Conscience: We attain our best through character and conscience.
Truth: Truth is our primary guide.

Brother's Keeper: We help others to achieve their best.

The school puts a high value on sincere effort. A student's natural ability and talent in academics or sports is a given; it does not change. But his or her attitude can change, and if it does improve, real learning and character development will result. The grading system assesses effort and attitude as well as achievement.

Among the students at Hyde there is a broad range of backgrounds and life experience. Some students are well-adjusted, successful young people who have come to Hyde for a rigorous, college preparatory education. Many, however, have struggled with problems ranging from substance abuse to chronic underachievement. Those who come to address particular problems and stay to graduate do so because the Hyde program awakens in them their own strength of character and their potential to lead meaningful, productive lives.

The Hyde approach is radical, perhaps unique, but it seems to work for most of the students who come to the school. Some run away and don't come back. But for those who stay, or who run away but return, Hyde often changes their lives and the lives of their parents. Their stories are poignant and powerful.

My campus guide, a broad-shouldered senior boy, recalls, "I came here after my sophomore year. I had gotten in trouble with drugs and had to go to a rehabilitation center. Coming here really helped me get my life back on track. I learned that I had to be honest with myself and with other people. I learned too that I had to take responsibility for my life. It has also helped my family. It's ironic, but we're closer and we understand each other better than when I was living at home."

A senior girl recounts her story: "My parents were divorced and I was barely getting by in school. I came here and hated it at first and ran away. I lived with my boyfriend and did a lot of drugs. But something told me that I had to come back, that I needed something that I could get only here. I guess it was self-respect and self-confidence."

Even though character is greatly emphasized at Hyde, academic standards are high. The classes and discussion groups I sat in on could have taken place at any elite New England prep school. Virtually all Hyde graduates are accepted by and attend selective colleges.

The Hyde School provides inspiring testimony that young people, even if they have had a lot of difficulty, can, with a supportive environment and help from peers and adults, turn their lives around. Character—that internal hidden quality that manifests itself in moral, creative, and socially beneficial behavior—can be learned even in adolescence.

"The students who come here and make it," says Paul Hurd, "go through a process. At first they only go through the motions of behaving well, of acting in an honest and responsible manner. They don't have much choice. But gradually as the students find they can meet the challenges of life at Hyde, the qualities and the principles the school stands for are internalized. The students become internally directed. They take charge of their lives."

There may be other schools like Hyde but Hurd does not know of them. There are some wilderness and adventure schools, like Outward Bound, that do something similar but on a short-term basis, in courses that are several weeks or a month long.

The demand for this kind of education is great.

For the past several years Hyde has been overseeing a program in the New Haven public school system called the Hyde Leadership School. Hurd observes, "It's not easy to establish this kind of program in a public school situation. It requires a total commitment on the part of parents, students, and teachers. But there is a steady stream of inquiries from public school systems around the country. And we are just about to open a second campus in Woodstock, Connecticut."

Resources

For More Information

Character Education Partnership (CEP)
809 Franklin Street
Alexandria, VA
Tel.: (703) 739-9515
Fax: (703) 739-4967

The Character Education Partnership, founded in 1992, is a broad-based, nonpartisan, nonprofit coalition of individuals and organizations dedicated to developing civic virtue and moral character in the nation's youth as a way of creating a more compassionate and responsible society. CEP holds that character is an identifiable set of characteristics—including courtesy, compassion, honesty, loyalty, tolerance, respect for others, self-respect, and patriotism—that does not develop automatically. It must be taught, modeled, learned, and practiced. CEP recognizes that while teaching character is primarily the responsibility of families, schools as well as religious and community groups also should teach character. CEP sees character education as essential to overcoming the moral crisis of the nation.

CEP campaigns against sex and violence in the media and opposes values clarifications programs, and while it does not support prayer in schools, it does support teaching about religion in the public schools. Several public school systems—Los Angeles,

Baltimore, and St. Louis, among others, have adopted a character education program, and CEP promotes similar programs for public and private schools.

On request CEP will send an information packet that includes an introduction to character education, an extensive bibliography listing books, articles, journals, magazines, and newsletters dealing with character education, and a list of organizations that promote character education.

School of Ethical Education
1000 Lafayette Blvd.
Bridgeport, CT 06604
Tel.: (203) 330-5052
email: Ethics@wisy.com

An organization founded in 1995 dedicated to promoting character education and to helping schools have effective character education programs.

Center for the Advancement of Ethics
 and Character
Boston University
School of Education
605 Commonwealth Avenue
Boston, MA 02215
Tel.: (617) 353-3262
Fax: (617) 353-3924

Founded in 1989, the Center's mission is to promote character education in the nation's elementary and secondary schools. Its approach emphasizes the curriculum as the primary vehicle for transmitting moral values to the young. The Center sees the school as a social environment where students can gain the enduring habits that make up strong character. It publishes the newsletter *Character*, helps keep parents and school personnel informed through its "Character Education Network," and provides services to school districts, universities, and other agencies.

Crossroads Academy
13 Dartmouth College Highway
Lyme, NH 03766
Tel.: (603) 795-3111

Crossroads Academy is an independent school that uses the Core Knowledge curriculum (see chapter 14). It is also strongly committed to character education. School director Mary Beth Klee and associates have developed a character education curriculum that is available to public and independent schools.

The Hyde School
66 High Street
Bath, ME 04530
Tel.: (207) 443-5584

The Hyde School in Bath, Maine, is a pioneer in education for character. It also has a campus in Woodstock, Connecticut.

Eagle Rock School and Professional
 Development Center
P.O. Box 1770
2750 Notaiah Road
Estes Park, CO 80517
Tel.: (970) 586-0600
Fax: (970) 586-4805

Eagle Rock School is a residential, independent secondary school for students "not experiencing success" in mainstream school situations. It uses a student-centered curriculum and pedagogy and has a strong character education program similar to that used at the Hyde School.

Outward Bound National Office
Route 9D-R2, Box 280
Garrison, NY 10524
Tel.: (800) 243-2141

The Outward Bound movement began in England after the Second World War and came to the United States in the early 1960s. Outward Bound courses use wilderness environments to help students develop certain character traits, including commitment, cooperation, a positive approach to physical and mental challenges, honesty, and generosity. The standard Outward Bound course is about four weeks. There are five Outward Bound schools in North America. They offer courses ranging from eight days to three months in length and in a variety of natural environments.

Sterling College
Craftsbury Common, VT
(802) 586-7711

Sterling College offers a two-year post–high school program combining outdoor adventure education; instruction and work in farming, animal husbandry, and forestry; and academic study.

FOR FURTHER READING

Bennett, William (ed.). *The Book of Virtues: A Treasury of Great Moral Stories.* New York: Simon and Schuster, 1993. Stories taken from many cultures portraying virtuous and heroic behavior.

Gauld, Joseph. *Character First: The Hyde School Difference.* San Francisco: Institute for Contemporary Studies, 1993. A description of the theory and practice of "education for character" by the founder of the Hyde School.

Kirkpatrick, William. *Why Johnny Can't Tell Right from Wrong.* New York: Simon and Schuster, 1992. A telling indictment of values-neutral education, of values clarification programs in the public schools, and of the schools' failure to help children develop moral standards and habits of moral behavior.

Kirkpatrick, William, Gregory Wolfe, and Suzanne Wolfe. *Books That Build Character: A Guide to Teaching Your Child Moral Values.* New York: Touchstone, 1994. An excellent practical guide and bibliography for character and moral education.

Kirschenbaum, Howard. *One Hundred Ways to Enhance Values and Morality in Schools and Youth Settings.* Needham Heights, Mass.: Allyn and Bacon, 1995. These one hundred ways also can be applied at home.

Lickona, Thomas. *Raising Good Children.* New York: Bantam Books, 1983. A helpful guide for developing character and habits of morality in children.

———. *Education for Character: How Our Schools Can Teach Respect and Responsibility.* New York: Bantam Books, 1991.

Minor, Joseph. *Outward Bound USA: Learning through Experience in an Adventure-Based Education.* New York: William Morrow and Company, 1981. An excellent recounting of the philosophy and origins of the Outward Bound movement and its establishment in North America.

Unell, Barbara C., and Jerry L. Wyckoff. *Twenty Teachable Virtues: Practical Ways to Pass on Lessons of Virtue and Character to Your Children.* New York: Perigee Books/Berkeley Publishing Group, 1995.

III

A GUIDE TO ALTERNATIVES
IN EDUCATION

11

Carden Schools

Mae Carden (1894–1977) was one of the outstanding educators in twentieth-century America. She developed an effective method for teaching reading, as well as a comprehensive elementary school curriculum that gives the child the basis for a broad liberal arts education. About eighty schools in the United States use the Carden method and curriculum today and do so with great success. But Miss Carden and her work remain a well-kept secret of American education. Even many experts have not heard of her, or if they have, know little of her educational methods. This is unfortunate, since the Carden reading methods and curriculum, and the schools that use them, comprise an important potential resource for American education.

Miss Carden was born in Hawaii into a wealthy family and received her early education in public schools there. She attended Vassar College and received her Bachelor of Arts degree in 1918. She then lived for several years in France and Italy, deepening her knowledge of art, music, and literature, and becoming fluent in French and Italian. Inspired by the great art museums and concert halls of Europe, she returned to the United States wanting to teach American children to appreciate classical art and music, but found that their reading and thinking skills did not allow

them to learn what she had to teach. Miss Carden enrolled for postgraduate work at Teachers College, Columbia University, and received her master's degree in 1927.

At that time, Columbia was the center of Deweyan progressive education, and Miss Carden found herself disagreeing with her professors. She later recalled, "I found that what they were saying about children and how they learn just didn't coincide with my experience of children and of teaching." Convinced that progressive methods were "child-chasing—running after the child as he does what he wants"—Miss Carden rejected them and resolved to develop her own educational technique.

Miss Carden was for a time head of the music department at the Ann Reno Normal School in New York City. Between 1929 and 1934 she was head teacher of the Whytehill School in New York. Then, in 1934, using her own money, she established "Miss Carden's School for Young Children" in New York City, which she ran as a laboratory school until 1949. During this time, she developed a distinctive method of teaching reading and spelling based on phonetics. She also wrote student readers and teachers' manuals for all the elementary grades and trained the teachers in her school in her pedagogical method. In this period too she developed a comprehensive, sequential curriculum for the elementary grades, which covered the usual subjects but in an integrated way. It stressed both mastery of content and the development of analytical thinking and problem-solving skills. The curriculum also was rich in art and music appreciation, artistic and musical activities, and drama.

At that time the dominant method for teaching reading was the "sight-recognition" or "look-say" method. With this approach, children are taught to recognize words by sight as whole words and to use clues and context to guess at words. Phonetic analysis and decoding of words play a minor role. Many children were not learning to read with this approach. Miss Carden found that with her method—based on phonetics but employing other elements as well—she could teach virtually every child to read (and not only with comprehension but with enjoyment), spell, and express him- or herself in writing and in speech, clearly and correctly. "Every child wants to learn," she said. "Every child is able to learn, some fast, some slow. There may be delay but there is not defeat. . . . If the child fails to learn, it is because the teacher has failed to teach."

As word of her method and its success spread, Miss Carden began to receive requests for help from school officials and teachers, mostly in nearby public school districts. In 1949 she closed her school, founded Mae Carden, Inc., and dedicated herself to disseminating her teaching methods. By 1960, ninety school districts in New York and New Jersey had adopted the Carden method. In that year Sibyl Terman and Charles Walcutt published a book called _Reading: Chaos and Cure_. In it, they termed Miss Carden a "ge-

> _"Every child wants to learn. If the child fails to learn, it is because the teacher has failed to teach."_
> —Mae Carden

nius" and praised her reading method, curriculum, and view of elementary and junior high school education. Miss Carden's work thus received national attention. Responding to requests from all over the country, she began to travel widely, lecturing to the public and giving training courses for teachers.

With the Carden reading method, children in kindergarten start to learn the consonants and vowels and the sounds associated with them. They also learn the various rules by which the sounds of vowels and consonants change. They acquire the ability to sound out almost any word by themselves. Miss Carden held that by age seven almost every child is capable of applying the rules of phonetics to analyze and sound out words and to read and comprehend sentences. In schools using the Carden method, children are reading the original _Peter Rabbit_ by Beatrix Potter by the middle of the first grade.

In Carden schools, a child also develops the ability to form a mental image of the word. The Carden readers do not contain pictures. Thus a child is expected to form a picture in the mind's eye of the meaning of each word and of each sentence and be able to describe that picture. The teacher works with children individually and in small groups, asking questions and making sure that each child is creating an accurate inner picture of what is being read. The text-only readers also give the children an opportunity to create their own illustrations for the stories.

Children also learn that there is a rhythmic grouping of words in a sentence. Thus when they read aloud a sentence such as "In the last days of Rome, there was a shortage of food," they read it with the words "In the last days of Rome" forming something like a musical phrase. Miss Carden emphasized that this rhythmic phrasing of sentences is essential to reading comprehension.

In the Carden method, grammar is used as a tool of comprehension. The children learn to analyze sentences. They learn to pick out the key word—the word that most carries the meaning of the sentence—and to emphasize it in reading and speaking. For example, in the sentence "Jack made a cake," "cake" is the key word. They also learn to identify the parts of speech, for example, the "who-word," the "what-word," and the "when-word."

Also as part of the Carden method, children learn to summarize sentences, paragraphs, and chapters and to give a title to groups of sentences. They thus learn to comprehend the meaning of the text and to express it in their own way.

Miss Carden was not interested only in teaching reading. She had a clear idea of the larger aim of education. She wanted children to become well-informed, cultured individuals who enjoy learning and life and who, as she said, "live triumphantly." She also felt that "the basic purpose of the school [is] to awaken in each student the desire to learn and to equip him with a solid foundation of learning skills and basic knowledge which will enable him to reach logical conclusions and to proceed with confidence through a lifetime of learning."

Miss Carden also held that a child's character formation is a primary goal of education. She believed that self-confidence and self-reliance can be developed in a child by careful teaching of key subjects. In 1946, she wrote:

> The purpose of the Carden Method is to develop well-adjusted, capable, confident, eager, alert, courageous, generous, just, compassionate, courteous, happy children, who have a sense of humor, who will be able to develop their ingenuity, who base their actions on the idea that we come to life to make a contribution to the welfare of the human race; children who realize that happiness is a by-product of doing for others; children who realize that the goal of living is not the amassing of money or possessions, but the attainment of the desires of the heart.

Reluctant to have her work compromised, Miss Carden shared her methods with and sold her books only to people she felt were devoted to applying her methods in a consequential manner. She found many such educators. Many private schools, most of them in Florida, Texas, and California and other western states, adopted the Carden method. A number of independent schools were founded specifically as Carden schools. Today, about eighty schools use the Carden approach.

Carden Memorial School

Salt Lake City, Utah

The Carden Memorial School was founded in 1969 by Anna Lou Jeffs and is run today by Jeffs and her husband Donald. Anna Lou Jeffs recalls, "At first, I was an active opponent of the Carden Method. Then I went to hear Miss Carden speak and I was converted. But you really had to convince her that you were serious about using her approach. You just about had to beg her to sell you the books." Today Carden Memorial is a thriving school with almost four hundred children from preschool to grade eight. It uses the Carden reading method and the comprehensive Carden curriculum.

The school is organized in "forms" rather than classes. The forms are based on level of academic skill rather than on age. Within each form the children are grouped again according to their skill level, usually into three groups. In a typical class period the teacher will spend time with each group while the other children are working on their own. This makes an intense interaction possible between the teacher and each student. The Carden pedagogy, especially in the language arts, is largely based on the teacher questioning the students, helping them discover what they know, and helping them express their knowledge and ideas clearly and precisely. Teachers also work with the class as a whole.

Reading and other language skills are a major focus. Anna Lou Jeffs remarks:

> The children in effect have two English classes a day, one for reading, writing, vocabulary, and spelling, and one for literature. From the early grades we read the classics of children's literature—*Bambi*, the Beatrix Potter books, the Thornton Burgess books, *Black Beauty* by Anna Sewell and the like. Older students read the King James Bible and authors like Robert Louis Stevenson, Mark Twain, and Shakespeare. By the eighth grade they are firmly grounded in the treasures of Western literature and have a rich vocabulary. Miss Carden said that an eighth-grader should have a vocabulary of about twenty thousand words.
>
> The children read a lot of poetry and memorize poems and excerpts from plays and books. They learn to speak with proper diction and enunciation. Miss Carden often said that the English language, spoken properly, is the most beautiful of languages.
>
> We read the classics not just because they are great literature, but because they help shape the character of the child. Carden education seeks to develop the child's emotional strength and moral character as well as the intellect. Miss Carden said that children deeply need inspiring role models

A teacher at the Carden Memorial School in Salt Lake City working intensively with a small group of students of similar ability levels. This "table work" is an important aspect of Carden education.

and uplifting ideas. The stories and books and poems the children read provide just that.

The curriculum at Carden Memorial is comprehensive and sequential. Throughout the grades, the children study history, geography, math, science, physical education, and art, as well as language and literature. They begin learning French in the first grade and Latin in the sixth.

"Art and music are very important," says Anna Lou Jeffs.

> Miss Carden was a lover of the arts. The children do art—they draw and paint—but they also study great art—Raphael, Rembrandt, Monet, Rodin, and the like. Museum-quality reproductions of great paintings and photographs of great sculpture hang in our classrooms and in our school hallways. The children are introduced to classical music and learn to sing on key. Miss Carden was a liberally educated and refined person. The education she designed is meant to help the child develop into a literate, cultured, and accomplished human being, who is capable of enjoying life.

Carden Memorial emphasizes decorum. All children come to school wearing a carefully prescribed school uniform. Boys wear white shirts, dark ties, gray slacks, and navy-blue blazers adorned with the school crest. Girls wear jumpers or dresses of Hamilton plaid (a maroon-and-blue wool plaid), a white blouse, and a navy-blue sweater, also with the school crest. Donald Jeffs observes, "When children come to school nicely dressed it gives them a sense of dignity and self-worth. It also tells them that school and what

they do there are important. Our school dress helps them behave well and to apply themselves to their studies."

Students at Carden Memorial must act according to clearly defined standards of politeness. As the school handbook states, "Courtesy is not optional." Students greet teachers and other adults with a direct look and a friendly "Good Morning, Mrs. ____," or "Good afternoon, Mr. ____." They stand up when a school director or guest enters the room. At the beginning of the day or when returning from an activity, the children stand quietly behind their desks until the teacher sits down or tells them they may sit. Students may not raise their hand when the teacher is talking and must sit in class with body straight, both feet on the floor, and head held up but "with no props."

The school handbook reminds parents to keep in mind the school's goal of "refinement" when they dress for a school visit. And it quotes Miss Carden:

> Oh parents! Please do not deny your children obedience;
> For if you deny them obedience, you deny them courtesy;
> If you deny them courtesy, you deny them deference;
> If you deny them deference, you deny them reverence;
> And if you deny them reverence, you deny them the ability to achieve their full stature, because they will never know humility.

The Jeffs call Carden Memorial "a nondenominational Christian school," and there is daily prayer, Bible reading, and weekly chapel. But Donald Jeffs emphasizes that in this respect Carden Memorial is not necessarily a typical Carden School: "At the core of the Carden approach is a particular educational philosophy and method. This can be used in different ways in different types of schools. Each Carden school represents the Carden method and curriculum but also reflects the personality and beliefs of its founders and directors. Even the curriculum is more a set of guidelines than a series of fixed lesson plans. Each school can adapt it to its own purposes. Carden schools are run in a variety of ways."

Nevertheless, Carden Memorial is probably similar to many other Carden schools. Schools such as the Jackson Carden School in Pearland, Texas, and the El Enconto Carden School in Santa Clara, California, seem to have a similar, conservative orientation. They also have strict uniform and behavior codes, emphasize decorum and moral values, and have a broad, content-rich, traditional curriculum.

Miss Carden actively promoted her method until her death in 1977. At that point David Merle Taylor, Miss Carden's longtime assistant, became her successor. Today the Carden Educational Foundation in Brookfield, Connecticut, carries on Miss Carden's work under Taylor's direction. The Foundation holds courses in the Carden method and publishes the Carden books and educational materials. It also provides information about existing schools and about procedures for adopting the Carden method in a new or established school.

Resources

FOR MORE INFORMATION

> Carden Educational Foundation
> P.O. Box 659
> Brookfield, CT 06894-0659
> Tel.: (860) 350-9885
> Fax: (860) 354-9812
> World Wide Web: http://www.cardenschool.org

This is the central organization for the Carden movement. It maintains a list of Carden schools around the country, promotes Carden education, and sells the Carden readers and other books and educational materials related to the Carden method. It also provides training for teachers and administrators.

> Carden Memorial School
> 1452 East 2700 South
> Salt Lake City, UT 84106
> Tel.: (801) 486-4895

FOR FURTHER READING

Carden, Mae. *Let's Bring Them Up Sensibly*. Glen Rock, N.J.: Mae Carden, Inc., 1967. A collection of observations, advice, and aphorisms about raising children. Interesting, but does not give a specific description of Carden education.

————. *Quality Teaching—Successful Learning*. Brookfield, Conn.: Carden Educational Foundation, 1985. A collection of general observations about education, but does not give a specific description of the Carden method.

There is also a thirty-minute video, *Carden Education*, which provides a general introduction to Carden education and includes interviews with parents and students. The books by Miss Carden and the video are available from the Carden Educational Foundation (see For More Information, above). While they introduce one to the spirit of Carden education, they do not give a clear, specific picture of the Carden curriculum and pedagogy. Interested parents should, if possible, get the name and address of a nearby Carden school (through the Carden Foundation) and pay a visit.

12

Christian Schools

The fastest-growing school movement in the country is the Christian school movement. The first Christian schools were founded in the 1960s as religiously based but nondenominational schools. In the late 1970s, there were still only a handful of these schools. In the early 1980s, however, the movement began to grow at a very rapid pace. Hundreds of schools were founded each year. This growth has continued: next to the Roman Catholic school system, the Christian school movement is the second largest group of schools outside the public school system. Today there are about 15,000 Christian schools with over 1 million students.

The fastest-growing school movement in the country is the Christian school movement.

Conservative Christians (fundamentalists, evangelicals, and charismatics) are the driving force behind the Christian school movement. They believe in the divine origin and literal truth of the Bible and try to use the Bible as a guide and inspiration in all areas of life. They see the intense personal experience of being saved by Christ, of being "born again," as a central religious experience. Fundamentalists tend to have a separatist attitude toward other Christian groups and toward society. Evangelicals and charismatics tend to be more open to other groups and to

society. For charismatics, ecstatic states linked to the indwelling of the Holy Spirit and the ministry of healing through faith are particularly important. Each of these groups has been active in establishing Christian schools, the fundamentalists particularly so.

Some Christian schools are very small, serving only the children of a particular church congregation. Some are large, with over a thousand students, educating children from various conservative groups, and unchurched children as well. Most Christian schools follow traditional teaching methods with classes where same-age children are taught as a group by a single teacher. Many of the smaller Christian schools, however, are so-called teacherless schools. In these schools children spend much of their school day independently working through textbooks and workbooks supplied by Christian publishing houses. An adult "coach" moves from cubicle to cubicle helping each student in turn.

Many of the first Christian schools were founded by Caucasian parents who wanted to avoid sending their children to newly integrated public schools. Today, however, virtually all Christian schools admit students regardless of race, color, or national or ethnic origin. Neverthe-

...se of geographic, social, and economic
...ost Christian schools are still largely or
...acasian. Christian schools, particularly
...reas, however, enroll many minority
...d there are Christian schools in which
...ost of all of the students are African-American.

Christian schools are based on strongly held
views of the world, human nature and destiny,
the aims of education, and the present-day public school system. Samuel Blumenfeld, historian
of education and commentator on the current
situation in the nation's schools, explains:

> Christian schools are based on the belief
> that an omnipotent, omniscient divine
> being created the world and mankind. In
> the Scriptures He has revealed the truth
> about the universe, about Himself, and His
> will for mankind. Man is fallen through
> original sin and can gain salvation only
> through the grace made available through
> the self-sacrifice of God in Jesus Christ.
> The Bible is the word of God and reveals
> God's will for humankind. Human nature
> is flawed. The child has to be taught what
> is right and wrong and has to be protected
> from harmful influences and ideas. There
> is a truth—an absolute, revealed eternal
> truth—that needs to be taught, in the
> home, church, and in the school. A Chris-
> tian school seeks to pass on this received
> truth and to help create a believing, virtu-
> ous, and responsible Christian member of
> society.

> The public school system is based on
> naturalism and on secular humanism. Nat-
> uralism sees the universe as a self-existent
> given, and the human being as the acci-
> dental product of evolution from lower
> forms of life. Secular humanism removes
> religion and any transcendent reference

> from every domain of human life. It holds
> that the human being is the measure of all
> things. We can create our own truth, cre-
> ate our own morality. Permissiveness,
> moral relativism, situational ethics, and a
> "do it if it feels good" attitude issue from
> naturalism and secular humanism. This
> view of and approach to life is manifested
> and taught in the public school. That is
> why chaos reigns there. The public school
> with its values-neutral approach creates an
> individual with no values except his own
> desires and impulses, a person who is for-
> ever engaged in the search for values and
> truth and never finds it.

> The conservative Christian parent sees
> public schools and most private schools as
> parochial schools for secular humanism
> and as a threat to the Christian family's
> beliefs and way of life.

These commonly held beliefs and attitudes are
manifest in certain characteristics shared by virtually all Christian schools. They include:

- Daily prayer, Bible reading, and Bible study
- Regular, at least weekly, and in some
  schools daily, religious worship
- Memorization of biblical verses and of
  other morally and spiritually edifying material
- Strong emphasis on honesty, integrity, responsibility, and love and respect for others
  and the use of biblical verses to support
  these as moral absolutes
- Emphasis on basic academic skills and traditional subject matter taught by traditional means (Child-centered curricula,
  teacher-as-facilitator pedagogy, and other
  elements of progressive education are not
  common in Christian schools.)
- Use of textbooks from Christian publishing

houses that present material from a Christian perspective
- Permeation of all subject matter with religious ideas and themes (In arithmetic, for example, the fact that numbers "work" may be presented as a sign of God's perfect wisdom; in history, the role of Christianity is emphasized as helping to realize God's will for humanity.)
- Teaching of creationism rather than of evolution as an explanation for the existence of the human race
- Strict dress codes that mandate neatness, cleanliness, and modesty (In many schools, students wear uniforms; girls usually have to wear jumpers or skirts and blouses.)
- Strict codes of manners and behavior (Students must obey and respect teachers and refrain from profanity. Often they must use "yes, sir" and "no, ma'am," and must stand when an adult enters the classroom. Students are not allowed to smoke or drink. They may be prohibited from coed swimming, from hand-holding and other displays of affection toward a member of the opposite sex, and from being alone with members of the opposite sex. These rules may pertain to life outside the school as well as in it.)
- Rejection of much of mainstream, popular culture (Many schools require that students not watch television, listen to rock-and-roll music, see certain movies, or play video games.)
- Strict enforcement of rules (In states where it is not prohibited by law, a mild form of corporal punishment may be used.)

- Emphasis on patriotic beliefs and values
- Daily saluting of the American flag and reciting of the Pledge of Allegiance
- Promotion of traditional family values and of traditional gender roles for boys and girls
- De-emphasis on competitive sports and absence of team athletics for girls
- Sex education either left to the family or presented as a topic in which moral and religious issues are paramount

There are more conservative and more liberal Christian schools, but in virtually all of them, the elements listed above are to some degree present. In curriculum, pedagogy, discipline, values, standards of lifestyle, and behavior, Christian schools are radically different from public schools.

The Christian school movement is especially strong in the nation's Bible Belt, which stretches across the southern part of the nation through the Southwest and into southern California. But there are now Christian schools all over the United States, in virtually every city and town and in many rural areas.

Many of these schools have modest facilities. They may lack the well-stocked libraries, the large gymnasiums, and the computer centers that public schools typically have. They cannot provide special services for the learning disabled.

Nevertheless, Christian schools offer an interesting alternative to parents who are Christians but who not may subscribe to conservative Christianity. Christian schools offer a safe, orderly, religiously informed learning environment, the teachings of basic academic skills and subjects, dedicated teachers, and an education that stresses self-discipline, morality, and spiritual values. Tuition at Christian schools

Christian schools offer an interesting alternative to parents who are Christians but who may not subscribe to conservative Christianity.

ranges from about $100 a year at the teacherless schools to $7,000 at well-equipped, large Christian high schools. But the average tuition is between $2,000 and $3,000, which is lower than tuition for most independent schools.

In looking at Christian schools, parents should be aware of certain differences between fundamentalists on the one hand and evangelicals and charismatics on the other. Christian educator David G. Cashin observes:

> The basic difference between fundamentalists and evangelicals is how they perceive themselves in society. Fundamentalists are "separatists" in the sense that they tend to separate themselves from the perceived corruption of society and from other Christian groups they perceive as having made compromises with corrupt society. Evangelicals are much more likely to remain within society's structures and to try to work through them. In the area of Christian schools, fundamentalist churches have been much more active. Many, though not all of their schools are restricted to members of the sponsoring church. In contrast, many evangelicals do not agree with the concept of separate Christian education. They believe that Christians should work in and through the public schools.

In other words, parents who are not conservative Christians but who are interested in a Christian school should be aware that the schools vary in their attitudes toward outsiders. Some may be quite happy to have children outside their immediate community, some may not.

The Valley Christian School
NORTHAMPTON, MASSACHUSETTS

Northampton, Massachusetts, seems an unlikely place for a conservative Christian school. It is perhaps the most liberal city in the nation's most liberal state and the capital of American lesbianism. Women walking hand in hand down the street and embracing and kissing in public are common sights. Jerry Falwell, chancing into Northampton on a Saturday evening, would think himself marooned in Sodom or Gomorrah.

But the revival of conservative Christianity and the spread of the Christian school movement have reached even Northampton. On a quiet residential street a few blocks from the center of town is the Valley Christian School, a school for children from kindergarten through the eighth grade.

The Valley Christian School is in a building that once housed the gymnasium and science laboratories of a private school for girls. College Church, an evangelical church, now owns the building and each Sunday uses the gymnasium as a sanctuary where about six hundred people worship. Former science labs and assorted other rooms have been converted into small but pleasant classrooms.

It is just before 9:00 AM on a Wednesday. About a hundred children are seated in folding chairs in a large carpeted room. Most of the girls are wearing dresses. Most of the boys are wearing collared shirts and slacks. No T-shirts emblazoned with cartoon or video game heroes are to be seen. Four days a week the school day begins with prayer and Bible study in the various classrooms. Each Wednesday all the children and teachers gather for chapel.

School director Carol Whiteley leads the children in a song that begins "This is the day that

The first-grade class at Valley Christian School in Northampton, Massachusetts. Small classes, emphasis on basic skills, and a strong moral and religious orientation attract many families to Christian schools.

the Lord has made. . . ." Several fourth-graders recite poems that they have memorized. One girl recites a poem she has written about her mother. It begins, "My mother is my very best friend. . . ."

Whiteley then introduces a visitor—Lydia—a member of College Church. Lydia is standing at the front of the room next to a table. On the table are a hand mirror, an ice-cream scoop with black-and-white "holstein" markings, and a rubber chicken. Lydia is seriously afflicted with cerebral palsy; her movements are spastic and her speech is hard to understand. The children listen attentively as Lydia talks about people who are different and how we should act toward them.

Lydia asks a teacher to come forward and to look into the mirror. It is a trick mirror that emits a burst of canned laughter in the teacher's face. "No one likes to be laughed at," Lydia says with a smile. "So if you see someone different, a boy in a wheelchair, for example, don't make fun of him. And don't be afraid, go and talk to him. Don't be a chicken." She picks up and shakes the rubber chicken. "You can always find something you have in common. For example, everyone likes

ice cream, don't they?" She picks up the ice-cream scoop, which in response emits a long "mooo." The children laugh and nod in agreement. "Well, you can always have an ice cream together."

Lydia has a child read a Bible passage from the first letter of the Apostle John: ". . . So we know and believe the love God has for us. God is love, and he who abides in love, abides in God and God in him. . . . There is no fear in love, but perfect love casts out fear. . . . If anyone says 'I love God' and hates his brother he is a liar, for he who does not love his brother whom he has seen, cannot love God whom he has not seen."

Later, Whitely talks about Valley Christian School: "The school was founded in 1974 and originally was part of College Church. Today there are about 140 children in the school. They live in Northampton and in various surrounding towns. Some commute a good distance. Virtually all of the families belong to a fundamentalist or evangelical church." She hands me a copy of the school handbook. At the bottom of the cover is the verse, "Jesus said, 'Let the little children come to me, and do not hinder them, for the kingdom of heaven belongs to such as these.'" On page 2 is "The Statement of Faith":

> We believe that the Scriptures of the Old and New Testament are the word of God and the only infallible rule of faith and practice. We believe that there is one true God eternally existing in three persons—Father, Son, and Holy Spirit—Who share equally all the attributes of deity and participate fully in the Divine essence; that God created Man in His own image; that Jesus Christ is the Son of God and Savior of the world and that through His life, death, and resurrection, atonement was made for sin and redemption was provided for all Mankind; that it is by God's grace that we are saved through faith, and not the result of our own efforts, that it is a gift of God; that through the indwelling power of the Holy Spirit the Christian is enabled to live a godly life in this present world; and that the Lord Jesus Christ will return in visible form to complete His saving work and establish His eternal kingdom.

Whiteley explains:

> The whole life of the school is based on God's will revealed in the Holy Scripture. For example, the Bible advises the Christian to dress modestly, with decency and propriety, so as not to cause anyone else to stumble into sinful thoughts. That injunction is the basis of our dress code.
>
> Our approach to discipline is based on the belief that all children need to be clearly and strongly directed in their behavior and to be disciplined as necessary. Biblical injunctions—such as "Train a child in the way he should go, and when

he is old he will not turn from it"—give guidance about how we should treat the children.

The grievance procedures of the school advise that a person having a problem with someone should go immediately to that person and try to resolve the issue. This is based on the verse in Matthew 18. The Gospel also tells the Christian not to let the sun go down on his anger with another person.

When I ask Whiteley why parents send their children to Valley Christian, she replies, "The main reason is that they want to get a strong Christian education for their child, one based on the Bible and Christian principles and teaching the Christian faith and way of life. Virtually all of our parents are members of Christian churches and subscribe to our statement of faith." Whiteley admits that there are other factors as well. Many parents, because of direct experience in the public schools or because of what they have heard about the public schools, do not want their child there. Sex education, the teaching of evolution, drugs and violence, and low academic standards in the public schools repel Christian parents.

I spend the rest of the morning visiting classes. They are small (ranging from eight to fifteen children), orderly, and purposeful. Instruction is teacher centered, and the children use textbook and workbooks in most classes. All of the teachers are women. The combined fourth and fifth grade is doing math problems from a workbook. The morning schedule is posted on the wall:

> 8:40–9:10 Bible
> 9:10–9:15 Math drills
> 9:15–9:45 History and geography

9:45–10:20 Science
10:20–10:40 Snack and recess
10:45–10:55 Reading aloud and penmanship
10:55–11:30 Language and journal
11:30–11:50 Spelling
11:50–12:30 Lunch and recess
Then grammar reviews and "Centers"

The seventh- and eighth-grade combined class is reading aloud from a history text on ancient Greece. At the end of the chapter, the teacher asks students about what they have just read.

In the first-grade class the children are busy writing their own stories, which they will later edit, rewrite, and publish. They are doing "process writing," which is part of the whole language approach. For the most part though, as in most Christian schools, the pedagogy and curriculum seem traditional, teacher centered, and textbook based.

Resources

FOR MORE INFORMATION

Association of Christian Schools International
P.O. Box 35097
Colorado Springs, CO 80935-3509
Tel.: (719) 528-6906

This is the largest of the Christian school associations. It publishes a directory of schools, which includes over 3,100 schools with about 540,000 students. It also publishes a survey of textbooks, which reviews textbooks and curricula of Christian as well as secular publishers in the full range of elementary and high-school subjects. The textbook survey helps schools and parents find educational materials that suit their point of view.

American Association of Christian Schools (AACS)
P.O. Box 2189
Independence, MO 64055
Tel.: (816) 795-7709
Fax: (816) 795-7462

AACS is a national association of fundamentalist and theologically conservative Christian schools. Its member schools enroll about 120,000 students. AACS offers various services to member schools and lobbies for Christian education at the national level. Many states have a state-level AACS, from which parents can get information about local schools. Information on state organizations is available from the national office.

Christian Schools International
3350 East Paris Avenue, SE
Grand Rapids, MI 49512-3054
Tel.: (800) 635-8288; (616) 957-1070
Fax: (616) 957-5022

This is an association primarily of Christian schools affiliated with the conservative wing of the Presbyterian church, although it increasingly has member schools that are connected with other conservative Protestant groups. See the end of chapter 28 for a full description of this organization's activities.

Many states have a state association of Christian schools. Call one of the national organizations for information about the association in your state.

FOR FURTHER READING

Carper, James, C., & Thomas C. Hunt. *Religious Education in America*. Birmingham, Ala.: Religious Education Press, 1984. Chapter 5, "The Christian Day School," by James Carper provides an excellent short treatment of the origins and present situation of Christian schools.

Cunningham, James. *Education in Christian Schools*. Colorado Springs: Association of Christian Schools International, 1987. A straightforward, readable presentation of the bases and practices of Christian education.

Gaebelien, Frank. *The Pattern of God's Truth: The Integration of Faith in Learning.* Colorado Springs: Association of Christian Schools International, 1995. Originally published in 1954 by Oxford University Press, this book is a classic treatment of the aims and means of Christian education.

Gangel, Kenneth. *Is Christian Education the Best Choice?* Colorado Springs: Association of Christian Schools International. A booklet comparing public education with Christian education.

———. *Christian Education: Its History and Philosophy.* Chicago: Moody, 1983.

———. *Called to Teach.* Colorado Springs: Association of Christian Schools International, 1995. A discussion of the special aspects of Christian education, such as the values and the moral and spiritual orientation. Meant for teachers in Christian schools but also helpful for parents.

Kienel, Paul, et al. (eds.). *The Philosophy of Christian School Education.* Colorado Springs: Association of Christian Schools International, 1995. A collection of articles dealing with various aspects of Christian education, including "Theology" and "Faith and Learning."

Parsons, Paul. *Inside America's Christian Schools.* Macon, Ga.: Mercer University Press, 1987. Although a bit dated, this is an excellent comprehensive survey of the philosophy, pedagogy, methods, and life-style embodied in the nation's Christian schools. Essential to understanding the Christian school movement.

Schindler, Bud. *Sowing for Excellence.* Colorado Springs: Association of Christian Schools International, 1987. A guide for Christian parents regarding Christian education.

13

Comer Schools

James P. Comer was born in 1934 and grew up in an African-American neighborhood in East Chicago, Indiana. Although his family was poor and not well educated, Comer succeeded in school. He went on to college and became a successful, respected psychiatrist and university professor.

In 1968, Comer was invited by the Yale Child Study Center to collaborate with the New Haven public schools in a school reform effort. In working with inner-city schools and considering the situation of the children there, Comer drew on his own life experience. Comer realized he had succeeded in school—and in life—largely because of the positive social environment in which he had grown up. His parents, as well as members of his extended family and other adults in the community, had provided care, love, discipline, guidance, and support. They had been positive role models, demonstrating in their behavior how one should live. They had also been legitimate authority figures who corrected and redirected him when he misbehaved. When he went to school his physical, emotional, and psychological needs were not at issue. He was ready to learn.

Comer, who is now Maurice Falk Professor of Child Psychiatry and associate dean of the Yale

The Comer approach brings school, parents, and community together in the collective enterprise of raising and educating children.

University Medical School, realized that "the same children who fail in a specific setting can become eminently successful if the adults in their lives can take the time to create a healthful climate."* He and his colleagues at Yale developed a concept of the school as supported by the whole "village" of the children—parents, teachers, school staff, and members of the community.

The program Comer developed, known both as the School Development Program (SDP) and as the "Comer process," helps parents, teachers, school staff and officials, and community members to make schools places for children to learn and to develop as whole human beings. Over six hundred schools in this country and abroad have adopted the program.

The Comer process is based on an innovative vision of what a school should be and what it should do. While acknowledging that schools cannot solve the problems of society, Comer holds that a school must minimize the effect these problems have on the teaching and learn-

*James P. Comer, et al., *Rallying the Whole Village: The Comer Process for Reforming Education* (New York: Teachers College Press, 1996), 1.

81

ing process. A school must work with families and the community to meet the needs of the children. It should address the children's physical, emotional, and psychological needs and development as well as promote their intellectual and academic growth. At the same time, the school should reach out to families and the community to strengthen and support them. It should involve families and the community in school life, drawing upon their strengths and resources in working with and serving the children. The Comer approach brings school, parents, and community together in the collective enterprise of raising and educating children. It manifests the truth of the African proverb, "It takes a whole village to raise a child."

There are a number of basic elements in the Comer process. These include:

- a concern with the child's overall development in six areas: physical, cognitive, psychological, linguistic, social, and ethical
- a proactive approach, in which measures are taken to prevent problems, not just to deal with them when they have arisen
- a focus on basic academic skills
- a site-based management (Parents, teachers, school staff, and administrators make the important decisions about life in the school.)
- parent and community education
- the involvement of parents and community members as helpers in the life of the school
- the application of three guiding principles—consensus, collaboration, and no fault—into every aspect of school life

Schools and school systems all over the country have adopted the Comer model. The Guilford County schools in Greensboro, North Carolina, did so in 1993. Superintendent Jerry Weast had done extensive research on the various approaches to school reform and decided that the Comer approach best combined on-site management with methods to help all children achieve academically.

New York City's Community School District Number Thirteen also has used the Comer model. Superintendent Lester W. Young, Jr. (writing in *SDP Newsline*, Winter 1996), notes that the Comer approach has helped the district's schools provide more opportunities (and hence increased motivation) for all of its students, including those with special educational needs. It has also helped the schools work with children at the critical transition into adolescence. Young writes, "It's a time when they can either go down one path or another, so schools need to become more responsive. For instance, when a youngster enters preadolescence or adolescence that's when they want to be known as an individual. If you place youngsters in a very large setting they become a number and lose their individuality. We are restructuring our middle schools so that adults assume greater responsibility for students with increased opportunities for youngsters to discuss issues."

When West Mecklenburg High School in Charlotte, North Carolina, adopted the School Development Program, attendance increased significantly, the number of students on the honor roll jumped 75 percent, and enrollment in advanced placement increased by 25 percent. School officials also reported a "renewed sense of community."

The Lincoln-Bassett Elementary School
NEW HAVEN, CONNECTICUT

In New Haven, Connecticut, virtually all public schools use the Comer approach to some extent.

The Lincoln-Bassett Elementary School is one of these. Lincoln-Bassett is located in a neighborhood of modest two-story frame homes. The houses are close together and abut narrow sidewalks, and there are almost no trees. Still, most of the homes and yards are well cared for and the neighborhood seems pleasant and quiet. It is in fact one of the most troubled areas in New Haven. I learn later that several blocks from the school is one of the main drug dealing areas in the city. Drugs and crime are both serious problems. The school itself is a long, low, yellow-brick building surrounded by a high chain-link fence.

Inside, the Lincoln-Bassett School is immaculately clean, orderly, and attractive. A long line of well-tended potted plants sits on a shelf next to a hallway window outside the school office. Nearby is a large poster honoring the "Read-Aloud Volunteers"—parents and community members who come in to read to the children. There is also a poster honoring the "student of the month" with a large photograph of the stu-

dent and a description of his work. A bulletin board features photographs of students and their project work. One of them is second-grader Ginnel Moore, who has done a study of "Wildflowers across America."

In the kindergarten and lower grades, almost all of the children are wearing school uniforms— dark blue jumpers and white blouses for girls and dark trousers, white shirts, and ties for boys. Margaret Best, a longtime teacher of music at the school, explains, "The parents decided years ago that Lincoln-Bassett would be a uniformed school. It's not mandatory of course, but it works pretty well in the lower grades. Later on, the children wear what they want, but still dress neatly." Best is wearing a navy cardigan emblazoned with the school's name and her own.

Lincoln-Bassett is managed by the members of the school community. Decisions affecting the life of the school are made not by state, city, or district administrators but by people in the school. The main governing body of Lincoln-

A computer lab at Lincoln-Bassett. In a school whose management is site-based, administrators, teachers, staff, parents, and community members decide together how to allocate resources for the education of the children.

Bassett is the School Planning and Management Team (SPMT). It includes the principal, representatives of the faculty, the parents, and the school support staff, and the members of the Mental Health Team—altogether about twenty persons. While district and local school boards set general goals and guidelines, the SPMT decides how to realize them. It makes all decisions about the curriculum, scheduling, staff hiring, and staff development and coordinates the activities of the various groups involved in the school. The SPMT has four subcommittees: Curriculum, Instruction, and Testing; Public Relations; Social (dealing with school and class "climate," staff morale, and student social development); and Staff Development/Parent Training. The operating principles for the SPMT and its subcommittees are a no-fault attitude; maximum use of school, family, and community resources; collaboration; and decision making by consensus.

Curriculum developer Carolyn Kinder remarks, "We try to address all the needs of the children—physical, emotional, psychological, as well as academic. Almost all the children eat breakfast as well as lunch here. We also have a 'latchkey program'—an after-school recreation and crafts program so if the parents are working the children are not at home alone or in the streets. The school and the gym are open until 8:00 PM."

At Lincoln-Bassett, as at all Comer schools, there is a group concerned with the school climate and morale and with individual children having problems. In many Comer schools this is called the Student Support Team. At Lincoln-Bassett it is called the Mental Health Team and consists of a psychologist, the special education teacher, the school nurse, the school social worker, and the principal. The Mental Health Team meets once a week to discuss schoolwide

issues but primarily to look at problems of specific children referred by parents or by school staff. The team views each case as a clinical challenge and recommends a course of action. This might include consultation with the classroom teacher, observation of the child, and perhaps direct counseling of the child. The Mental Health Team tries to deal with a child's difficulties before a major problem has developed.

The school also has a social development curriculum (see chapter 7). This program teaches children how to deal with stress and how to get along with others; it also builds self-esteem. In one of the kindergartens I visited the teacher asked, "What do you do if you feel angry?" Immediately a barrage of answers came from the children. "Take ten deep breaths." "Go for a walk." "Scream." "Take it out on a pillow."

Lincoln-Bassett has an aggressive program to help students develop basic academic skills. Every child who falls below the fiftieth percentile on the Metropolitan Achievement Test—a standardized test of reading and other basic skills—receives special tutoring, either from a human or computer program tutor. In the "Essentials of Literacy Program," twenty third-graders with low reading scores spend two hours each day working with a team of four adults, including a teacher, a parent volunteer, and two paraprofessionals. The children work intensively in small groups, focusing on phonics, comprehension, spelling, vocabulary, and writing.

Parents are brought into the life of the school as much as possible, both as decision makers and as support persons. They come and work in the classrooms and tutor individual students as volunteers. They are on the SPMT and all its subcommittees. They are welcome in the school at all times, and their input on all issues is invited and appreciated. Parents also organize school activities. In a typical recent year, Lincoln-Bassett parents organized an African-American history exhibit and presentation to which other schools were invited, a book fair, a roller-skating party, and an October harvest fair. The parent group also runs a "publishing company" that laminates the covers of the "books" that the children write and bind in class.

Lincoln-Bassett actively addresses the needs of parents. There are twice-monthly question-and-answer meetings about topics such as child health and the meaning of standardized test scores. Teachers and staff members make home visits to help with child rearing and other issues. The latchkey program offers after-school adult supervision for children and takes pressure off working parents. It includes arts and crafts, sports, and reading activities.

The school also involves the larger community as much as possible. "Everyone is affected by how the children turn out," Kinder observes. Student volunteers from Yale come once a week to teach instrumental music. During the summer, nearby Albertus Magnus College offers special courses for the children. Patients from the Veterans Administration Hospital, mainly those with post-traumatic stress disorder, work with the children as part of the community service element of their therapy program. The school's adult education classes are open to all community members. And there are plans to open in the school a medical and a dental facility that would serve the entire community.

The stated aim of Lincoln-Bassett is to teach children basic academic skills—reading, writing, and arithmetic—and "to help them to be curious learners, creative problem-solvers." Just as the school is free to realize its goals in the way it chooses, individual teachers can choose the pedagogical approach that suits them best.

Most teachers seem to use a traditional teacher-centered approach that emphasizes basic skills and a standard curriculum. In one kindergarten, the children were learning to sit "like first-graders," with "eyes open, mouths closed, and hands in lap," and then were assigned to one of several learning centers. In a fourth-grade class the children spent the last half-hour of the day at different learning centers but were assigned to the one the teacher thought they needed most. Fifth-grade teacher Kim Francis drilled her students in mental arithmetic. "Seven plus twelve times two minus ten equals what?" she said slowly, giving the children time to calculate. The buzz of discharging neurons was almost audible.

The recently established "Constructive Center" at Lincoln-Bassett is introducing student-initiated in-depth project work. Each term two children from each class go to the center several hours a week. They do a research project based on a personal interest and then make something as part of the project. The day of my visit, two boys, both aspiring to be police officers, were completing their project work about police life by building a police car out of cardboard and other materials.

Carol Damsky, project coordinator of the Construction Center, observes, "The hope is that the children will go back to the classroom and bring the principles of projects and hands-on work to the other students and to the teacher. Some teachers are responding positively to this, but most prefer to continue to work in the way they are used to. It involves looking at children and teaching in a totally new way. Here each teacher is free to work as he or she wants, and each does what seems to work."

The Comer process has helped make Lincoln-Bassett a vital center of learning for its children and for the community. Lincoln-Bassett, like many of the schools using the Comer process, is in a disadvantaged area. But the family and community problems that are endemic in places like New Haven are today present in more affluent communities as well. There, also, children do not necessarily arrive in school washed, brushed, neatly dressed, and well fed, ready and able to learn their ABC's and times tables. They do not come with their basic physical, emotional, and psychological needs met. They may be hungry, angry, upset, feeling unloved, deeply distressed by something happening in their home life, needing some adult who will take a personal interest in them, needing also positive role models. Today, family and community problems are present at every level of the social and economic ladder, and this is reflected in schools everywhere.

Shortly after visiting Lincoln-Bassett, I read an article in the local newspaper of a well-to-do, privileged community. The town has a well-respected, well-financed school system, but according to the article, both the town and its schools have serious problems. The writer, a local therapist who has served on the junior high school's "Discipline Advisory Committee," points out that most of the students come from single-parent homes or from homes where both parents are working. These parents have limited time and energy to devote to the care, discipline, support, and education of their children. Also, the children have few positive role models and few adults whom they respect as authority figures.

While most of the students are conscientious and well behaved, there are many students with problems. The writer says that there is a small group of potentially violent students who can't be dealt with until they actually hurt someone. There is another larger, more benign group of apathetic, uninvolved, chronically truant students who just get by. The school deals with discipline

problems by punishing students with detention or expulsion. The therapist points out that there is mistrust and lack of cooperation between the school and the parents and that there are no in-school or after-school programs to challenge the students to develop self-discipline and positive interests.

The principles and practices of the Comer model that work in schools like the Lincoln-Bassett School in New Haven may also be needed and appropriate for schools in affluent, privileged communities. In fact, many of the schools the School Development Program now works with are suburban and rural rather than inner-city schools.

As the authors of *Rallying the Whole Village* observe, "The program originally addressed the need of urban students and schools, but experience has shown that it can benefit all children. The program is now being implemented in a broad array of diverse communities" (Comer et al., 4).

Resources

FOR MORE INFORMATION

> The Yale Child Study Center/School
>   Development Program
> 55 College Street
> New Haven, CT 06510
> Tel.: (800) 811-7775

This organization (part of Yale University) provides information to and supports parents, teachers, and administrators who are interested in implementing Comer's principles and approach in their schools. It helps schools and school districts apply the Comer school model to their particular situations. It welcomes inquiries from parents, teachers, school staff, and administrators.

The School Development Program (SDP) sells a

"Comer School Development Program" video series with an accompanying "Discussion Leader's Guide." It also publishes a quarterly newsletter called *SDP Newsline* and a "Summary of SDP Documentation and Research."

The SDP has a web site on the World Wide Web at http://info.med.yale.edu/comer. This site provides an overview of the program, a staff and a national SDP network directory, a bibliography of publications produced by the SDP staff since 1990, and other information.

For Further Reading

Comer, James. *School Power: The Implications of an International Experiment.* New York: Simon and Schuster, 1993. Comer's analysis of the problems besetting most public schools and his prescription for improving conditions by transferring decision-making power to the local school community.

Comer, James P., Norris M. Haynes, Edward T. Joyner, and Michael Ben-Avie. *Rallying the Whole Village: The Comer Process for Reforming Education.* New York: Teachers College Press, 1996. An in-depth description of the School Development Program and its implementation in schools throughout the country.

Comer, James, and Alvin Poussaint. *Raising Black Children.* New York: NAL-Dutton, 1993. A guide for parents, counselors, and teachers, focusing on the needs of African-American children.

14

Core Knowledge Schools

In *Cultural Literacy: What Every American Needs to Know*, published in 1987, E. D. Hirsch, a professor of English at the University of Virginia, asserted that the United States shares a common cultural heritage that is the basis of national life. This body of shared knowledge—concerning geography, history, literature, science, politics, government, art, and music—helps create and support the life of all Americans. Hirsch believes that to participate in the economic, political, social, and cultural life of American society, a person must be familiar with this cultural legacy. Thus a primary aim of education should be to transmit this shared national culture to children so that they can participate in, continue, and enrich the national culture.

Hirsch criticizes American education for failing to effectively pass on this national literate culture to students today. In his view, the educational system focuses too much on developing so-called higher cognitive functions through "content-neutral" curricula. Children learn research techniques, problem solving, analysis, and synthesis. They do intensive projects on specific topics, such as daily life in the colonial United States or saving the rain forest. But they do not acquire a comprehensive view of history, geography, literature, science, mathematics, art, and music.

They are encouraged to explore their particular personal interests but are not asked to master significant bodies of knowledge. They learn to read using current imaginative literature, often books of their own choosing, rather than the classics of children's literature or informative nonfiction. As a result, a student can graduate from the eighth grade or even from high school and not know when the Civil War was fought, or who Macbeth was, or who discovered the vaccination for smallpox.

Hirsch also charges that the fragmented, content-neutral curriculum in American schools is responsible for the declining literacy in the American population. Reading is not just a process of decoding words or using contextual clues to recognize them. It is comprehending their meaning. To read with true understanding a child must have a vast store of cultural references in his or her memory. For example, a student may encounter the sentence, "Harry Smith, rich as Croesus and dressed like Paul Bunyan, walked into a room full of the loveliest young women of the Yukon, and looked around." The child may be able to sound out all the words and recognize almost all of them. But if the child does not know that Croesus was very rich, that Paul Bunyan was a lumberjack, and that the Yukon is in northern

Canada, he or she will not grasp the sentence's meaning. To master the national language one must master the national cultural heritage.

Hirsch charges that both privileged and underprivileged American children today are not getting in school the cultural and scientific information they need to be able to read, to write, and to communicate in the national mainstream culture. Disadvantaged children suffer more, since more affluent children are likely to acquire much of what they need at home.

Hirsch offers a remedy for this situation. He suggests that the body of essential or core knowledge be made explicit and that it be incorporated into the curriculum of all primary schools in the nation. Young children love to learn, he asserts, and have a tremendous capacity to learn and retain factual material. By the age of thirteen all children can be taught that body of knowledge that will enable them to be literate, informed, and capable members of society. Hirsch suggests that this core knowledge comprise 50 percent of the curriculum and that the rest of the curriculum deal with topics of particular interest to the community and the school. Higher-order skills should also be taught, Hirsch asserts, but these will be more easily acquired if the children have a broad foundation of knowledge.

Hirsch holds that the restructuring of the curriculum is important not only for children as individuals but also for the various ethnic and racial communities that comprise the nation and for the nation as a whole. Each child needs this body of core knowledge to take part successfully in national life. The various ethnic and racial minorities need this knowledge to improve their situation in society and to be able to make their

Hirsch suggests that the body of essential or core knowledge be made explicit and that it be incorporated into the curriculum of all primary schools in the nation.

own contributions to it. Without this cultural vocabulary they will remain economically and socially disadvantaged and culturally outside the national discourse. And the nation benefits, since it is held together by the glue of a common cultural language. The stakes are high. An extensive curriculum based on cultural literacy can break the cycle of illiteracy and poverty, help realize social justice, make the United States more of a participatory democracy, and keep the nation competitive in the world economy.

After the publication of *Cultural Literacy: What Every American Needs to Know*, Hirsch was criticized for asserting the primacy of Caucasian, male-dominated, European-based culture and for undermining multicultural education and awareness. Despite these attacks, which Hirsch strongly rebutted, his book became a national bestseller. Hirsch used his earnings from the book to establish the Core Knowledge Foundation in Charlottesville, Virginia. This is a nonprofit organization promoting cultural literacy in the schools. With the help of experts in many fields, Hirsch produced a series of books containing the essential knowledge appropriate for the various grades. They are entitled *What Every First-Grader Needs to Know*, *What Every Second-Grader Needs to Know*, and so on, for grades one through six.

Since 1990 the Core Knowledge Foundation has been publishing a *Core Knowledge Sequence: Content Guidelines for Grades 1–6*. This thick, large-format book presents in outline form what should be covered in each grade—what poems and stories children should read, and what they should learn about literature and language, world history, world cultures, American history and civilization, geography, the visual arts, music, mathematics, and science. Since this is commonly held, specific knowledge to be presented in a certain sequence, teachers are advised not to change the basic curriculum. What the *Content Guidelines* suggest is not meant to be a complete curriculum, though, but only one-half of the total content of the curriculum. Thus there is much room for other material, such as multicultural topics, and teachers are encouraged to add elements that pertain to local conditions and that meet students' interests.

The Core Knowledge curriculum for first-graders as it appears in the 1995 edition of the *Content Guidelines* includes the following:

- Poems, folktales, fairy tales, and fables such as *My Shadow* (by Robert Louis Stevenson) and *Wynken, Blynken, and Nod*, and fairy tales such as "The Frog Prince," "Sleeping Beauty," and "The Boy Who Cried Wolf"
- Letters of the alphabet, capitalization, contractions
- History, geography, and art of ancient Africa, Egypt, Mesopotamia, pre–Columbian North and South America, and of modern Mexico
- Judaism, Christianity, and Islam
- American colonial history through independence
- Elements of color, line, shape, and texture in art
- Self-portraiture, still life, and murals
- Basic elements of music, singing, and music appreciation, including works by Bach, Mozart, Tchaikovsky and Grieg, and a variety of popular songs such as "Oh Susannah" and "Yankee Doodle"
- Numbers, patterns, addition, subtraction, measurement, and basic geometry
- Living things and their environments

- Systems of the human body, the idea of matter, and the properties of matter
- Introduction to electricity and to the solar system, and the earth
- Lives of scientists such as Thomas Edison, Edward Jenner, and Louis Pasteur

A partial list of the fifth-grade curriculum includes:

- Poetry of Emily Dickinson
- *The Adventures of Tom Sawyer, Little Women, Little House on the Prairie*
- Abraham Lincoln's "Gettysburg Address" and Chief Joseph's "I will Fight No More Forever"
- Grammar rules about direct and indirect objects, agreement of pronouns, etc.
- Comedy, tragedy, metaphors, similes
- European exploration, trade, and the clash of cultures
- The Renaissance and Reformation, England's Golden Age, the English Revolution, early growth and expansion of Russia, feudal Japan
- Westward expansion, the Civil War and Reconstruction
- The political geography of Europe, geography of Russia, Japan, and Indochina
- Perspective in art, the art of the Renaissance, nineteenth-century American art, the art of Japan
- Three-part singing, recognition of chords, jazz, music of the Harlem Renaissance
- Probability, statistics, algebra
- Classification of living things—for example, kingdom, phylum
- Cell structure and processes, photosynthesis, life cycles, reproduction, the endocrine system

- Chemistry of matter
- Energy transfer, models of the universe, speed, power, and work in physics

Even these partial lists are impressive and convey the breadth and depth of the Core Knowledge curriculum.

Although Hirsch's rigorous, content-rich approach to education runs counter to some strong trends in American education, it has appealed to a great many school officials, teachers, and parents. Over 150 schools all over the country, both public and private, have adopted the Core Knowledge concept and curriculum.

Crossroads Academy

LYME, NEW HAMPSHIRE

Crossroads Academy is an independent school, founded in 1990 as a Core Knowledge school. Founder and director Mary Beth Klee, who has a Ph.D. in American history and has taught at the college level, had serious questions about the educational system even before she came upon the work of E. D. Hirsch. She recalls:

> The time I spent teaching undergraduates—and to be candid, the time I spent reflecting on my own over-long educational career—made me very aware of how inefficient our educational system is. The undergraduates I taught were bright people who had been through decent schools, but they hadn't learned much. They had been learning how to learn, but the content wasn't there. They lacked a context in which to place new information. I once gave a lecture on the Protestant Reformation. A student came up afterward and asked why I kept leaving off Martin Luther King's last name.

Klee's interest in early education became more active when her son reached kindergarten age. Although the schools in Hanover—the town where Klee lives and the home of Dartmouth College—are reputed to be among the best in the country, Klee felt that their programs were largely skills based and content neutral.

Klee began a kindergarten in the basement of the local Catholic church and used songs, poems, and games to introduce material about the American presidents, the solar system, and other topics. The next year she had a kindergarten and a multi-age class, with a total enrollment of sixteen children. Articulate and energetic, Klee worked hard, giving talks, having school open houses, and writing articles for local papers to spread the word about her little school. Soon it outgrew its basement home.

Crossroads Academy now has nearly one hundred students and is housed in a large and spacious brick building in a pleasant rural setting. Crossroads is not typical of most Core Knowledge schools. It is a private school, while most others in the movement are public schools. It also has several elements that, while they do not contradict the Core Knowledge approach, are not necessarily part of it. These include a strict dress code, a moral education program (see chapter 10), and a nondenominational but explicit commitment to the Judeo-Christian religious and philosophical tradition. Yet Crossroads is typical in its commitment to the rigorous, content-rich Core Knowledge curriculum. This is clearly the major force shaping the school.

In the second-grade classroom, the day begins with a minute of silence, after which the teacher reads aloud a story illustrating the importance of perseverance. The children recite from memory a poem by A. A. Milne, and then, also from memory and with accompanying hand motions, sing a song about the history of ancient India. The class spends the rest of the morning studying phonetics, language arts, and math for periods of thirty or forty minutes. The children sit in rows facing the teacher and the blackboard. An assistant teacher moves quietly about giving individual help. For math, the class breaks up into four groups, each with its own teacher. In the afternoon the children study French, history, and music.

When I ask the second-grade teacher why parents send their children to Crossroads, she replies, "I was a teaching assistant at a local elementary school for some time, and the program here is just a lot more rigorous. The children really learn a lot more, from kindergarten on. Plus the classes are small, and the children receive a lot of individual attention."

For the other classes as well, the day is divided into periods during which they study a particular subject. Thus, at 10:30 AM the combined fourth and fifth grade is getting a spelling test. Next door the third-grade children are reciting from memory Brutus's speech to the Romans, "Friends, Romans, countrymen, lend me your ears . . .," and down the hall the combined sixth- and seventh-grade class is doing mental math. The students seem interested, engaged, and enthusiastic. When the teacher asks a question, many of them eagerly and quickly raise their hands to answer.

After lunch, the classes are less structured. Klee has a ninety-minute session on medieval history with the combined fourth- and fifth-grade class. She begins by drawing a time line on the blackboard and marking it with three dates: AD 476, AD 800, and 1215. Some of the children almost leap out of their seats to volunteer what happened in each year (the Roman Empire fell; Charlemagne was crowned emperor of the Holy

Roman Empire; the Magna Carta was signed). The children then rehearse a play about the Norman conquest of England. Later, with Gregorian chant music playing in the background, the students use clay to fashion chess pieces—knights, bishops, kings, and queens.

The program at Crossroads is clearly academically rigorous and content rich, but it is not dry or one-sided. As is clear in Klee's class, the material is presented in imaginative and interesting ways, and the students have many opportunities for self-expression. Next to the science room downstairs is a large and much-used art and projects classroom.

In our final conversation Klee remarks:

> There is an important piece missing from most of the efforts at educational reform today: content. Critical thinking, problem solving, and decision making are important, but the children also need the basic academic skills and a knowledge of our cultural heritage. It is not a matter of either/ or. We can and must give them both. I think that the Core Knowledge approach represents the cutting edge in education today. This is the type of education that will serve us best in the twenty-first century. That's why some families living in this area, families that pay thousands of dollars in property taxes to support a public school system, send their children to Crossroads.

The Monhegan School
BRONX, NEW YORK

The Monhegan School is a public elementary school located in a disadvantaged, minority area in the South Bronx. All of its students are poor;

99 percent are African-American. Monhegan is one of the large and growing number of public schools using the Core Knowledge curriculum.

In 1988, Jeffrey Litt took over as principal of what was then called Public School 67. The school was a disaster, both as a physical facility and as a place for learning. Litt managed to spruce up the school and to instill some pride and confidence in faculty and students. But in 1990 he still lacked a curriculum that inspired and really educated the children. He attended a conference on Core Knowledge, heard Hirsch speak, and decided to try the approach.

The following year, Monhegan School adopted the Core Knowledge curriculum. There, as in many similar schools, it has been a signal success. Reading scores have increased (13 percent in one academic year), as have math scores. Monhegan has become a magnet school attracting children who have been in parochial schools or in schools in nearby districts.

Of the Core Knowledge curriculum, Litt says, "It is the great equalizer. When inner-city kids feel challenged instead of written off, they learn. And that's their way out of the ghetto, their way to a better life."

For More Information

Core Knowledge Foundation
2012-B Morton Drive
Charlottesville, VA 22903
Tel: (804) 977-7550

The Core Knowledge Foundation was started by E. D. Hirsch. It provides information on the Core Knowledge approach and helps schools wishing to adopt the program. It has a list of schools around the country that are working successfully with the Core Knowledge approach and that will welcome inquiries.

The foundation publishes a newsletter called *Common Knowledge* and holds regular conferences dealing with the Core Knowledge curriculum to education.

For Further Reading

Core Knowledge Foundation. *Core Knowledge Resource Series.* New York: Doubleday, 1991/1991/1992/1992/1993/1993 This is a series of books—one for each grade through grade six. They are titled *What Your First [through Sixth] Grader Needs to Know,* and give the basic knowledge—in literature, science, math, history, music, and other areas—that a child at that age should have.

———. *Core Knowledge Sequence: Content Guidelines for Grades K–6 (Revised 1995).* Charlottesville, Va.: Core Knowledge Foundation, 1995. This presents in outline form the suggested curricular content for grades K-6.

Hirsch, E. D., Jr. *Cultural Literacy: What Every American Needs to Know.* Boston: Houghton Mifflin, 1987. Academic in tone, *Cultural Literacy* is nevertheless a readable and convincing justification for content-rich education. This book launched the Core Knowledge educational movement and includes a list of about five thousand names, phrases, dates, and concepts that is an attempt to make explicit the shared background of American literate culture.

——— (ed.). *A First Dictionary of Cultural Literacy: What Our Children Need to Know.* Boston:

Houghton Mifflin, 1991. An illustrated reference guide with easy-to-understand explanations of some two thousand names, places, events, and ideas that are part of American culture's common knowledge.

————. *The Schools We Need and Why We Don't Have Them.* New York: Doubleday, 1996. Hirsch charges that bad ideas and failed theories have come to dominate American education. The result is an inadequate education for all children and especially for children from disadvantaged backgrounds. He presents a new model for education, inspired in part by the educational systems in countries like Japan, France, and Germany. The book contains "A Critical Guide to Educational Terms and Phrases" and a glossary of such terms as "child-centered education," "multiple intelligences," and "critical thinking skills."

Hirsch, E. D., Jr., and John Holden (eds.). *What Your Kindergartner Needs to Know.* New York: Double-

day, 1996. Stories, poems, a "friendly" introduction to history and geography, and activities in science, music, and the arts.

————. *Books to Build On: A Grade by Grade Resource Guide for Parents and Teachers.* New York: Bantam Doubleday Dell, 1996. Quality books, tapes, and educational materials in language arts, history and geography, visual arts, music, science, and math.

Hirsch, E. D., Jr., Joseph Kett, and James Trefil (eds.). *The Dictionary of Cultural Literacy.* Boston: Houghton Mifflin, 1993. A comprehensive reference guide (with maps, charts, and illustrations) with entries discussing the important names, places, and ideas that make up the body of necessary knowledge.

Ravitch, Diane, and Chester Finn. *What Do Our Seventeen-Year-Olds Know?* New York: Harper and Row, 1987. An analysis of the failure of our schools to give students the basis of cultural literacy.

15

Essential Schools

Between 1979 and 1984, Theodore Sizer, a former dean of Harvard's School of Education, directed a study of American high schools. He found that in most schools something approximating the following situation prevailed.

The school is large and impersonal. There may be as many as 5,000 students and 300 teachers. The teachers are overworked and demoralized. Each has to teach as many as 150 students and has little freedom in what and how they teach. Curricula are mandated by the state, are textbook based, and are oriented to standardized tests. Each subject is treated as an isolated discipline, to be studied in its own forty-five minute period with a teacher specialist. Much of the students' learning involves their memorizing facts to be regurgitated on tests. Students are classified, labeled, and segregated according to age and to academic ability, or, more accurately, according to their ability to take written tests. Pen-and-pencil tests, usually multiple choice or fill-in-the-blank, are virtually the only means of student assessment and evaluation. Many students are unmotivated, with little interest in school, and are only "serving time" until they graduate.

Schools must have a clear vision of what they want to accomplish, that is, what kind of person they want to send into the world.

Even the school principal has little power to change the school. There is a powerful bureaucratic hierarchy, composed of officials at the local, district, state, and federal levels, that determines most of what goes on in the school. There are also various special interest groups—teachers' unions, schools of education, textbook publishers, purveyors of goods and services to the schools—each with a stake in the status quo and not enthusiastic about significant change.

This situation, which perhaps has not changed substantially in the past decade, was intolerable to Sizer. The schools, he felt, were not fulfilling their mission to educate children to become thoughtful, decent, happy citizens.

After finishing the study, Sizer published *Horace's Compromise*, which described the problems besetting America's high schools and proposed a rethinking and reform of the schools to address those problems. In that same year, he founded the Coalition of Essential Schools, an association of schools committed to their own restructuring and reform. In a second book, *Horace's School: Redesigning the American High School* (1992), Sizer reiterated and developed his program for change in the schools.

Sizer maintains that, above all, schools must have a clear vision of what they want to accomplish, that is, what kind of person they want to send into the world. School reforms based on corporate and government concerns about economic competition in the world are not necessarily based on the best interests of the student.

Sizer has a clear image of the kind of human being he thinks schools should strive to develop. Most of all, this person is a "thoughtful" human being, an individual with an informed, balanced, and responsibly skeptical approach to life. This person has strong intellectual skills and healthy intellectual habits. These include a keen analytical ability, a broad perspective, communication skills, and the capacity to see an issue from another person's point of view, as well as imagination and a sense of commitment to the world. Dependability, practicality, courage, a sense of humor, a sense of social justice, and aesthetic sensitivity are also important. But as an aim of education, the quality of thoughtfulness is paramount.

Sizer asserts that to realize these objectives, the educational system must change radically—in organization, pedagogy, and curriculum. To this end, he makes a series of proposals:

- The size of the group of which a student is a member should be small. Ideally, a school should have no more than two hundred students. If it is larger, it should be broken down into "houses," "teams," or "schools within a school," each with its own group of students and teachers. Each student should be part of a yet smaller group and have a faculty advisor.
- The number of students a teacher teaches should be reduced to a maximum of eighty. This would allow teachers to get to know

students better, to help them more effectively in their studies, and to evaluate their work in a more reflective manner.
- The classroom model in which the teacher is the dispenser of information and the student is the passive recipient should be replaced by a model in which the student is an active, self-directed learner and the teacher is a guide, facilitator, and inspirer. The teacher creates opportunities for the students to learn. Teachers must look on themselves as learners who are growing, developing, and creating along with the students.
- Teachers should have both autonomy and responsibility in educating the children. The principal should be a coordinator and support person rather than an overseer.
- The curriculum should emphasize depth rather than breadth. In mainstream schools, students are rushed through a lot of content without time to reflect on it or to develop proper habits of mind. Rather, one important though limited topic should be studied deeply over a long period of time. For example, students might study the history of the United States and the experience of Americans in the world rather than the whole of world history.
- Grouping should be multi-age and, in terms of ability, heterogeneous. Thus teams and classes should include students from several age groups and with various levels of ability. There should be no tracking. Each student should have as much academic stimulation and challenge as possible.
- Cooperative and collaborative learning among students and group problem solving should be emphasized, rather than compe-

tition for grades and for class rank.

- Long-term, in-depth projects leading to exhibitions should comprise most of the student's work. Students choose a theme or topic or are presented with one and then do an interdisciplinary study that culminates in a public presentation or exhibition demonstrating the skills and abilities they have acquired.
- Students should be assessed on the basis of a portfolio—a collection of their written and artistic work, video and audio tapes, and other products of their activity in school. The portfolio should be the basis of promotion and graduation.
- Higher-order critical thinking skills such as analysis, synthesis, and evaluation rather than lower-order skills such as memorization should be emphasized.
- The decision-making power about what goes on in a certain school should be invested as much as possible in that school. Teachers, school administrators, parents, and students should decide together what kind of school and what kind of curriculum they will have. District school boards, state supervisors, federal officials, and other distant administrators should only be sources of advice and help, not authorities who make decisions and then impose them from above. The community in which the school is located should be brought into the decision-making process so that it can support and nourish the school.
- There should be regular interaction with the community through field trips, community service, and student apprenticeships and internships.
- The school year should be lengthened from thirty-six to forty-two weeks. The school

day should be lengthened to eight hours, to last from 8:00 AM to 4:00 PM. Each house or team within a school should have control over its own schedule. Teachers should be allowed time for meetings and collaborative planning.

When Sizer founded the Coalition of Essential Schools in 1984, nine "charter" schools committed themselves to this program of reform. As of December 1995 there were 220 member schools, 469 schools exploring the organization's program, and 263 schools actively planning to implement it. The schools involved include inner-city, suburban, and rural schools, public and private schools, and middle schools as well as high schools.

The Ralph B. O'Maley Middle School
GLOUCESTER, MASSACHUSETTS

The Ralph B. O'Maley Middle School is a massive, small-windowed brick structure overlooking acres of grass playing fields. It is less than a mile from the ocean, and standing in front of the school, one can smell salt in the air.

Despite its typical public school appearance, O'Maley is a relatively rare bird. Out of the eight hundred public schools in Massachusetts, it is one of the eleven that is a member of the Coalition of Essential Schools. Nevertheless, Principal Sue M. Gee says that what O'Maley is doing is not an "alternative" to the educational mainstream. "This is the wave of the future," she avers:

With the educational reform and restructuring bill passed in Massachusetts in 1993, every school in the Commonwealth will be going down this path. Site-based management, a student-centered curriculum, and an end to tracking have all been mandated by the legislature.

Besides, the kind of hands-on experiential learning that we promote is supported by the latest educational research. Studies indicate that children remember 2 percent of what they listen to in a lecture, 20 percent of what they see, but 75 percent of what they are involved in in a participatory, active way, and 90 percent of what they teach to others.

A short time later I am in a sixth-grade classroom. Karen MacAulay is one of two main teachers for the class, teaching math and science while a colleague covers language arts and social studies. The desks of the twenty or so children are arranged in clusters of four with the students seated facing each other. Some of the children have a "geo-board," a piece of wood about ten inches square with nails arranged in a tight grid. They are using long "elastics" (or rubber bands) to form various geometric shapes on their geoboards. Others have used a ruler and compass to construct a rhombus on a piece of drawing paper and now are using crayons to add an illustration and a definition.

"What's a rhombus?" asks a plump boy of the teacher. "Brandon, look it up or ask a neighbor," replies MacAulay, declining to play the role of teacher as encyclopaedic source of information. Brandon sighs in exasperation, then queries the nearest possible source. "What's a rhombus?" he asks me.

Then there is a quiz. "Everyone form a rhombus on your geo-board," instructs the teacher. The children do so, then hold up the boards for inspection. "Now a polygon!" "Okay, a trapezoid!" At each command the children rearrange their elastics on the pegs with intense concentration.

Later, in a seventh-grade social studies class, the children are studying the conflict in the former Yugoslavia. A student is leading a question-and-answer session about the geography of Serbia and Bosnia. The teacher, Ann Ziergiebel, remarks later, "We do a lot of project work. The children work in small groups and together produce an exhibition. It helps them use their research, language, and organizational skills but in a real situation with a real goal rather than in an abstract situation. Recently, a class did a study of the World Bank. They had to design a program for economic development for a third world country and make a proposal for funding to the World Bank. They worked in pairs and in small groups, and used teachers and members of the community as resources."

Later I ask Gee about the process of becoming a Coalition school. She replies:

> First a school signs up as an exploring school, which means that it is seriously looking into the Coalition approach. Then usually a group of faculty members will go on a "trek," a week-long intensive orientation in the Coalition's principles and practices. The trek we attended was at Brown University. The school then begins to implement changes, often with the help of experienced teachers and administrators from an established member school. The school may apply for membership when a majority of the faculty vote in favor of the move and when a prospectus for change is written by a steering committee. There is no charge for joining the Coalition but schools do need money for professional development. O'Maley received a grant from the State Department of Education and

also has used local professional development funds to make the transition.

Staff development is the major challenge. Teachers have to learn to work with the children in a different way. It can be difficult and anxiety producing to adopt a new approach to teaching that, for example, addresses different learning styles and uses cooperative learning groups.

Parents are important collaborators in school change. They take part in the management of the school as members of the screening committee which hires teachers and as members of the site-based management team which creates policies and explores continuing changes.

The Central Park East Secondary School
NEW YORK, NEW YORK

One of the flagship schools of the Coalition of Essential Schools is the Central Park East Secondary School (CPESS) in East Harlem in New York City. It was founded according to Coalition principles in the mid-1980s by Deborah Meier and other New York City schoolteachers who felt the need for a new and workable vision of education. The school has been a signal success and much has been written about it.

At CPESS all students take the same set of core courses. There is no "smorgasbord curriculum" as at a large comprehensive school. All students, even those with learning disabilities, are mainstreamed and expected to master the standard curriculum. The focus is on developing positive intellectual habits. The students learn to ask questions like "What do we know?" "How do we know what we know?" "What is the evidence?"

"What is the viewpoint behind the person giving the evidence?"

Classes meet in two-hour blocks. Students do research projects on a given theme in each subject. Art and music are woven into the academic subjects. There is both individual and cooperative work and students are assessed based on the exhibitions and presentations that emerge from their projects. Promotions and graduation take place based on careful review of student portfolios, which contain various work products.

Each student has an advisor, who is their personal advocate in the school, and the two meet every day for ten minutes. There are longer group meetings between advisors and all of their advisees, as well as longer individual sessions. Advisors read student journals, tutor advisees, and serve as a resource for the students.

The school is organized to create a sense of community. It is open from early in the morning until early evening. During these hours, students are free to use the school and its facilities, including the library. Parents are consulted and involved in all areas of school life.

CPESS is in a disadvantaged, inner-city area. Forty-five percent of the students are African-American and 30 percent are Hispanic. In New York City, these groups normally have a drop-out rate of 78 percent and 72 percent, respectively. There are virtually no dropouts at CPESS, and the students do well on standardized tests.

Various schools have joined the Coalition of Essential Schools. The Coalition emphasizes that it does not propose a specific recipe for reform, it only provides certain basic ideas about educational aims, methods, and modes of organization. Each school can and should implement these principles in ways that are appropriate to its particular identity and situation.

There are "Nine Common Principles" of the

Coalition, which are the shared guidelines for all Coalition schools:

1. The school focuses on helping adolescents to use their minds well.
2. The school has a simple goal: to help each student master a limited number of essential skills and areas of knowledge. The aim is mastery and competence rather than coverage of a large amount of material.
3. The school seeks this goal for all students. It applies different means to achieve it.
4. Teaching and learning are personalized. Curricular and scheduling decisions are made by the principal and faculty. A teacher should have responsibility for no more than eighty children.
5. The student functions as an active, largely self-motivated learner, the teacher as a coach and guide.
6. The basis for graduation is an exhibition in which a student demonstrates the knowledge and central skills the school aims at. Credits earned or time spent at school have no value.
7. There is an explicit and nurtured relationship of trust and respect among parents, students, and teachers.
8. Teachers and principals are generalists, committed to the school and willing to take on various roles in the school.
9. The operation of the school according to Coalition principles will not increase the operating budget by more than 10 percent. Some nonessential services may have to be reduced or eliminated.

The principles and practices of the Coalition of Essential Schools are basically those of classical Deweyan progressive education, supplemented by a concern for site-based management, size reduction, limitation of educational goals, and debureaucratization. The Coalition is essentially a grassroots, up-from-below movement. The impetus for a school becoming a Coalition school most often comes from a principal or group of teachers, not from educational officials higher up in the bureaucracy. Of course, parents may initiate the process by calling the attention of local school board members, administrators, and teachers to the Coalition and its program.

In the early years of the Coalition, Sizer realized that some of the major obstacles to reforming individual schools were state rules and regulations concerning education. Thus in 1988, the Coalition cooperated with the Education Commission for the States—a commission created by the state governments—to form Re:Learning. This organization tries to create a supportive environment for educational change, one that reaches from the local school to the statehouse. A state can join if the governor and the chief state school official, such as the commissioner of education, approve and if the state agrees to support reform efforts in up to ten Coalition schools for five years. Eleven states are now members: Arkansas, Colorado, Delaware, Illinois, Indiana, Maine, Missouri, New Mexico, Pennsylvania, Rhode Island, and South Carolina. In these states, parents, teachers, and local officials have an advantage in initiating the reform and restructuring of a school, since the state is formally committed to change according to the Coalition pattern.

Resources

For More Information

Coalition of Essential Schools
Brown University
Box 1969
Providence, R.I. 02912
Tel.: (401) 863-3384

The Coalition of Essential Schools is the central organization for the Essential School restructuring and reform movement. It offers help and guidance to parents, teachers, and administrators who want to learn about the Essential School approach. It offers regular workshops, forums, and conferences.

The Coalition publishes and sells a number of research studies and short articles, as well as back and current issues of *Horace: The Journal of the Coalition of Essential Schools.* Back issues are $1.50; subscriptions are $20 per year (five issues).

The Center for Collaborative Education
1573 Madison Avenue, Room 201
New York, NY 10029-3899
Tel.: (212) 348-7821
Fax: (212) 348-7850

This is the New York City affiliate of the Coalition for Essential Schools; it promotes Coalition concepts actively in New York City.

Grant, Gerald. *The World We Created at Hamilton High.* Cambridge, Mass.: Harvard University Press, 1988. An account of the transformation of one high school into an Essential School.

Lightfoot, Sarah Lawrence. *The Good High School.* New York: Basic Books, 1983. A study of the factors that make a high school work.

Meier, Deborah. *The Power of Their Ideas.* Boston: Beacon Press, 1995. The story of the successful application of the Coalition principles of the Essential School to the Central Park East Secondary School located in East Harlem in New York City.

Sizer, Theodore. *Horace's Compromise: The Dilemma of the American High School.* Boston: Houghton Mifflin, 1984. Sizer's initial analysis of the ills besetting secondary public school education in the United States and his recommendations for reform.

———. *Horace's School: Redesigning the American High School.* Boston: Houghton Mifflin, 1992. A sequel to *Horace's Compromise.* Sizer describes the state of most American high schools and offers his fully developed program of reform.

Wood, George H. *Schools That Work: America's Most Innovative Public Education Programs.* New York: Dutton, 1992. A survey of schools that have been successfully reformed and restructured. Wood points out that it is helpful to look at healthy schools to see what they are doing. Most of the schools he discusses are operating according to the guidelines of the Coalition of Essential Schools, the Comer model, and other progressively oriented approaches.

16

Foxfire

꧁

In 1966, Elliot Wigginton, a young English teacher at a high school in Rabun County, Georgia, was looking for a way to motivate his students. Inspired by the idea of experiential, student-initiated learning that was then receiving widespread attention, Wigginton decided to have his students create a magazine about the local Appalachian culture and history. The students conducted interviews, did research, wrote and edited articles, and designed, published, and distributed the magazine. It was called *Foxfire* after a luminescent fungus found in the area that grows on dead trees and gives off a bluish-green light at night.

Foxfire was an educational, literary, and commercial success. Through their work on the magazine, students acquired the skills they were supposed to develop as students in an English class. At the same time they learned much about their local area and also produced an informative and attractive magazine. *Foxfire* gained national distribution and recognition. Anthologies of its articles were published by a major publishing house and the magazine is still being published.

Out of his experience with the magazine, Wigginton developed and articulated an approach to education which he called the Foxfire approach. It is based on classical Deweyan, progressive ideas and incorporates some of the neoprogressive addenda. Its core principles and practices—as currently presented by the Foxfire Institute—are as follows:

The goal of schooling and of the Foxfire approach is a more effective and humane democratic society.

Students must become thoughtful participants in their education and develop so that they can guide their own learning for the rest of their lives. The aim is independence, responsible behavior, and wisdom.

1. All work that teachers and students do together flows from student desire and student choice. Students must be involved in solving the problems that arise in the classroom.

2. The teacher is a collaborator, team leader, guide, and model of behavior, attitude, and values, rather than a boss.

3. There must be academic integrity. The children must master all the mandated academic skills but also go

> *Students must become thoughtful participants in their education and develop so that they can guide their own learning for the rest of their lives.*

꧁

deeper into the material and relate it to other material.

4. The work is characterized by student action, not by the passive reception of processed, predigested information. Students must be led into new work and unfamiliar territory. They must constantly apply newly won skills. Since they are always working at the edge of their competence, failures are seen as occasions for constructive change.

5. Peer teaching, small group work, and teamwork that involves and gives importance to each student are central. These approaches usually eliminate discipline problems.

6. Connections between classroom work and the surrounding communities and the outside world are clear. Larger issues are understood as having implications for the local community.

7. There is an audience beyond the teacher for student work—an individual, a group, or a community that affirms the importance and worthiness of the work.

8. New activities gracefully spiral out of the old.

9. Teachers acknowledge the worth of aesthetic experiences and of the imagination. Aesthetic experiences give us a sense of wholeness and completeness and help us to express ourselves and to break out of restrictive ways of thinking.

10. There is time set aside for reflection that can lead to further insights and to revisions.

11. There is honest, ongoing evaluation of the skills acquired and content mastered—by the student himself or her-

self, by fellow students, and by the teacher.

Using funds earned by the publication of _Foxfire_, Wigginton and his colleagues and students established the Foxfire Institute to develop and spread the Foxfire approach. In 1986, the institute received a five-year grant from a private foundation. It has since developed Foxfire programs in schools all around the country. The Foxfire Institute now has ten full-time staff members in its home office in Georgia. There are also coordinators in various parts of the country who work to spread Foxfire methods.

In each region, training in Foxfire methods is available for in-service teachers. Some of the courses are graduate-level courses offered through colleges and universities. Some are part of staff development programs sponsored by school districts or educational agencies. But most are one- or two-week courses held during the summer that have follow-up sessions during the school year. These are for-credit courses for practicing teachers taught by teams of teachers who themselves use the Foxfire approach. The instructors demonstrate and explain the Foxfire approach, relate it to past and present educational reform movements, and examine with teachers in the course the state-mandated educational goals they must fulfill. They help the aspiring Foxfire teachers design classroom activities that will fulfill the goals in a way that is consistent with the Foxfire approach.

Over four thousand teachers have been trained in the Foxfire approach. Some of these teach in schools that have completely gone over to the Foxfire method. Many are teachers who alone or with a few colleagues have brought Foxfire into their schools.

Marylyn Wentworth of Kennebunk, Maine,

works to introduce Foxfire methods to public and private schools in the state. She explains:

> Foxfire is very much a grassroots movement. The main initiators are individual teachers who want to try an approach that puts more of the learning and decision making into the hands of the children. I give courses for in-service teachers, from kindergarten to the high-school grades, mostly through the University of Southern Maine in Portland. Foxfire originally was an approach for high-school students. But it can be used very effectively in elementary and middle school classrooms as well.
>
> The Foxfire approach is not a simple recipe, with easy-to-follow step-by-step directions. Rather it is a set of principles which must be applied differently in each situation. It requires teachers to make fundamental changes in their approaches to teaching.

Teachers who have adopted the Foxfire approach can receive ongoing support from local and regional networks of Foxfire teachers. These networks offer periodic meetings, newsletters, collegial visits, informal gatherings, and opportunities for professional development.

Foxfire is spreading. There are Foxfire initiatives at about a dozen inner-city schools around the country. At several universities, undergraduate teacher training in the Foxfire approach is available.

The Skillin Elementary School
SOUTH PORTLAND, MAINE

The Skillin Elementary School is an attractive school—spacious, bright, and colorful. In terms of its curriculum and pedagogy, it is a fairly typical American elementary school. Students study English, history, geography, math, and science. For the most part they learn in traditional ways, through teacher presentations, workbooks, and textbooks and readers.

Life in Maggie Allen's classroom, however, is different from life in other Skillin classrooms. The children are learning the same skills and covering the same subject matter but doing so in a different way. They spend very little time listening to their teacher present information or working with textbooks and workbooks. They spend a lot of time planning and carrying out their own research projects and preparing public presentations for audiences outside the classroom.

Allen's second-floor classroom looks out over playing fields and tennis courts bordered by trees, almost leafless now in late autumn. The room is neat and tidy and the children sit facing each other in groups of four. At a top corner of each desk is a list of the personal goals that each child has set for the year. "Improve handwriting and spelling. Reduce talkouts," reads one.

A major portion of the window-side wall is covered with round pieces of colored paper. Above them are the words "Does your work. . . ." Each "balloon" has a phrase written in it:

> Flow from your own interests and concerns?
> Spiral out of previous work?
> Involve your own action?
> Have academic integrity?
> Have an audience beyond the classroom?
> Use teamwork?
> Relate to your own life?
> Have ongoing and honest assessment?

Below the balloons are colored paper strips that describe the student this classroom hopes to develop. These "learner outcomes" include:

Children in the Foxfire program at Skillin Elementary School in South Portland, Maine, confer on a research project. Student research leading to a class presentation is an important element in the Foxfire approach.

Knowledgeable person
Effective communicator
Collaborative learner
Involved citizen
Critical thinker
Quality producer
Self-directed lifelong learner

In all their studies the children in this class play a major role in deciding what and how they learn. For example, the previous year, as fourth-graders, the children studied the state of Maine. Allen started the project off with a "carousel" exercise. There were several stations, such as "History and Geography," "Nature and Wildlife," and "Famous Mainers." The class was divided into groups and each group spent time at each station brainstorming about what it knew about that topic, writing down the relevant names and words, and thinking about things it would like to research.

During the course of the year the class studied each broad topic in turn. For each topic students formed groups. Each group chose a research

theme, carried out a project, and prepared a presentation. One group prepared a poster about the birds in Maine. Another researched the role of Maine in the Civil War, sponsored a visit from two representatives of the Maine Civil War Reenactors, and held a bake sale to fund the visit. Another group studied the World War II liberty ships, which were built in Maine, and invited outside speakers to talk about the war years in Maine. For the "Famous Mainers" projects, individual students chose a notable Maine native, did research about the person, and made a presentation to the class. They were allowed to use any medium—a skit, a commercial, a song—anything except a straight oral report. One girl studied Margaret Chase Smith and, wearing a black dress and a signature red rose, gave a speech the former United States senator had once delivered.

Much of the work took the children outside the school and into the community. Some students did a community survey to find out who the best-known Maine natives were and discovered that horror-writer Stephen King is by far the most well-known, with Henry Wadsworth Longfellow a distant second. The class took a trip to the state capital and with the help of political lobbyists staged a mock legislative committee meeting.

The study of folktales is also part of the standard fourth-grade curriculum in Maine. The class took as the "essential question" the focal issue of the project: "How do folktales reflect their culture?" Children with interest in the same country worked together in groups. They studied folktales of England, Japan, China, Germany, Scandinavia, the United States, and Native American culture within the United States. They studied how the folktales of each country reveal something about that culture. One boy decided that the importance of self-sacrifice in Japanese stories might be related to the smallness of the country. Two girls concluded that the Paul Bunyan stories of early America were related to the need to get things done in a huge and untamed land.

In a class meeting about their folktale projects, a boy observed that he learns better when he is physically active. So each group designed a game that went along with its country, and the class set up a "Folktale Town" for the whole school. There was a soccer game with "the Black Forest" and a German castle as goals. There was a pitcher-batter game with the home-run wall being a cardboard model of the Appalachian Mountains. The Folktale Town was so successful that the class was invited to present it to a statewide conference of Maine educators.

Allen evaluated all the work of all the children. But the children also evaluated their own work and that of other students. Whenever possible the presentations were made to an audience beyond the class.

The class carried out these projects as fourth-graders. When I visit they are just beginning fifth grade, looking ahead to another year of research

and presentations. They have Allen as their teacher for a second year because they sent a petition to the principal to have her again.

Besides the in-depth project work, Allen's students work hard on basic academic and critical-thinking skills. The day starts with two analogies and a math problem. Allen writes on the board, "drill:bore as ——:sew." There is a lively discussion of the various possible answers. A large part of the morning is devoted to a writing workshop in which the children work in twos and threes on reading comprehension, vocabulary building, and writing.

The class functions largely democratically. Allen takes the role of facilitator and guide rather than of authority figure. The children not only have a large voice in deciding what and how they study, they also play a role in grading. They de-

Students help each other read and write during the daily language arts period of the Foxfire class at Skillin Elementary School.

signed a grading rubric that specifies what level of effort and achievement is involved with each of the four possible assessment grades—1, 2, 3, and 4.

They also formulated the guidelines for classroom behavior and created a "being," who represents ideal behavior. On one wall is a huge outline drawing of a human figure. Within the figure are words and phrases such as "telling the truth," "kindness," "consideration," and "responsibility." Outside the figure are written "lying," "teasing," "bullying," "cheating," "stealing," "causing a disruption," and other less-than-ideal behaviors.

Allen's approach seems to work. The children are interested, engaged, and enthusiastic. They seem to be acquiring the basic academic skills, and although the IQ range is from 60 to 140 they all do well on standardized tests. Children from opposite ends of the IQ spectrum work harmoniously together. Before entering the class, one boy with learning and behavioral problems had been considered for placement in a special education class. Now he is a steady, hard-working, well-behaved student. The boy himself wrote in a composition that what he is doing in school now is interesting and important so it is easy for him to behave well and to learn.

A two-minute's walk away from the Skillin School is the Memorial Middle School. One of the teachers there is Mary Weber, who, like Allen, has studied and adopted the Foxfire approach. Her eighth-grade social studies class is engaged in a project on maps and map reading. The "givens," that is, the requirements of the project (a basic Foxfire concept), are that the students learn the different kind of maps, the different parts of maps, how the landforms are represented, and how to use maps. The essential question is, "How can maps be used to represent a community?"

Small groups have formed, each with a specific interest and corresponding project. One group is studying a local housing development that was built about thirty years ago. They are looking through old hand-drawn maps of South Portland and at photographs taken thirty years ago. Another group is preparing an enlarged map of a local shopping mall. When these and the other projects are finished they will be displayed in public places outside the school. The housing-development project will be hung up in the town hall; the mall map will be displayed at the mall itself. Weber goes from group to group answering questions and offering advice.

A new teacher at Memorial, Weber talks about introducing her students to the Foxfire approach and to student-centered learning:

> At first they didn't know what to make of it. They were used to being told what to learn and how to learn it, and of being the passive recipients of knowledge spouted by the teacher. And on some days, I was at a loss and asked myself, "Is this going to work here?" But I have just kept handing them the ball and making them take responsibility.
>
> Earlier in the map project they wanted to learn how to do orienteering, so they contacted the L. L. Bean store in Freeport and found out that they offer group courses. But it costs $100 for the class. They asked me, "How are we going to get $100?" I said, "I don't know." So they decided to have a bake sale. They can do it. They just have to break the habits of passivity and realize they can take responsibility for their own learning. When they do that, learning becomes fun and exciting.

Foxfire

FOR MORE INFORMATION

For information about Foxfire and its Rabun County (Georgia) activities, contact:

> Hilton Smith, Executive Director
> Foxfire
> P.O. Box 541
> Mountain City, GA 30562
> Tel.: (706) 746-5828
> Fax: (706) 746-5829

For information about courses in the Foxfire approach and about teacher networks around the country, contact:

> Kim D. Cannon, Executive Assistant
> Foxfire
> P.O. Box 541
> Mountain City, GA 30562
> Tel.: (706) 746-5318

FOR FURTHER READING

DeYoung, Alan. "Today Kentucky, Tomorrow America? Linking the Foxfire Approach to Teaching to Contemporary American School Reform," in *The New American School: Alternative Concepts and Practices*, ed. Bruce Jones. Norwood, N.J.: Ablex Publishing, 1993.

Ensminger, Gene, and Harry Dangel. "The Foxfire Pedagogy: A Confluence of Best Practices for Special Education," in *Educating Students with Mild Disabilities*, edited by Edward L. Meyer. Denver, Colo.: Love Publishing Company, 1993.

McDonald, Joseph P. *Teaching: Making Sense of an Uncertain Craft*. New York: Teachers College Press, 1992.

Teets, Sharon, and Janet Mobley. *Assessment in the Second-Grade Classroom: A Foxfire Story*. New York: Teachers College Press, 1992.

Wigginton, Eliot. *Sometimes a Shining Moment*. New York: Doubleday, 1985. An account of the origins, philosophy, and practice of the Foxfire approach.

———. "Culture Begins at Home," *Educational Leadership* 49 (December 1991/January 1992): 60–64.

Wood, George. *Schools That Work: America's Most Innovative Public Education Programs*. New York: Dutton, 1992. A survey of various progressively oriented public schools, including some that are using the Foxfire approach or similar student-centered approaches.

17

Free Schools

As mentioned in chapter 2, the 1961 publication of A. S. Neill's *Summerhill* in the United States was an important event in the history of American education in the second half of the twentieth century. The book describes Summerhill, an experimental primary and secondary boarding school that Neill founded in Leiston, Suffolk, England, in 1921. It presents in a concrete, compelling way the ideal and the practice, in a modern setting, of humanistic education based on the philosophy of Jean-Jacques Rousseau. Neill writes, "My guiding principle is that the child is innately wise and realistic. If left to himself without adult suggestion of any kind, he will develop as far as he is capable of developing."

Neill also maintains that happiness is "an inner feeling of contentment with life, of well-being, a sense of balance," and that it is the goal of life and education. Freedom is the means to achieve happiness. Thus at Summerhill the children have almost complete freedom in their education and in all aspects of their lives. They are free to establish their own limits in all areas, as long as they do not endanger their own health or safety or impinge on the rights of others.

The school is self-governing. All decisions are made at a general meeting at which all students, including first- and second-graders, have an equal voice and vote. The curriculum focuses more on contemporary needs than on classical education, and teaching methods vary. Arts and crafts are emphasized. Students are free to go to class or not go to class, to study or not to study, to remain at the school or not to remain at the school.

Children are free to establish their own limits in all areas, as long as they do not endanger their own health or safety or impinge on the rights of others.

When there is possible therapeutic or pedagogical value in a situation, this freedom may even extend to the destruction of property. Neill recounts that he once came upon a boy throwing stones at the school. Rather than reprimand him, Neill joined in the activity! At the same time Neill began to ask the boy what the trouble was, why he was angry. In the end, the encounter turned into one of Neill's "private lessons," a one-on-one session in which he helped a student deal with a problem.

Summerhill helped stimulate radical humanistic-progressive criticism of American education. The very concept of school came under attack. John Holt, for example, charged that what goes on in schools is confusing, boring, demeaning, and oppressive. The idea of school as a place separated from the world and reserved for "learning" is false and ridiculous. Children want to learn and are good at it. In fact they are learning all the time in games, sports, conversations, and other daily activities. Traditional, formal schooling only interferes with natural learning. Rather than marching children into schools against their will, adults should make the world accessible to children, let them explore it as they will, answer their questions, and otherwise stay out of the way. And Ivan Illich in *Deschooling Society* attacks schools as based on a variety of false ideas: that the world consists of educational and noneducational realms; that learning requires instruction in a school and that grades and certificates attest to learning and ability; and that the self-taught person is neither competent nor professional.

This intense criticism of mainstream education in the United States led to the establishment in the late 1960s and early 1970s of hundreds of small, "alternative" schools. Some, such as the school started by Jonathan Kozol (author of *Death at an Early Age*) in Roxbury, Massachusetts, were in the inner city and primarily served African-American children. Most were in suburban and rural areas—many in intentional communities—and were founded by white, middle- and upper-middle-class educated people who were disaffected from mainstream culture.

These were grassroots schools usually founded and run on a shoestring by a group of parents, teachers, and community members. They were small, independent, and cooperatively run. The schools were inclusive—admitting every child regardless of ability, circumstances, and behavioral or other problems. Tolerance, concern for the environment, and social justice were often central themes in school life.

Curricula and teaching methods varied. Most alternative schools adopted progressive principles

and practices, often in the radical form advocated by Neill, Holt, and others. They emphasized self-motivated, self-directed learning and allowed time for a lot of games, free play, and exploration of the natural environment and the community. Academic skills were taught but not pushed upon the children. The prevailing belief was that children will learn to read and do math when they are ready for it and ask for it. Children decided what they were to study and learn, and in many schools, whether they were to study and learn at all. They also were commonly given a voice in the running of the school. Because of the great freedom the children enjoyed, these schools were sometimes called "free schools." Because they were community based they were also called "community schools."

By the late 1970s there were over a thousand of these renegade schools in the country. Maine, a state with fewer than one million inhabitants, had more than forty such schools at that time.

Most of these schools have disappeared. Financial difficulties, disagreements over educational goals and the means to achieve them, and the decline of idealism in American society have taken a toll. But some survive and even flourish. There are about 350 free schools in operation today in the United States. Each is an expression both of the ideal of freedom in education and of the particular group of people or community who create and support it. Thus while these share some common characteristics, they vary greatly in particulars. The Sudbury Valley School in Framingham, Massachusetts, for example, is a relatively large school with close to two hundred students. Parent's participation is not encouraged; in fact, parents have to ask permission to visit the school. Students are free to attend class or not and are full participants in the decision-making processes that determine school life. Students help decide which teachers are to be re-hired. The two schools described below are also distinctive expressions of a commonly held philosophy and practice.

The School Around Us

ARUNDEL, MAINE

The School Around Us (SAU) in Arundel, Maine, was founded in 1970 by parents interested in community life, an ecological life-style, and a new type of education for their children. It is housed in an attractive, steep-roofed, cedar-shingled wooden building with a kitchen, dining room, and classroom on the ground floor and a large meeting room on the second floor. Next to the school is a railroad track that is still in use. Behind the building is a stream and beyond that dense woods. Near the school are a number of tall, thick-trunked pines with massive, bare, low boughs. Several harbor rough tree houses, and all show signs of being much climbed.

Two of the founding parents, Marylyn and Stacy Wentworth, donated the land for the school and they, other parents, and community members built the building. The five Wentworth children attended the school and all went on to successful college careers. Their daughter, Leah, returned to become a teacher at the school. The Wentworths still live on their farm, which is adjacent to the school. Stacy Wentworth recalls the idealism of the early years: "At first the school was heated by wood, and the children were responsible for keeping the fire going. Then it was decided to put in a propane furnace and we got into the fossil fuel business!"

Parent founded and parent built, SAU has also been parent run. At certain times in the school's history, parents, working as volunteers, have been the only teachers. Even in periods when there were paid, full-time teachers, parents have played an important, even dominant role in school life. Decisions about business matters as well as curriculum and pedagogy are made by consensus at meetings of all adults affiliated with the school. Helen Thorgalsen, whose two children are in the school and who is there herself most days, says, "In some free schools, the parents are not always very welcome. Here, though, we are an important part of the school. I come nearly every day and help out with the teaching and other activities."

There is no established curriculum at SAU. The students decide what they would like to study, and the teachers teach it or help the children conduct their own research and do their own projects. One day a week students teach classes of their own, on tree climbing or "magic cards," for example. The children are free to come to class or not. If they decide not to come to class, they must be respectful of others and do something constructive or worthwhile with their time. They also play a role in making decisions about school life.

An important part of the school day is the morning gathering. On most days it consists mainly of announcements and group singing, but on Wednesday—the day I visit—it is a formal meeting to deal with school issues. About twenty children between five and thirteen years old and six or seven adults form a loose circle in the large upstairs room. Some children sit on the floor, some on benches; a few stretch out on the floor. A few smaller children sit in the laps of adults or of older children. The atmosphere is informal, warm, and familial.

Audra, one of the older girls, is the moderator. She calls for agenda items and then writes each on a blackboard. A letter from Maine Senator William Cohen is read, acknowledging the children's concern, expressed in a letter to him, about cutbacks in Amtrak service. Then a letter from singer/songwriter Tom Lehrer is read, giving the class of older children permission to use a song of his in their video on recycling. The children and teachers together discuss several issues: the use of magic cards in the school; a table-and-blanket "fort" downstairs, which some of the boys are using for private meetings; and the dangers involved in tree climbing.

The meeting is well run and orderly. The children are self-confident and articulate and do not hesitate to contradict the adults. When one teacher suggests that they institute a height limit on tree climbing (a girl has recently fallen and hurt herself) a boy replies simply, "That is a bad idea!" Finally, it is decided that no child will climb to a height at which he or she feels uncomfortable. After the meeting there is a snack, and then most of the children and teachers and their visitor gather on the grass playground for the "morning activity"—a spirited game of "Capture the Flag."

After lunch the second of the three multi-age classes—which includes children between the ages of eight and ten—has a gardening class. After the gardening class, this group of children heads to the corporate headquarters of Tom's of Maine in nearby Kennebunk to take down an exhibit of their artwork. Tom Chappell, the owner of the natural body-care product company, was a founding parent of SAU. Meanwhile, at the school the older children are discussing the marketing of their recycling video, and the younger children are having a reading class.

The reading class takes place in a small room next to the kitchen. Seven children between six and eight years old and their teacher gather around a lilliputian table. The teacher, a woman in her forties, announces that she will read the class a story. Two of the boys immediately adjourn to a loft in the room to play magic cards and to, as they say, "listen from there." The children who remain discuss what story they would like to hear. After several minutes, they decide on a Doctor Seuss book and on two chapters from a book in the "Goosebumps" series called *Monster Blood II*. The teacher then carefully confirms the decision with each child. "Are you comfortable with that, Shanta? Does that work for you, Devon?" And so on around the table.

Shortly before school is over this same teacher is standing next to a tall pine tree, peering up into its branches. "Nicholas, come down, please." I look up also and see a figure about twenty feet above the ground.

"No. I'm okay," comes the reply from above.

"But I don't feel comfortable with how high you are."

"Well, the rule says that I have to feel comfortable, and I do." The discussion ended there.

Later there is a clean-up time—each student has a daily responsibility—and the day ends with a journal writing session.

Claudia Berman, associated with SAU for sixteen years both as a parent and a teacher and author of a book about the school and its history, says:

> Parents send their children here for a variety of reasons. They are repelled by the public schools, by the passivity, regimentation, the academic pressure, and the competition. They want their children to be active learners. They want to have more control over their child's education. They like the community that forms around the school and they share the values of the school.
>
> It can be difficult for parents, though. If they really don't understand the principles

behind this kind of education, sooner or later they start saying, "Well, what is my child really learning?" They have to realize that the children are learning basic skills, but at their own pace, and they are learning how to learn. Besides that they are gaining self-confidence and acquiring life skills, skills that will help them get along in the world: problem solving, decision making, conflict resolution, consensus building, and how to live in a community. In fact, right now there is a group of parents that is calling for more structured, rigorous academic work. But we have been through this before. A school like this is always going through changes, adjustments, and crises, but it always lands on its feet.

The Free School

ALBANY, NEW YORK

The Free School is located in a former parochial school building in downtown Albany, surrounded by three- and four-story tenements. It is another alternative school that has stood the test of time. Founded in the 1970s, the school now has about forty-five students, ranging in age from two to fourteen. There are three multi-age classes and a preschool group. Some of the children come from distant suburbs but most come from the neighborhood. Many are from single-parent homes. Tuition is based on income and ranges from fifty to four hundred dollars a month.

Each morning, most of the children and teachers gather in a morning meeting. They sing songs, play games, share news, and do some stretching, dance, or other movement to start the day. Afterward the several classes go to their own rooms or other venues for their activities. The day is loosely structured. If they wish, children may take part in the activities of other classes or may pursue their own interests.

The council meeting is central to life at The Free School. It is an ad hoc gathering of all teachers, staff, and children and can be called by anyone in the school. A student is chosen to chair the meeting, which is run by Robert's Rules of Order (the standard protocol for parliamentary

Chris Mercogliano, a teacher at The Free School in Albany, New York, shucks corn with students during a field trip. Free schools emphasize child-centered and experiential learning.

procedure). The meetings fall into two broad categories. Some (about 25 percent) are called to discuss a school policy. Someone may wish to change a certain school procedure or rule. A majority vote of all school members—children and adults—determines the decision. The meetings are a real-life exercise in democracy and self-government. The rest of the meetings are called to help a person or persons resolve a problem or conflict. As teacher Chris Mercogliano says, in such meetings the children learn that the resources of a community can be called on to solve a problem and that in a conflict situation there are many ways to find a solution. Anger and fighting are not the necessary or only possible result of conflict. The council deliberates until the proposal is decided or the conflict in question is resolved.

As is fitting in a school so named, the children at The Free School have a great deal of freedom. Mercogliano explains:

> We try as much as possible to give the children freedom of choice, but sometimes things have to get done. If, for example, we are out at our land in the country and firewood has to be unloaded, then everyone works, like it or not. But otherwise, the children can do what they want as long as it doesn't destroy anything or hurt anyone. They can take part in what their class is doing, or go to another class, or do something on their own.
>
> Learning in The Free School is based on the children's interests. In following those interests, inevitably the students develop the same basic academic skills they would acquire in a conventional school. Many of the older children do internships or apprenticeships out in the community. Last year one girl worked with a dancer in a

local dance company and got an inside view of what a dancer's life is like. Also, we do a lot of field trips. Right now the older children are raising money to go to Puerto Rico later in the spring to help poor people rebuild their homes destroyed by the recent storms.

In the tiny yard behind the school is a sturdy and space-efficient playground with ramps, walkways, and wooden structures. Nearby is a small barn with goats and chickens. Mercogliano takes some of the children out to feed the animals and to look at a pregnant goat that is about to give birth. On the walk back he reflects:

> What we are doing is different and unusual. We really give the children space to be themselves and to explore the world, to find themselves. Some of our kids come here because every other type of schooling has failed them. They start to straighten out and then the parents panic because they want something more like regular school. It kills me to lose a kid; even after twenty years it kills me to lose a kid whom I know the school is helping. But sometimes I get a letter years later and a kid who has been here only a few months writes how much the experience has meant.

The Free School is run and supported by a core community of about twenty people. It consists of Mary Leue, the principal founder of the school, now in her very spry seventies, Mercogliano and other teachers, and a number of friends of the school in the area. Some school parents are also members of the core community, but school parents are not required to join.

Boys at The Free School, an inner-city, racially diverse school open to all children regardless of their family's financial resources.

Family Life Center. Recently it has started to publish a magazine called the *Journal of Family Life*. It offers workshops on topics such as self-development, Reichian therapy, and Native American culture. The community helps support a Buddhist peace pagoda in nearby Grafton, New York.

Leue, an energetic and outspoken woman, says with a sparkle in her eye,

> We are radicals. We want to get down to the root of things. So we are happy to live and work outside the monied establishment. As soon as you get money from the government or somebody else you lose your freedom. Here we want to act and react as we see fit in the moment. We don't have an ideology. You have to respond to each child as a unique being and to each situation as a new one. We were inspired by Summerhill, but we do not imitate it. There is no recipe for this school. We have maybe one firm principle: We never turn away any child for any reason.

Each Wednesday evening members of the community meet as the "group." They share concerns, insights, and ideas, not just about the school but about a wide range of personal and social issues. "We have developed a deep level of intimacy and commitment over the years," says Leue, "in spite of the fear of commitment and of bonding that most people have in our society."

The Free School community has other projects that extend outside the school. For years it has published *SKOLE: The Journal of Alternative Education.* It runs a natural foods co-op and a birthing-support and family health center called the

Resources

FOR MORE INFORMATION

National Coalition of Alternative Community Schools (NCACS)
P.O. Box 15036
Santa Fe, NM 87506
Tel.: (505) 474-4312

A coalition of about three hundred schools, groups, and individuals committed to local (student, parent, and staff) control of education. The coalition provides opportunities for networking, holds conferences, and publishes a "National Directory of Alternative Schools" and a newsletter called *National Coalition News.*

National Association for Legal Support of
    Alternative Schools (NALSAS)
P.O. Box 2823
Santa Fe, NM 87504-2823
Tel.: (505) 471-6928

A sister organization of NCACS that accredits Coalition member schools. It also offers legal information and services to alternative schools.

The Sudbury Valley School Press
2 Winch Street
Framingham, MA 01701
Tel.: (508) 877-3030
Fax: (508) 788-0674

The Sudbury Valley School is one of the first and most successful of the democratic and libertarian schools in this country. The school's press publishes and sells books, pamphlets, and audio and video cassettes; it also offers a "New School Starter Kit."

The Free School
8 Elm Street
Albany, NY 12202
Tel.: (518) 434-3072

A free school in the center of Albany that has been operating for about twenty-five years and is willing, as its resources permit, to help parents and teachers apply its principles and ideals. Call for information.

Down to Earth Books
72 Philip Street
Albany, NY 12202
Tel.: (518) 432-1578

Run by members of The Free School community. Publisher of *SKOLE: A Journal of Alternative Education* and the *Journal for Family Life*.

FOR FURTHER READING

Berman, Claudia. *The School Around Us: 25 Years.* Kennebunk, Maine: School around Us Press, 1994. The philosophy and history of an alternative school that has survived and thrived.

Dennison, George. *The Lives of Children: The Story of the First Street School.* New York: Random House, 1969. Dennison, a writer who started and ran a free school, has here written a classic on education based on freedom.

Greenberg, Daniel. *Free at Last: The Sudbury Valley School.* Framingham, Mass.: The Sudbury Valley School Press, 1991. An account of life in a well-established and successful libertarian and democratic school.

———. *A New Look at Schools.* Framingham, Mass.: The Sudbury Valley School Press, 1991. Greenberg critically examines the presuppositions, ideas, and practices on which most schools are based and asserts that these are neither the only nor the best foundation for educating children.

Kozol, Jonathan. *Death at an Early Age.* New York: Houghton Mifflin, 1967. Kozol's initial description of how public schooling puts minority children at a disadvantage and keeps them in a low social-economic level.

———. *Free Schools.* Boston: Houghton Mifflin, 1972. Examines how political and economic factors affect the education of poor children.

Leue, Mary. *Challenging the Giant: The Best of SKOLE.* Albany, N.Y.: Down to Earth Books. Selections from a journal on alternative education. Volume 3 appeared in October 1996. Can be obtained from the publisher (For More Information, above).

Neill, A. S. *Summerhill.* Boston: Hart Publishing Company, 1960. The classic account of Neill's libertarian school in England, a book that has had a great influence on education in the United States.

18

Friends Schools

⚬

Members of the Religious Society of Friends, commonly known as Friends or Quakers, have played an important role in American religious, cultural, and educational life since colonial days. The first Quaker schools were founded in the 1680s. Today there are 92 schools in 20 states founded and run by Quakers according to Quaker principles. Friends schools are known for their academic excellence and for the moral and spiritual values they embody. They educate both Quaker and non-Quaker students. In fact, in most Friends schools, non-Friends are in the large majority.

George Fox, founder of Quakerism, was born in Leicester, England, in 1624, the son of a weaver. As a young man he had personal religious experiences that led him to a view of human nature, God, and the moral and religious life which, for that place and time, was radical and dissenting. The Puritans then ruled England, and the orthodox faith was a strict Calvinism that emphasized the authority of the Bible and of the clergy, the innate sinfulness of human beings, the salvation only of those elected by God, and the eternal damnation of all others.

In contrast, Fox taught the following:

Each human being has a divine, pure "Inner Light."

God can directly reveal His will and truth to every human being in and through this Inner Light.

The human being is capable of moral and spiritual improvement and perfection.

True worship is gathering together in silence.

God intends for all human beings to be saved.

The sacrament of a "life well-lived" is sufficient for salvation.

Every believer is a priest and every building can be a house of worship.

Violence and war are a direct violation of Christ's teaching.

As a religious organization, the Religious Society of Friends organized by Fox is very unusual. It has no formal creed or statement of beliefs, no churches, clergy, sacraments, ritual, or hierarchy. It is opposed to war and to oath-taking (a truthful person, Fox held, does not have to swear in order to tell the truth) and is devoted to a simple and modest life, to individual development, and to the improvement of society. Because in the early years communal worship often led to states of religious ecstasy accompanied by physical effects, the Friends also came to be called "Quakers."

Fox and his followers were persecuted for their beliefs and for their missionary activities. One of the first Quakers in the United States, Anne Hathaway, was hanged by the Boston Puritans. In 1681, Quaker leader William Penn founded Pennsylvania Colony as a haven for Quakers and other persecuted religious groups. Within a few years the Friends had established three schools in the colony. Abington Friends School, which is still in existence, was founded in 1697. Each local "meeting" or congregation strove to have its own school. By 1800 there were seventy Friends elementary schools in Pennsylvania and thirty-five in New Jersey. Between 1860 and 1890, the larger monthly and quarterly meetings founded over fifty secondary schools or academies.

During this period, most Quakers lived in tightly knit insular communities, distinguished by their simple lifestyle and conservative ways of speech. For example, Quakers retained the honorific forms of the second-person pronoun—"thee," "thou," and "thine"—far longer than other Americans. Their schools were meant to prepare Quaker children for a "life apart." The schools were coeducational and emphasized practical skills, nature study, and science. The early Quaker schools eschewed art, music, and drama, considering them unnecessary ostentations. Since Quakers believed that all labor is sacred, physical work was usually part of daily school life.

In the late nineteenth and early twentieth centuries, Quakers became more integrated into American life, and public education gained wide acceptance. Many Quaker schools closed, and those remaining accepted more and more non-Quaker students. By the 1930s, there were only thirty-one Quaker schools in the country.

Since that low point, Quaker education has enjoyed a renaissance. Many new Quaker schools

The religious element of Friends schools is presented in a relaxed, nonsectarian, nondogmatic way, so students of other faiths usually feel comfortable.

⎯⎯⎯✥⎯⎯⎯

have been founded; the ninety-two now in the United States educate about sixteen thousand students. Most (thirty-seven) are in Pennsylvania, and many of these are in the Philadelphia area. But there are seven Friends schools in both New York and New Jersey, and six in California. New schools, particularly schools for young children, are being founded each year.

The Friends schools vary greatly. Some are large, affluent, and on the surface at least, look like typical, upper-class private schools preparing the next generation of Ivy Leaguers. Many, especially the newer ones, are small, struggling schools, geared toward early childhood and elementary education. There are inner-city Friends schools in Brooklyn, Philadelphia, and Washington, D.C. There are also many suburban schools and several rural farm-based, boarding schools. Some schools are for children with above-average intelligence but with learning disabilities. Most Friends schools primarily serve families of well-to-do white families, but all seek out and enroll children from minority or disadvantaged backgrounds. Some have diverse student populations. At the Greene Street School in Philadelphia and at Landsdowne School in Landsdowne, Pennsylvania, for example, more than half of the students belong to a minority group.

It is hard to generalize about these schools, but some common elements are shared by most or all of them. Life in a Friends school has a strong moral and spiritual component. A regular, usually weekly, silent communal Meeting for Worship takes place in all Quaker schools, both for Quaker and non-Quaker students. In some schools, each class period begins with a moment of silence. This religious element is presented in a relaxed, nonsectarian, nondogmatic way. For this reason, students of other faiths, as well as students with little or no religious background, usually feel comfortable in a Friends school.

Quakers have long been leaders in social welfare and reform movements, and this interest is often manifested in the curriculum and in school life. Multicultural studies, concern about minorities and the disadvantaged, community service projects, and studies of war and peace issues are likely to play an important role in school life.

Quakers share with humanistic-progressive educators an optimistic view of human nature, a belief in the human capacity for further evolution, and a faith in the democratic process. Earlier in the century, many leaders of the Progressive Education Association were Friends, and Quaker schools were among the first to adopt progressive ideas and practices. Today most Friends schools (particularly at the elementary level) are in many respects progressive schools. The typical progressive and neoprogressive elements are present: a democratic, open classroom; a child-centered curriculum; individual and group in-depth, long-term research projects based on student interests; an emphasis on the arts, dramatics, puppetry, and music (the earlier antipathy to the arts having been overcome); use of the community as a laboratory for learning; emphasis on group work and problem solving; a de-emphasis on tests, grades, and competition; and a whole language approach to reading and writing.

Another valid generalization about Quaker schools is that only a small percentage of the teachers and students actually are Quakers. There are only one hundred thousand Quakers in the country. In some schools children from Quaker families may comprise 15 or 20 percent of students, but more typically they comprise 5

percent or less. Quakers also make up a tiny percentage of the faculty and in some schools even the director is not a Quaker. Many schools struggle with the questions "What makes us a Quaker school?" "How can we retain a Quaker identity if there are so few Quakers on the faculty and as students?"

The Moses Brown School
PROVIDENCE, RHODE ISLAND

The Moses Brown School is located on a 32-acre, in-town campus that is both impressive and beautiful, with ivy-covered red brick buildings, tasteful modern structures, broad playing fields, magnificent old elms and oaks, and a splendid gymnasium. In one corner of the campus stands a simple but striking brick Quaker meetinghouse. The school was founded in 1784 in Portsmouth, Rhode Island, as a Quaker school and moved to Providence in 1819.

Moses Brown has a kindergarten and a lower, middle, and upper (i.e., high) school, and serves about eight hundred students. Almost all of them are day students from the greater Providence area. In appearance, ambiance, facilities, curriculum, pedagogy, and faculty and students, it seems a typical New England private elementary and college preparatory school. About 5 percent of the students and 10 percent of the faculty are Quakers. Jim English, a teacher in the middle school, is a member of the Providence Meeting. I asked him in what sense Moses Brown is a Quaker school. He replied:

> The school is owned by the New England Yearly Meeting, and about half of the members of the Board of Overseers are Quakers. But their influence is more indirect than direct.

While the school is not in the business of converting people to Quakerism, all new members of the faculty, administration, and Board of Overseers are introduced to Quakerism in a special workshop each fall. And all freshman in the upper school take a three-week seminar on Quakerism.

The use of silence as a tool for personal growth is very important here. Quakers believe that there is a divine inner light in each person, and in silence and introspection each can perceive this inner light. The class day opens with a period of silence. The lower grades have a longer meeting once a week in their classroom. The students of each grade of the middle and upper schools gather once a week for a forty-minute Meeting for Worship. The long-range benefit of this is incalculable. It gives each student the opportunity for quiet, undisturbed introspection. For many this becomes an enduring practice and resource. Alumni write us all the time that the ability to sit quietly and in reflection has been an invaluable, lifelong gift.

Fifteen minutes later, English and I are walking—or rather, being blown by a strong New England wind—across campus toward the meetinghouse. We are going to the weekly Meeting for Worship of one of the three "teams" that comprise the middle school. Small groups of sixth-, seventh-, and eight-graders are being blown in the same direction.

Two girls carrying backpacks come up alongside us. English asks, "What do you girls think about going to Meeting every week?"

"Oh, I like it a lot," responds one. "It gives me time to think about things and to settle down. Otherwise life is so hurried. I sit away from my friends so I'm not distracted."

Five minutes later I am sitting on a long white wooden bench, one of many identical benches arranged in concentric squares around an unadorned space in the center of a large room. The room has a high ceiling, tall windows, and an austere, compelling beauty.

Students and teachers—about seventy persons in all—sit alone or in small clusters. At one point, a faculty member shares a memory of his grand-

A class meeting in the lower school of Moses Brown School in Providence, Rhode Island. Friends schools typically emphasize democratic decision making and social awareness.

mother and how she valued education. Otherwise, except for some shuffling of feet and clearing of throats, the room for the next forty minutes is perfectly quiet. Virtually all the students seem alert, awake, and introspective. Finally, a teacher shakes the hands of the person on his right and left, and everyone in the room does the same. The Meeting is over. As we file back out into the windy day, students and teachers alike seem pensive and peaceful. There is little talk.

Later I ask the head of the school, Joanne Hoffman, about the role of Quakerism at Moses Brown. Hoffman, who is in her first year at the school, replies:

> Of course the practice of silent reflection is very important. It gives students the habit and the benefit of introspection. There is in general a special atmosphere in the school. In part, it is a result of the Meeting, in part the result of the explicitly stated and practiced Quaker values. It is an atmosphere of mutual respect, tolerance, and trust among students, among faculty, and between students and teachers. The students feel free to stand up and to speak their minds. They are comfortable with open exchange, with disagreement. They know they will be listened to and accepted, whatever their point of view. I am not a Quaker, but I think the Quaker idea that God is in every person and can speak through every person permeates the life of the school.
>
> Also, Quakerism informs our decision-making processes and our attitude toward conflict resolution. In the lower and middle schools, the children are taught to resolve conflicts without resorting to angry words or fighting. In the upper school, the Discipline Committee, which consists of faculty and students, makes its decisions by consensus. And the social service element of Quakerism is very much present too. Each upper school student has to do forty hours of community service a year.

A woodworking class at Moses Brown. Photograph by Janet Woodcock.

The Meeting School

RINDGE, NEW HAMPSHIRE

The Meeting School is a hundred miles or so north of Moses Brown in Rindge, New Hampshire. While also a Quaker school, it is quite different from its sister school in Providence.

The Meeting School is housed in a cluster of buildings on either side of a country road. The school owns 132 acres of woodland and fields and includes five houses, a barn, several yurts, a cabin used primarily for individual retreats, and a garden house. The school was founded in 1957 by Quaker families who wanted to live communally and to provide a meaningful education for their children. Today there are about thirty high-school students and twelve faculty. Students and teachers live together, family-style, in the five residences and cook, eat, study, and work together. Adults and teenagers share housekeeping chores, and students must in addition do four hours a week of school service work.

The school day begins in the large living room of an old farmhouse. Through a large picture window at one end of the room, the shallow cone of Mount Monadnock, majestic even at a distance, juts into a gray morning sky. A barefoot, bearded man with a banjo and a tall man with a guitar are playing a lively Irish jig. A teenage boy with a stripe of purple hair down the middle of an otherwise shaved head comes in, curls up in an easy chair, and closes his eyes. A teenage girl wearing a rustic, full-length dress, her hair still wet from washing, enters. She is carrying a flute and soon joins in the playing. Adults, teenagers, and several small children drift in until there are about thirty people on chairs, couches, the floor, and in laps. The atmosphere is informal, intimate, and warm, like that of a large multigenerational family.

A teacher calls the meeting to order; the day's schedule is reviewed; and announcements and comments are solicited. The time and place of class meetings are set. A song is sung. Then there is a period of silence that lasts several minutes. At its close each person takes the hand of the person to the right and to the left so that a circle is formed, and a gentle squeeze is passed from hand to hand. The students scatter, some directly to a class in a house basement or living room, some first to an outdoor "designated smoking area."

At the Meeting School, students must fulfill credit requirements in order to graduate. Students have to take courses or display competence in mathematics through advanced algebra. They must do ongoing work in English and writing and have to take credit hours in social studies and science. Courses in "Wellness" and in "Sexuality and Relationships" are required.

But there is a strong orientation to student-centered and experiential learning. Teachers enjoy full autonomy and can tailor courses to the interests and needs of the students. During the current term, a class fulfilling the persuasive writing requirement in English has been focusing on film criticism. A life sciences class the previous year studied wolves and took a trip out to the National Wolf Research Institute in Minnesota. All students do an intersession project each year in the four weeks between the fall and spring terms. They leave campus for a "learn by doing" experience. Foreign travel, volunteer work, art or crafts projects, and apprenticeships are some of the things that occupy students during the intersession period.

There also is an alternative graduation system, by which a student can bypass the usual requirements. A student who has demonstrated basic academic skills and an ability to manage time can create a checklist of academic and life-skill objectives. Fulfillment of these objectives qualifies the student for graduation.

Mendalara Van Wick, a teacher at the school, comments that "a lot of our students have been homeschooled or were in alternative schools or just couldn't handle a regular school. We are more interested in process and personal growth than in content-heavy academic achievement." Another teacher comments, "We are trying to achieve a balance among the academic, communal, practical, and spiritual dimensions of life, both for ourselves and for the students."

Six of the twelve faculty are Quakers—perhaps the highest percentage in any American Quaker school—and the Quaker influence is strongly felt. Each school gathering includes a period of silence. There is a silent Meeting for Worship each Wednesday afternoon from 1:00 to 1:45. When they feel it is necessary, students and faculty can take a "Bartlett Day"—a day of solitary retreat and reflection at an isolated cabin on the property. School and residence-house decisions are made by consensus, all present having to agree to the final decision.

Quaker social awareness and social activism are also important in school life. On the day of my visit a political activist spoke to a history class about the Food Not Bombs movement and then gave an all-school workshop on the philosophy and practice of "formal consensus."

The "clearness process" is a traditional Quaker means of dealing with difficult personal and group situations and is an important element of life at The Meeting School. When a person can say "I am clear," it means they have reached a clear understanding of the right things to do in a situation. A clearness meeting aims to bring the person to that clarity. It involves one facilitator, and sometimes more than one, helping an individual, two people, or a group to come to clarity about an issue.

At The Meeting School, an individual struggling with a personal decision, or two or more people in conflict with each other, can call a clearness meeting. The clearness process is also used when a student has broken an important rule. It can help determine why the student broke the rule, what can be done to heal the situation, and what can be done to meet the future needs of the student.

Resources

FOR MORE INFORMATION

> The Friends Council on Education
> 1507 Cherry Street
> Philadelphia, PA 19102
> Tel.: (215) 241-7245

This is the central source of information on Friends education. It has "A List of Schools, Colleges, and Study Centers under the Care of Friends" available on request and free of charge.

> The Philadelphia Yearly Meeting Library
> 1515 Cherry Street
> Philadelphia, PA 19102
> Tel.: (215) 241-7220

The library will send a list of books and pamphlets about Friends education. The books and pamphlets can be borrowed by mail.

> Pendle Hill Bookstore
> 338 Plush Mill Road
> Wallingford, PA 19086-6099
> Tel.: (800) 742-3150; (215) 566-4514

Pendle Hill is a Quaker center for study and contemplation near Philadelphia. It also publishes books and pamphlets on various aspects of Quaker thought and life, including education. A catalogue is available on request.

Friends Schools

Brinton, Howard. *Quaker Education in Theory and Practice.* Wallingford, Pa.: Pendle Hill, 1967. (Pamphlet)

Heath, Douglas. *The Peculiar Mission of a Quaker School.* Philadelphia: The Friends Council on Education, 1979. (Pamphlet)

Kenworthy, Leonard. *Quaker Education: A Sourcebook.* Kennett Square, Pa.: Quaker Publications, 1987? A collection of readings about the history, philosophy, and current reality of Quaker education.

Lester, John A. *The Ideals and Objectives of Quaker Education* and *The Place of the Quaker School in Contemporary Education.* Philadelphia: The Friends Council on Education. (Pamphlets)

Palmer, Parker T. *Meeting for Learning: Education in a Quaker Context.* Wallingford, Pa.: Pendle Hill, 1976. (Pamphlet)

19

Holistic Schools

Holism is a worldview that has been present in most cultures and religious traditions. Hinduism, Buddhism, Taoism, Shintoism, and the worldview of the so-called primitive peoples contain strong and explicit expressions of holism. In the Jewish, Christian, and Islamic traditions, holism has appeared primarily in esoteric and mystical circles outside the mainstream, but it has been present. Holism has been espoused by such philosophers as Aldous Huxley, who expressed it in what he called the "perennial philosophy."

While holism has long been present in American culture—Transcendentalism can be understood as a holistic worldview—it started to become an important element in American life in the late 1960s and early 1970s. It is the philosophical foundation for various spiritual movements such as Zen Buddhism and yoga, for humanistic and transpersonal psychology, the human potential movement, the ecological movement, various nonallopathic medical approaches, and for other elements in the alternative, non-mainstream culture.

Holism views the world and the universe as an integrated organism, in which all parts—the mineral, vegetable, animal, human, energetic, and spiritual—are intimately related, each affecting and each affected by all the others. All existence is ultimately a unity, is related, has meaning, and is evolving toward higher forms.

Holism also views the human being as an integrated organism of equally important, interrelated functions and dimensions—physical, emotional, intellectual, artistic, social, moral, and spiritual. Also, holism holds that human life has spiritual, cosmic, transpersonal, and archetypal dimensions that cannot be grasped or understood by logical, scientific analysis alone. It rejects the materialistic, rationalistic, and reductionistic views that understand the human being as a biological processor of information, an aggregate of scarcely controlled physical passions, or the victim of economic and social forces. Holism affirms the freedom and transcendent dignity of the human being as a being with an inherent, unfolding spiritual nature.*

Thus holism rejects the dualism that has dominated much of Western thought and experience, a view that perceives a separation between matter and spirit, mind and body, reason and intuition, intellect and emotion, science and art, individual and community, the sacred and the profane, and

---

* This definition is based on the exposition of holism that appears in Ronald Miller, "Holistic Education in the United States." (See listing in Resources section at the end of this chapter.)

humanity and nature. Holism sees these pairs not as opposites but as complementary phenomena, each real and each vital and necessary to the other.

A holistic view of the world, of the human being, and of the child has been an important element of the humanistic-progressive tradition in education. Rousseau, Pestalozzi, Froebel, Emerson, Parker, Dewey, and others all emphasized the importance of educating the whole child. Many of the alternative, free, and progressive schools founded in the late 1960s and early 1970s had an implicit or explicit holistic basis and holistic intent. But since the 1970s, holism has developed into a specific educational movement with its own identity apart from its historic predecessors.

Ronald Miller, a historian of education, founder of the *Holistic Education Review*, and a leading advocate of holistic education, comments on the essential qualities of holistic education:

> Holistic education aims to nurture and develop the varied but interrelated capacities of the human being. Thus while it addresses the intellectual development it is equally concerned about the child's development as a physical, emotional, artistic, social, moral, and spiritual being. It aims to create a person who is well-rounded and—in a broad sense—healthy, a human being who has developed each aspect of his or her humanity. The aim of education is not merely to fill the child with information, to develop academic and job skills, and to prepare the child to fit into the prevailing economic and social system. Rather it is to help the young person develop into

"Holistic education gives young people a real sense of the interrelatedness of all things, a deep ecological awareness, as well as a sense of social responsibility."
—*Ronald Miller, founder of* The Holistic Education Review

---

a free, creative, compassionate being who can participate fully in the life of the community.

Holistic education includes most or all of the elements of classical progressive education as well as the recent neoprogressive addenda. It is child centered and largely experiential. Cooperative learning, the use of developmental models of childhood, multicultural education, and democratic and consensual decision making typically are incorporated into holistic schools.

Holistic education has enough in common with progressive education that the distinction between a progressive school and a holistic school sometimes is not immediately obvious. Miller agrees, but explains that there are real differences.

> Both progressive and holistic education focus on the whole child and emphasize developmental learning, cooperative strategies, experiential approaches, and the like. But holism goes deeper and sees the human being in an ecological and spiritual context. Holistic education attempts to nurture a deeper connection between the inner life of the person and the surrounding environment. A holistic school is not sectarian or even religious, but it does try to cultivate the spiritual dimension of life. It seeks to help the child develop a sense of reverence for life and an appreciation for life's meaningfulness and value. This can be done in various ways—by including quiet time for reflection or by encouraging self-expression through art, by presenting

the teachings of diverse religious faiths, and so on. Ultimately, holistic education gives young people a real sense of the interrelatedness of all things, a deep ecological awareness, as well as a sense of social responsibility—a commitment to making the world a better place.

The Global Alliance for Transforming Education (GATE) is an organization committed to holistic education. According to GATE, holistic education's vision "fosters personal greatness, social justice, peace, and a sustainable environment" and has ten basic components:

1. It aims at human development.
2. It honors students as individuals.
3. It is experiential, immersing students in the natural, social, and inner world.
4. It seeks to develop all dimensions of the human being—physical, artistic, emotional, intellectual, and—in a nonsectarian way—spiritual.
5. Its teachers are co-learners and facilitators.
6. It involves freedom for the learner in the educational process and for the family in choosing a school.
7. It educates for participatory democracy and tries to develop critical thinking skills, empathy, and a sense of justice.
8. It educates for global citizenship, teaching students their role in the human family and encouraging an appreciation and respect for cultural diversity.
9. It educates for earth literacy, teaching that the welfare of all beings and phenomena is interrelated and that it is the responsibility of each individual to care for the planet.

10. It includes spirituality, teaching that there is a deep and meaningful connection between one's self and others, that daily life has meaning and purpose, that all life is interconnected, and that we can find within ourselves a respite from the restlessness of the world and an independent source of meaning.

The Bellwether School
Williston, Vermont

The Bellwether School is located outside Burlington, Vermont, in the northeast corner of the state. It opened in September 1995 with Ronald Miller as its primary founder and mentor. The school is spacious, bright, and airy, includes two acres of lawn and playground, and looks out to cornfields and rolling hills. In its first year, Bellwether had a large preschool class and a class for children ages five through eight, with a total of about thirty-five children. Almost all the children came from middle-class, professional families.

Beth Stadtlander, the teacher for the large preschool class, ran a holistically oriented kindergarten in her home before helping found the school. Diane Davison, teacher for the older class, explains that she uses an "emergent curriculum," one that comes out of the interests of the children. The children start the day with discovery time, during which they are free to choose what they do. Some draw; some playact with costumes; several build mazes from blocks and see how Squiggle, their new guinea pig, manages to negotiate them.

For the rest of the day the children do group activities, are read stories that they then discuss, play, do arts and crafts, and have elementary instruction in reading, writing and arithmetic.

Around the room there are learning centers for each of the seven "multiple intelligences" (see chapter 26); each center is named for a famous person who exemplified that particular aspect of human function. Thus there is a Mozart center, an Emily Dickinson center, and a Benjamin Franklin center. Davison encourages each child to spend time at each center.

The fledgling school is still developing its identity, but Miller has a visionary goal. He believes that a holistic understanding of human development and learning means children should not be isolated in self-contained school buildings and that the entire community should be involved in their education. At Bellwether there is a room set aside as a Family Resources Center, containing books on education, homeschooling, and child development.

Miller talks of the future: "We would like the school to become a resource for the parents and for the wider community, where people can learn about and exchange ideas about education, child development, and ecological and social issues. We want to involve the students, teachers, and parents in a supportive and caring school community that is concerned with the larger community and with the world."

The Robert Muller School

ARLINGTON, TEXAS

The Robert Muller School is founded on an explicit holistic approach to life and to education. Its founder, Robert Muller, was for many years an assistant secretary general of the United Nations and is deeply interested in fostering a global and holistic consciousness. In his book *New Genesis: Shaping a Global Spirituality*, Muller writes:

Reason suddenly is unable to give us the answer to the complexities of creation. That is why at this juncture, we need to turn to other values which women possess instinctively and naturally. . . . A woman who has a child is not reasoning with herself about her relation with the child. It is all expressed very simply and beautifully in the word *love*. It is a relationship which one cannot define, which goes totally beyond all reason. Since women nurture the family and the child, this is her speciality. What we need today on this planet is more love than reason. We must now fashion a world based on the great virtues of truth, love, compassion, and beauty. And when it comes to love, it is increasingly apparent that the main challenge for our age is to live with the entire creation, to love our planet, to love the human family, to love each other, and to love the mysterious creator.

Muller has developed a curriculum called the "World Core" curriculum. Its purpose is to help children develop an awareness of the interdependencies that exist among all human beings and among all beings and phenomena in nature and in the cosmos. The curriculum places all academic work into one or more of the following categories:

1. Our planetary home and our place in the universe
2. The family of humanity
3. Our place in time
4. The miracle of the individual human life

The curriculum develops the child physically, emotionally, mentally, and spiritually, from birth through adolescence. It also seeks to nurture a consciousness that is aware of the whole family of humanity and of the entire globe, and that is characterized by love.

The Robert Muller School was founded in 1980 as a tuition-free, independent school supported by voluntary donations. It is fully accredited and has a volunteer staff. The school implements the World Core curriculum and has become the coordinating center for similar schools in Mexico, Russia, Argentina, Holland, England, Brazil, and Australia.

Resources

For More Information

> Resource Center for Redesigning Education
> P.O. Box 298
> Brandon, VT 05733-0298
> Tel.: (800) 639-4122
> Tel. and Fax: (802) 247-8312

The Center regularly publishes *Great Ideas in Education*, a book and video catalogue that also reviews new books and videos. It features materials concerning holistic education, Montessori education, whole language, and alternative education.

> Global Alliance for Transforming Education
>   (GATE)
> P.O. Box 21
> Grafton, VT 05146
> Tel.: (802) 843-2382

GATE works with teachers, educators, educational organizations, United Nations Organizations, child advocates, local communities, business leaders, and government officials as well as with schools and families to promote holistic education. It has issued its own statement of educational goals for the year 2000, *Education 2000: A Holistic Perspective.*

> *Holistic Education Review*
> P.O. Box 328
> Brandon, VT 05733-0328
> Tel.: (800) 639-4122

This journal is published four times a year and contains articles and book reviews dealing with progressive/humanistic/holistic education. It is academic in tone but readable and informative (one-year subscription, $35).

> Robert Muller School
> 6005 Royal Oak Drive
> Arlington, TX 76016
> Tel.: (817) 654-1018
> Fax: (817) 654-1028

The Robert Muller School has a resource catalogue that contains materials about the World Core curriculum as well as books by Robert Muller.

For Further Reading

Flake, Carol, ed. *Holistic Education: Principles, Perspectives, and Practices.* Brandon, Vt: Holistic Education Press, 1992. This is a book of readings based on *Education 2000: A Holistic Perspective* (GATE's statement of educational goals; see For More Information above). It includes sections on "Educating for Participatory Democracy," "Educating for Cultural Diversity and Global Citizenship," and "Spirituality and Education."

Miller, John P. *The Holistic Curriculum.* Toronto: Ontario Institute for Studies in Education, 1988. A concise and informative introduction to holistic education that also traces the history of holistic thinking in science, psychology, religion, and social theory.

Miller, Ronald. *What Are Schools For? Holistic Education in American Culture.* Brandon, Vt.: Holistic Education Press, 1990. A readable and informative account of the humanistic/progressive tradition in the United States. Also an exposition of holism in education. Miller traces the history of humanistic and holistic education in the United States and describes the origins and aims of public education.

———. "Holistic Education in the United States: A New Paradigm or a Cultural Struggle." First printed in *Holistic Education Review* 6, no. 4 (Dec. 1993): 12–18. An article on the philosophy and history of holistic education, available as a reprint from the author at P.O. Box 818, Shelburne, VT 05482.

———. "Holism and Meaning: Foundations for a Coherent Holistic Theory." *Holistic Education Review*. 4, no. 3 (Fall 1991): 23–32.

Mintz, Jerry. *The Almanac of Education Choices: Public and Private Learning Alternatives and Homeschooling*. New York: Macmillan, 1995. A comprehensive directory, listing by state over six thousand alternative schools, programs, and learning resources across the United States.

20

Homeschooling

⌘

The rapid growth of homeschooling has been an important phenomenon in American education in the last decade. Ten years ago, only a handful of American children were being educated outside the public and private schools. Today there are at least a million children being educated at home, and the number is growing very fast. In 1990, Vermont—a state with half a million inhabitants—had two hundred homeschoolers registered with its department of education. In 1995, there were over one thousand registered homeschoolers.

Today there are at least a million children being educated at home, and the number is growing very fast.

⌘

Until the public school system came into being, parents had the responsibility and the right to educate their children. Most parents taught their children to read, write, and do arithmetic at home, and also taught practical and vocational skills. Well-to-do families might have engaged a tutor or sent their children to a private academy. For most families, though, the education of children at home by parents and other family members was the norm, as it had been in all cultures, literate and nonliterate, throughout human history.

The public school movement took from parents both the right and the responsibility to educate their children. In effect, the state said to its citizens, "Your children must be educated. But don't worry, the state will do it for you. Pay your taxes to build schools and to pay professional teachers, and the state will do the job for you. And don't be concerned about what your children should learn and how they should learn it. The state will decide that."

Not all parents were happy with this arrangement, as was apparent in the resistance to mandatory, universal, public education in many areas. But the law was hard to resist. Besides, the process of industrialization was taking many men out of the home to work in factories, making it difficult for women left alone all day both to run a household and to tutor their children. From the late 1800s until the 1970s, homeschooling virtually vanished from the American cultural landscape. Such an approach to education, which had helped produce many great men and women—for example, George Washington, Benjamin Franklin, Louisa May Alcott, Mark Twain—as well as thousands of literate, informed, and freethinking citizens, seemed irrelevant in twentieth-century life.

But from the mid-1970s and continuing today, homeschooling has enjoyed a renaissance. Critics

131

of public education have attacked public schools as rigid, regimented, repressive, demeaning, dehumanizing, and unable to really educate or let the child develop. Some have attacked the concept of school itself.

John Holt, a teacher in Boston, was a leading critic of schooling and an articulate and influential advocate for homeschooling. In widely read books such as *How Children Learn*, Holt maintained that children have a natural desire and ability to educate themselves. All they need is access to the real world and to educational materials; the freedom to explore; emotional support; and time to think about and assess their experiences. Schools, Holt argued, provide none of these key elements of learning. In fact, schools thwart the education and development of the child. For Holt, the home and the real world outside the classroom constitute the ideal learning environment for the child. And the parent, sensitive to the special needs and abilities of the child, is the best possible teacher.

Such ideas, rooted in the Romantic and humanistic tradition, inspired and have continued to inspire many parents to homeschool, or perhaps more accurately, to let their children educate themselves at home. Today probably two hundred thousand children are being homeschooled according to Holt's philosophy and methods. Most of the parents involved are white, well educated, and affluent, with a lifestyle that in some way puts them outside mainstream culture. Many are members or former members of intentional communities. While some of these anti-schooling or de-schooling families are in cities and suburbs, most are found in rural areas.

About the time that parents inspired by Holt and others began keeping their children out of school, another homeschooling movement began, based primarily on conservative Christian-

ity. The Christian homeschool movement has its own distinct rationale and educational approach and has grown rapidly since the 1980s. About 80 percent (at least eight hundred thousand) of all homeschooled children are from conservative Christian families. Most of the 10 to 15 percent annual increase in the number of homeschoolers in the country probably comes from Christian homeschooling families.

Evangelical and fundamentalist Christians believe in the literal truth of the Bible as the Word of God. For them, the account of the creation of the world and of the human race in the Book of Genesis is true as given. The Ten Commandments and other injunctions found in the Bible are unequivocal moral absolutes. Conservative Christians tend to have conservative social attitudes. They observe traditional sex roles for men and women and reject homosexuality as a violation of biblical law.

In addition, many conservative Christians feel alienated from and threatened by the public school system in the United States, even as they feel alienated from and threatened by much of mainstream culture. They see the public schools as antireligious, dominated by materialism, secularism, humanism, and moral relativism, and plagued by violence, sexual promiscuity, and drug use. For the conservative Christian, the public school is a place where prayer is prohibited; the mention of religion is banned; homosexuality is presented as a normal, acceptable lifestyle; drugs are bought and sold; and condoms are distributed for free. Because they do not wish to send their children to such a place, hundreds of thousands of Christian parents enroll their children in so-called Christian schools (see chapter 12). And at least an equal number educate their children at home.

The Holtian, de-schooling type of homeschoolers and the Christian homeschoolers make up the vast majority of homeschoolers in the United States today. These two groups represent the left and right extremes of the philosophical, religious, political, and educational spectrum. But it is possible to educate children at home without subscribing to the laissez-faire approach of the Holtians on the one hand or the conservative Christian approach on the other. There are excellent, nonsectarian, content-rich, skills-based elementary and junior high homeschool curricula available. These allow a family to give a child a broad-based, well-rounded liberal arts education at home.

Regardless of their reasons and their particular approach, families that homeschool find that homeschooling has advantages and disadvantages. Homeschooling greatly strengthens family life. Parents spend much more time with their children than they would if their children were in school six or seven hours a day. Parents also interact much more closely with their children in the daily teaching and learning process. Homeschooling provides an education or reeducation for parents, too. They themselves must always be in a process of learning or relearning. Homeschooling also gives parents some control over the information, beliefs, values, language, and behavior patterns to which their children are exposed.

Parents as teachers can tailor the materials, pace, and style of teaching to the needs of the individual child. They can be much more sensitive to a child's progress and problems than a public school teacher might be, and they can give personal attention as needed. It is not surprising that homeschooled children invariably do better on standardized tests than their public school peers. Homeschooling also may nurture self-motivation and creativity.

Homeschooling is convenient and inexpensive.

There is no time-consuming commute to school, and schedules can be adapted to suit the day's activities. Even a family that relies on published curricula and other mail-order educational materials will seldom spend more than five hundred dollars a year on homeschooling. Learning does not have to be suspended for the summer months. Children can experience the fact that learning can be something that goes on all the time.

A common objection to homeschooling is that it isolates children socially and deprives them of the opportunity to learn social skills. Homeschoolers reply that a typical school classroom in which a child is isolated with thirty children of the same age and one adult is scarcely a normal social situation. The standard classroom situation is one that exists almost nowhere else in society. Homeschooling advocates maintain that schools create an unhealthy social environment that helps foment bullying, elitism, exclusionary behavior, teasing, and conformism to peer pressure.

For a child without siblings, however, and for children living in a sparsely populated area, the lack of social contact can be a valid issue. Some families meet regularly with other homeschooling families to provide social contact for children and parents. Homeschooled children can take part in community recreational and sports programs and be active in groups like the boy scouts, girl scouts, and church youth groups.

In general, school officials have not been helpful to parents who were homeschooling, viewing them as having rejected the public school system. Today, however, more and more school districts allow homeschoolers to come to school on a pick-and-choose basis to take art, music, and other classes and to use the library, gym, and other school facilities. A few school districts even allow homeschooled children to join school athletic teams.

Parents should not be surprised if their own aspiration to homeschool is overwhelmed by their child's desire for peer contact. Particularly as they near adolescence, children may strongly prefer public school over being homeschooled, irrespective of their parents' beliefs.

One of the principal hardships often involved in homeschooling is economic. While the cost of curricular materials usually is modest, homeschooling generally keeps one parent out of the work force. Economic conditions today almost require that both parents work. A family that wants to homeschool probably will have to make some sacrifices in lifestyle. Homeschooling for single parents who work outside the home is impossible, but single parents who work at home or who are on public assistance would find it possible.

Some proponents of homeschooling have suggested that homeschooling families be given the money that the government spends per child in the public system, or at least that they get a tax break. In a country where homeschooling has become legal only in the last two decades, such a suggestion seems unlikely to be implemented, at least in the near future. But the climate in education is changing rapidly, and such provisions may not be as farfetched as they sound.

Another important concern is the legality of homeschooling. Twenty years ago when the homeschooling movement began, the pioneering families had many problems with the public authorities. Homeschooling contradicts the assumption on which the present public system is founded, that is, that education can only happen and should only happen in public schools under the eyes of state-certified teachers. Homeschooling is a clear threat to the monopoly of compulsory public education. Early homeschooling parents were legally threatened, arrested, and often brought to trial as abettors of truancy and sometimes even as child abusers. It took many long and difficult legal suits to establish the right of parents to educate their own children.

Today that right is clearly established in all the states, but the conditions for homeschooling vary. In some states it is easy to homeschool. One may only have to write a letter of intent to the state department of education. In other states, it is much more difficult. Parents may be required to prove that they are qualified to teach their children, or they may be forced to incorporate as a school to avoid trouble with the authorities.

Parents interested in homeschooling should clearly establish the legality of what they plan to do. Fortunately, each state has homeschooling associations that can give advice about pertinent requirements. There are also numerous national organizations that will help with the legal and other aspects of homeschooling. (See Resources.)

The Hackett-Ellis Family
CHELSEA, VERMONT

Kimberly Hackett and Kevin Ellis and their four children live in an enlarged and renovated solar-powered farmhouse high on a hillside in the village of Chelsea, Vermont. The dirt road to their home is steep, deeply rutted, bounded by stone walls, and free of power lines. It seems to be leading into another historical era.

Kimberly and Kevin both come from upper-middle-class families. Kevin graduated from Amherst College and Kimberly studied writing at a junior college and took adult education courses at Harvard. They met in Washington, D.C., and seven years later moved to Vermont—choosing what Kimberly calls family health and unity over life in the suburbs. Kevin works as a lobbyist–political consultant in Montpelier, a thirty-five-minute drive from their home. None of their children goes to public school.

The Hackett-Ellis home is spacious, bright, and on the splendid spring morning I visit, filled with children and adults. Kimberly explains, "Today is a little more hectic than usual. Once a week some other homeschooling parents in the area come over with their children. It gives the children a chance to do some projects together and to play together. They've been doing a lot of art and craft work, and today there is a drama teacher here. We parents have a chance to get together, to share experiences, and to support each other. We are trying to build an ongoing, supportive community that includes adults and children."

The day begins with a large group of children and three adults sitting in a circle on the floor in a large, sunny room. The children range in age from about five to about twelve. They are bright eyed, alert, and talkative as they relate news and stories of the past week. They then divide into two groups. The younger children head outside to play in the sunshine. The older children go into the attached barn to do theater exercises with the visiting teacher.

Kimberly talks about homeschooling:

> I knew from the beginning that I was going to homeschool my children. Public schools are warehouses. They are day care and bureaucracy at their worst. If a child is from a dysfunctional home and needs structure and maintenance, schools are helpful. Both otherwise, public schools have nothing to offer. Unless one of my kids insists on it, none will ever go to school.
>
> I believe that children have a natural de-

sire to learn and to acquire skills and that when they are ready to learn something they will do it on their own or they will ask for help. My son Jackson is eight and loves to read. There's a list on the wall of the books he has read lately. He's not interested much in writing yet, but I don't push. He'll be ready for it sometime. I am pretty laissez-faire about what he and the younger children do. Some of the other mothers here, though, use a more structured approach. Anita, for example, who drives here each week from Plymouth, New Hampshire, about ninety minutes away, does some daily instructional work with her daughter.

Homeschooling is not for everyone. It takes a big commitment by both parents to the family. It requires a lot of time and energy. It is really a life-style choice as much as an educational choice.

Terry is another mother in the group who homeschools. She talks about her eight-year-old daughter: "She was in public school for kindergarten and first grade. But she learned faster than the others and was frustrated at the slow pace. At first when I had her at home she missed the structure and didn't know what to do. I was worried, and kept asking myself, am I doing the right thing? Now, though, she's always motivated and busy. She reads a lot, does arts and crafts, plays math games, writes poetry, and just explores. I'm convinced this is the best thing for her right now. But it might change later."

Two of the children in Kimberly's Friday support group plan to attend the elementary school in Chelsea because, as their mother reports, "They feel isolated and want to be with a lot of other children."

The Wood Family

Hartford Village, Vermont

Tony and Dayna Wood and their sons Nicholas, nine, and Jordan, seven, live in a trim ranch house high above Hartford Village, Vermont. Below is the spring-full White River and in the distance the asphalt north-south ribbon of Interstate 91. When Nicholas was six, Dayna decided to assume responsibility for her sons' educations. While the boys model with clay at the kitchen table, I sit with her in the living room. Dayna talks about her reasons for homeschooling. She is not opposed to schools per se but is concerned about what her children may be exposed to in the local public schools. She explains:

> Nicholas was in the kindergarten in town, and I often went to help out. Even at that age the children were using profanity and making remarks with sexual innuendos. And already there was peer pressure to wear certain kinds of clothes and to act in

a certain way. I got very concerned about putting him in that kind of environment.

I was also concerned about the health studies program that he would be exposed to, which included sex education. About that time there was the big controversy in New York City about the "inclusive curriculum," which presents homosexuality and lesbianism as normal, acceptable alternatives—you know, *Jenny Has Two Mommies*, that kind of thing. My husband and I are both Christians; we believe that the Bible is God's word and is absolutely, literally true. And the Bible says that homosexuality is *not* normal and acceptable. That doesn't mean that I dislike homosexuals. I treat them with the same respect I show every human being. It just means I don't want my children to be taught that their lifestyle is an acceptable one.

Also, we knew that in the schools, evolution would be taught as the explanation for the existence of the human race. We believe, as the Bible says, that God created

Homeschooling parent Dayna Wood of Hartford Village, Vermont, reads a children's version of The Count of Monte Cristo *with her sons Nicholas and Jordan. Homeschooling gives parents and children an opportunity to learn together.*

the world and everything in it. He created human beings as human beings. We are not descended from the primates.

At first, my husband wanted to send the boys to the public school anyway. The Bible says that Christians should not "hide their light under a bushel." But I convinced him that children are too impressionable to have to deal with a world that is so different from and hostile to our way of thinking and living.

Dayna's approach to teaching her two sons is highly structured. She works with them Monday through Friday from 8:30 AM until around noon. She uses curricula from a Christian publishing company in Pensacola, Florida. For each subject—English, mathematics, history, geography, health, science, art, and music—there is a textbook and workbook for the boys and a teacher's guide for Dayna.

The texts have a clear though not overbearing religious perspective. The history textbook, for example, contains biographies of notable Ameri-

cans, and each one describes that person's religious beliefs and religious and devotional life. Biblical passages are interpolated into the text at many points.

Dayna remarks, "A number of families from our church homeschool and they told us at the beginning, 'Get a good, structured curriculum and follow it closely.' That was good advice. At the outset I was pretty unsure of myself. Now I'm more confident and experiment a bit more. I've ordered a history curriculum for next year that uses real books rather than textbooks. We have a computer and some educational software that the boys like." Dayna is taking one year at a time and is planning to send her boys to the local Christian school, Mid-Vermont Christian, when they are a bit older and if the family can afford it.

The Woods have received little help from the town. Dayna describes how she wrote the school superintendent and asked if she could use the school library. "He wrote back that I would be welcome in the library as soon as I enrolled my boys in the school," she says. "I've learned,

Homeschooler Jordan Wood makes his daily journal entry. While some homeschooling families do not follow a schedule, the Woods use the period from 8:30 A.M. to about 12:00 noon each day for learning activities.

though, that the best way to get a positive response is to go in with a very friendly, nonjudgmental attitude. The school board is in the process of developing a policy on how to deal with homeschoolers and the situation will most likely improve."

Homeschooling has created a financial challenge for the Wood family. Dayna, who is a trained beautician, comments, "Things would be much easier financially if I worked. But even if the boys were older I doubt I would want to work more than half-time. My family will always be more important to me than the finances."

Vermont requires only a letter of intent to homeschool and an annual report. Dayna recounts that if she files the report properly, the state leaves her alone. "Actually, I have found the state officials to be quite helpful," she says. "The paperwork is very time-consuming, but the personnel at the education office have been encouraging."

Today most homeschooling parents belong to the Holtian de-schooling movement or the Christian right. But every parent, regardless of religious, philosophical, or political orientation, is free to keep a child out of school and to educate that child at home as long as state requirements are fulfilled. There are many home study curricula—including mainstream, standard ones—available to help parents who decide to homeschool.

Resources

For More Information

John Holt's Bookstore
2269 Massachusetts Avenue
Cambridge, MA 02140
Tel.: (617) 864-3100
Fax: (617) 864-9235

This bookstore, established by the founder of the modern homeschooling movement, offers a variety of books, videos, and homeschooling materials. Holt's organization also publishes *Growing without Schooling*, a bimonthly journal that Holt founded in 1977. It contains stories, news, and information about learning outside school. *Growing without Schooling* is also available on-line via CompuServe (call the bookstore for details). The bookstore offers information by phone on homeschooling and also offers forty-five-minute private consultations about homeschooling issues.

Each year *Growing without Schooling* publishes in its December issue a directory for homeschoolers, covering all fifty states. The directory lists private "umbrella schools" that enroll homeschooling children (to avoid legal difficulties), homeschooling support groups and organizations, correspondence schools, curriculum suppliers, homeschooling magazines, and related organizations. The listings include the entire philosophical, religious, and educational spectrum, so that all homeschoolers—including Christian and other religiously or traditionally oriented homeschoolers—will find it useful. The directory is a unique and valuable resource for all homeschoolers and is available from the bookstore.

Home Education Magazine
P.O. Box 1083
Tonasket, WA 98855
Tel.: (509) 486-2477

Home Education is a bimonthly magazine with useful articles and information.

Home School Legal Defense Association
P.O. Box 159
Paeonian Springs, VA 20129
Tel.: (540) 338-5600

This organization provides legal advice to homeschooling parents. Upon request, parents can receive a free one-page synopsis of the homeschooling laws in their state.

The Teaching Home
Editorial and Advertising Departments
P.O. Box 2029
Portland, OR 97294
Tel.: (503) 253-9633

The Teaching Home is a bimonthly magazine that focuses on Christian homeschooling. Each issue lists currently operating state Christian homeschooling organizations (numbering about forty-three at this time). The list is updated four times a year. These organizations can supply information about Christian schools in a particular state and locale. Each issue also advertises about seventy suppliers of Christian curricula, books, and educational materials. The magazine offers a trial subscription and distributes a free question-and-answer brochure about Christian home education.

Bob Jones University Publishers
Bob Jones University
Greenville, SC 29614-0001
Tel.: (800) 845-5731

A major distributor of textbooks and educational materials for Christian schools, Bob Jones also has curricula and books designed for Christian homeschooling.

Abeka Books
Box 18000
Pensacola, FL 32523-9160
Tel.: (800) 874-2352

A major distributor of curricula, books, and educational materials for Christian schools and for Christian homeschoolers.

National Home Education Research Institute
Box 13939
Salem, OR 97309
Tel.: (503) 364-1490

Institute Director Brian Ray conducts research into the effects of homeschooling on academic performance and collects the results of other research in the field, which he publishes in a bimonthly newsletter. He distributes free of charge a fact sheet summarizing important recent research.

Blumenfeld, Samuel L. *The Alpha-Phonics Book: A Primer for Beginning Readers.* Boise, Idaho: Paradigm Company, 1983. A guide to teaching children to read using the traditional phonics approach.

———. *How to Tutor: For Parents and Teachers, a Manual That Works.* Boise, Idaho: Paradigm Company, 1973, 1993. A guide to teaching the three Rs in the traditional manner.

Guterson, David. *Family Matters: Why Homeschooling Makes Sense.* Orlando, Fl.: Harcourt Brace and Company, 1992. An engaging reflection on and description of homeschooling by a father and high-school English teacher.

Gorder, Cheryl. *Home Education Resource Guide.* Tempe, Ariz.: Bluebird Publishing, 1989. Lists hundreds of valuable resources for homeschoolers, many of them free.

———. *Home Schools: An Alternative.* Tempe, Ariz.: Bluebird Publishing, 1990. An excellent survey of homeschooling as a viable alternative to public schooling. Includes legal advice; many helpful addresses.

Holt, John. *Teach Your Own.* New York: Delacorte/ Seymour Lawrence, 1981. Holt was for years the leading figure in the homeschooling movement. This is a practical handbook for parents wishing to educate their own children.

Peterson's Guide to Independent Study. Princeton: Peterson's Guides. Revised and reissued every year, this book lists a large number of correspondence and home study courses, ranging from the unstructured, laissez-faire to the highly structured and content rich. The book is available in most public and school libraries.

Spietz, Heidi Anne. *Modern Montessori at Home: A Creative Teaching Guide for Parents of Children Ages Six through Nine.* Rossmoor, Calif.: American Montessori Consulting, 1989. See chapter 25 for more about the Montessori approach.

———. *Modern Montessori at Home: A Creative Teaching Guide for Parents of Children Ages Ten through Twelve.* Rossmoor, Calif.: American Montessori Consulting, 1990. See chapter 25 for more about the Montessori approach.

21

The International Baccalaureate

For many teenagers, life in high school is too narrowly academic, too competitive, and too much governed by exams and grades. These students might be better off in a progressive educational environment that includes an emergent curriculum, student projects, cooperative learning, and arts-based learning. Or they may be happier as "liberated" teens, taking responsibility for their own education in the way Grace Llewellyn describes in *The Teenage Liberation Handbook* (see chapter 31).

But some young people are discontent in high school for quite different reasons. They want more rigor, more academic challenge, more material to master, and more skill development. They are tired of the smorgasbord of fluff courses designed to attract students rather than to challenge them as learners; they are tired of inflated grades; and they are tired of an environment in which to be smart is to risk being socially ostracized. They want to be challenged and measured.

Most high schools do offer some courses that are especially rigorous and challenging. Many, for example, offer advanced placement (AP) courses in various subjects. AP courses are college-level courses that juniors and seniors take and for which they receive credit when they get to college.

The International Baccalaureate is a broad liberal arts program that challenges high-school students to work at a college level in every academic subject.

But there is another widely available program for the academically motivated high-school student: the International Baccalaureate (IB), a broad liberal arts program that challenges students to work at a college level in every academic subject. The two-year IB program includes rigorous comprehensive exams. Students who pass these receive a diploma that is recognized around the world as a sign of high academic achievement at the secondary school level.

The idea for the International Baccalaureate began among the so-called international schools. In many of the world's national capitals and in other major cities, there are private schools that primarily educate the children of foreigners living in the particular country (e.g., children of diplomats, business executives, and officials of international agencies). The typical international school goes through the twelfth or thirteenth grade and has students from many countries. English is usually the language of instruction, examination, and social interaction.

Most students in these schools return to their native country for college or university studies. But admission requirements for these colleges and universities vary greatly from country to country. Some schools require broad knowledge in all academic subjects. Others require specialization and in-depth study of two or three subjects. Thus, at the high-school level, the international schools have a difficult, almost impossible task—to prepare each student for university entrance in that student's respective country. In the late 1950s and early 1960s, high-school teachers in certain international schools began to address this problem.

These teachers envisioned a standardized two-year curriculum and a set of examinations that would lead to accreditation acceptable to any college or university in any country. They designed such a curriculum, making it both general and specialized, and developed comprehensive examinations that would test a student's mastery of the curriculum. Students who passed the exams would demonstrate that they have the academic skills and knowledge to study at virtually any institution of higher education in the world.

This standardized curriculum was the origin of the International Baccalaureate. It was first used at international schools in Copenhagen, Frankfort, New York, Barcelona, and a few other cities. Foundation grants in the late 1960s allowed the founding teachers to organize and to formalize their activities. A central office was set up in Geneva, Switzerland.

In the 1970s, the International Baccalaureate program was adopted by many international schools and by some elite private schools. The private schools were more interested in the scope and rigor of the program than in the international diploma that it led to. During the 1980s and 1990s, the IB has spread rapidly. As of Sep-

tember 1, 1995, 603 schools in 84 countries offer the IB. In the United States, the IB has been adopted by many public schools. There are now 184 schools that offer the IB in this country. Of these about 75 percent are public schools, including suburban, inner-city, comprehensive, and specialized high schools. About eleven thousand American high-school students are enrolled in International Baccalaureate programs. In the United States, the two-year IB is usually offered in grades eleven and twelve. Some schools have IB preparatory programs beginning in the ninth and tenth grades.

The IB curriculum consists of six subject groups:

> Language A (the student's best language plus the study of selections from world literature)
>
> Language B (second language) or, for a bilingual student, another language at the A level
>
> Individuals and societies: History, geography, economics, philosophy, psychology, social anthropology, business and organization
>
> Experimental sciences: Biology, chemistry, physics, environmental systems
>
> Mathematics
>
> Electives: Art/design, music, theater arts, Latin, classical Greek, computer studies, and others (the elective requirement can also be satisfied by taking another course from language A, language B, individuals and societies, or experimental sciences)

Each year students take one course from each subject area. Each course presents the methods and assumptions of the particular academic discipline and treats a small number of topics in great depth. Rather than superficially surveying a lot of material, the students study in depth a few topics in each field.

Of the six required courses, three are studied and examined at the higher course level. Higher-level courses are two years in length, requiring a minimum of 240 classroom hours. Higher-level examinations are taken at the end of the second (i.e., senior) year. The other three courses are studied and examined at the subsidiary level. Subsidiary level courses require a minimum of 150 classroom hours. They can be taken in one year, and up to two subsidiary level exams can be written at the end of the first (i.e., junior) year.

Subsidiary level courses are not inferior to higher-level courses; they are simply broader in their approach. Because the courses are organized in this way, IB students can explore their strengths in depth but also are required to pursue academically challenging curricula in areas of lesser interest or expertise.

Students take comprehensive exams on each of the subjects studied, most of them at the end of their senior year. The exams consist of essay questions and questions that require a student-generated answer. Unlike the Advanced Placement exams, which are largely multiple choice questions, the IB exams very seldom contain any multiple choice questions.

These are international exams. The exam for each subject is given on a particular day or days in May or November, depending on which hemisphere the school is located in. The exams are immediately mailed outside the school to be graded. They are graded on a single standard with 1 as the lowest grade and 7 as the highest. Students must acquire a total of 24 points (out of a possible 45) from the six exams, an extended

The International Baccalaureate has been immensely successful at raising the academic standards and level of achievement in both private and public schools, and is spreading rapidly.

essay, and a course called "Theory of Knowledge." The extended essay is a four-thousand-word independent research paper. Theory of Knowledge is a course that explores the relationships among the various academic disciplines and engages students in the analysis of and critical reflection on the knowledge acquired within and outside the classroom.

To receive the IB diploma students must also spend 150 hours over the course of their junior and senior years in what is called "CAS" (Creativity-Action-Service). Creativity can include music, art, drama, or work on a newspaper. Action involves activities such as sports, dance, environmental cleanups, and walkathons. Service includes tutoring, hospital work, helping out at a camp for the handicapped, and work with the homeless.

The IB program is demanding and difficult. About 70 percent of the candidates earn the diploma, yet the program seems a boon to both the schools and the students taking part in it.

To establish an IB program, a school must apply to International Baccalaureate North America (IBNA), located in New York City. IBNA then studies the school's ability to run the program. The school must be able to offer the full IB curriculum and have enough qualified teachers to teach high-level courses in their field. If the school does not have such teachers, it must recruit and hire qualified teachers. Faculty who will teach in the IB program attend orientation and training courses to learn about the purposes and methods of the IB program. Once a school has been approved, it can start to offer IB courses. Some schools open IB courses to all students. Others limit courses to students who are taking the full program.

The program is not inexpensive. The school must pay an application fee of $2,500, an annual subscription fee of $7,000, plus about $120 for each student enrolled and taking the exams. But as Paul Campbell of IBNA points out, the costs are comparable to costs of other educational programs in public and private schools.

The IB seems a good investment. Apparently it can have a trickle-down effect on an entire school. A recent study showed that students who attended an IB school but didn't take part in the program did better than similar students from a non-IB school. The high expectations and rigor that surround the IB rubs off on non-IB students and teachers in a school.

Parents whose child might be interested in an IB program can contact IBNA for a list of schools around the country (see Resources at the end of this chapter). They may find that a public or private school in their area is offering the IB. They might also approach local high-school teachers and officials and suggest that they look into the program. The IB has been immensely successful at raising the academic standards and level of achievement in both private and public schools and is spreading rapidly. Nevertheless, not all educators know about it.

The IB program is also offered at the United World colleges. Located in New Mexico, British Columbia, Wales, Italy, Norway, Argentina, Hong Kong, Singapore, and Zambia, these are two-year colleges for students in the twelfth and thirteenth grades. English is the language of instruction and examination. All students follow the standard IB curriculum and take the qualifying exam.

United World colleges offer a cultural as well as an educational experience. Each college has about 250 students. About half the students and half the faculty are from the host country. The others are from as many as fifty different countries around the world. Each student, in addition to working toward the IB Diploma, has an opportunity to meet and work with students and teachers from many cultures.

Lincoln Park High School
CHICAGO, ILLINOIS

Lincoln Park High School was among the first public schools in the country to adopt the IB program. In 1979 when the school began to consider the program, its student population was about 78 percent African-American and 12 percent Hispanic. When the program was adopted in 1980 it was hoped that it would help create an integrated, multiracial school in which all students, whether or not they participated in the IB program, would strive for academic excellence. In both respects the program has succeeded. The student body is now 44 percent African-American, 26 percent Caucasian, 23 percent Hispanic, and 7 percent Asian. Of the IB students, who number about 280 out of a school population of about 1,750, approximately 50 percent are Caucasian, 15 percent African-American, 15 percent Hispanic, and 20 percent Asian. Of the over 300 seniors in the class of 1995, 93 percent went on to college. Each of the 60 IB graduates went on to college.

Mary Tookey, IB program director at Lincoln Park, comments:

> The IB program is the most rigorous and challenging pre-university program that there is. In each course students study the basic approach which informs that academic discipline—be it literature, history, or biology—and focus on a few topics important for an understanding of the disci-

pline. Thus they acquire the skills and knowledge which will allow them to continue their studies in that discipline at the undergraduate level. They develop efficient work habits. They learn how to think and to express themselves orally and in writing. In college, IB graduates distinguish themselves as motivated, sophisticated, and successful learners.

It is often said in American educational circles that the best exam is one the students cannot prepare for. In the IB, the approach is totally different. Both teachers and students know what content and skills have to be learned for each subject area. The exams and the whole assessment process reflect these requirements.

The clear standards in the IB create strong motivation in both students and teachers, and put the teachers in the position of coaches. Students work together in groups and help each other out with their studies. Because the tests are criterion-referenced, not norm-referenced, one student's high grade does not lessen another student's chance to get a high grade. The IB students work in a real community of learners, comprised of motivated students and committed teachers, where curiosity, intellectual rigor, and hard work are appreciated.

But the students don't become academic machines. They engage in sports, drama, other extracurricular activities, and do service in the community. They regularly go out to help in nursing homes, hospitals, day-care facilities, centers for the disabled, and similar places.

Nor are the students separated from the rest of the student body. Through homeroom, through art, music, and gym classes, and through sports they are integrated into the life of the school. They are very active

in athletic and extracurricular activities, and are liked and respected by students in other programs. IB students are often student leaders, class and club officers, and sports team captains.

About 75 percent of the students in the IB program at Lincoln High earn the full IB diploma in addition to their regular high-school diploma. Those who don't get enough points for the diploma earn certificates for the individual subjects and thus receive college credit and advanced placement for their work.

Students in the International Baccalaureate program at the Richard Montgomery High School in Maryland work on a housing project for the homeless. Students do community service as well as take a set of rigorous academic exams to receive the IB certificate.

Richard Montgomery High School

ROCKVILLE, MARYLAND

Carol Dahlberg, IB director at Richard Montgomery High School in Rockville, Maryland, also has high praise for the IB:

> Our school was losing enrollment when the IB was established. Now we have a very strong enrollment with about five hundred of the fifteen hundred students in the IB program. We can take one hundred ninth-graders in our IB preparatory year and we have over eight hundred applicants. Between 90 and 100 percent of the students in a given year earn the IB diploma.
>
> The IB is for the academically oriented student who is willing to work hard, to be self-disciplined, to learn and practice time management, to study in an interdisciplinary way, and to be measured against a demanding, international standard. In the IB, it is okay to be smart, to be interested in school, and to work hard.
>
> Teachers like it because they have a lot of freedom in the selection and presentation of the content. The IB provides subject guides and general guidelines, not specific lesson plans. Within a given course a teacher can choose to concentrate on particular topics. Thus in a history course the teacher selects a particular region such as Europe and may emphasize certain topics such as the Enlightenment or the Holocaust. Also teachers use different teaching methods, including lectures, seminars, discussions, theme projects, role-playing, response journals, and panels. There is a lot of interaction and cooperation among teachers and much interdisciplinary treatment of themes.
>
> The students are definitely challenged. Almost all of them go on to college and, when they come back to visit, they say how glad they are they took the IB. They have the basic tools to work in every subject. I often get letters from students at Yale or Stanford or another university that say something like, "The IB taught me how to manage my time and to study effectively and gave me the skills I need in college. You know, Mrs. Dahlberg, I'm the expert in the dorm on writing papers."

International Baccalaureate students at Montgomery High School socializing with senior citizens.

FOR MORE INFORMATION

International Baccalaureate North America
 (IBNA)
200 Madison Avenue, Suite 2007
New York, NY 10016
Tel.: (212) 696-4464
Fax: (212) 889-9242

This is the main administrative organ of the International Baccalaureate in North America. Upon request, it sends out an information packet that includes a directory of all schools in North America that offer an IB program. The organization helps schools prepare to initiate IB programs and sells study guides and other materials. IBNA also schedules meetings and conferences for teachers and educators interested in becoming involved with the IB movement.

IBNA publishes a magazine called *IB World*. It is available through:

International Baccalaureate Organization
15, route des Morillons
1218 Grand-Sacconnex
Geneva, Switzerland
Tel.: (41) 22-791-0274
Fax: (41) 22-791-0277

IBNA also has a list of the United World colleges around the world. Three of the world colleges are:

United World College of the American West/
 Armand Hammer
P.O. Box 248, Route 65
Montezuma, NM 87731
Tel.: (505) 454-4217
Fax: (505) 454-4274

United World College of the Pacific/
 Lester B. Pearson
R.R. 1, Victoria, British Columbia V9B 5T7
Canada
Tel.: (604) 391-2411
Fax: (604) 391-4212

United World College of the Atlantic
Saint Donat's Castle, Llantwit Major
South Glamorgan, Wales CF61 1WF
United Kingdom
Tel.: (44) 1446-792-345
Fax: (44) 1446-794-163

FOR FURTHER READING

Petersen, A. D. C. *Schools across Frontiers: The Story of the International Baccalaureate and the United World Colleges.* Lasalle, Ill.: Open Court Press, 1987.

The University of Virginia, Case Western Reserve University, and Bryn Mawr College have all published studies on the International Baccalaureate. International Baccalaureate North America can provide information on how to obtain these studies (see For More Information, above).

22
Islamic Schools

Islam is one of the world's great religions. Its history began in the seventh century in what is now Saudi Arabia with the revelation received by the prophet Muhammad. An active missionary religion, it began to spread soon after its founding. Islam is now the dominant religion in the Middle East, North Africa, much of sub-Saharan Africa, Turkey, Iran, Iraq, Pakistan, Indonesia, and several of the former republics of the Soviet Union. There are substantial Islamic communities in India, China, Malaysia, Canada, the United States, and in some countries of eastern and western Europe. There are nearly 1.5 billion Muslims in the world, and the number is growing rapidly.

Most Americans know very little about the history or the beliefs of Islam. What we do know is largely determined by the generally negative representation of Islam in the American media. In that representation, being a Muslim is usually equated with being an Arab terrorist or a radical African-American separatist.

The basis of Islam is the Holy Qur'an, which Muslims believe is the literal word of Allah, Creator and Lord of the universe, and which represents His will for humanity. The Qur'an was revealed in Arabic to Muhammad through the archangel Gabriel and contains 114 suras or chapters. Muslims honor as true prophets of Allah the prophets of ancient Israel as well as Jesus of Nazareth. But they believe that Muhammad is the "seal of the prophets," the last communicator of Allah's word and will. With him Allah's redemptive work for humanity is complete.

The Qur'an, as the will of Allah for humanity, contains many laws and rules regarding personal, family, and community life. In English the word "Islam" means "submission" (to Allah's will). A Muslim is a person who submits his or her life to the will of God. The so-called Five Pillars of Islam are the duties incumbent on the devout Muslim. The Muslim must recite the profession of faith—"There is no God but Allah God, and Muhammad is his prophet"; perform the five daily prayers; observe a fast during daylight hours in the lunar month of Ramadan; give alms to the poor and unfortunate; make a pilgrimage to Mecca, the center of Islam; and strive to spread the faith. Muslims do not eat pork or drink alcohol.

There were very few Muslims in the United States prior to the twentieth century. In the 1930s, W. D. Fard, a Muslim immigrant, began to proselytize in the African-American community. Fard was especially active in Detroit and Chicago between 1930 and 1933.

In 1933, Fard handed the mantle of leadership of the small but growing Islamic community to Elijah Muhammad. Under Elijah Muhammad the community came to be called "The Nation of Islam." Temples were founded—Temple Number One in Detroit, Temple Number Two soon afterward in Chicago, and more over time.

Elijah Muhammad advocated racial and religious separation. When he died in 1975, his son, W. Deen Mohammed, was elected as his successor. W. Deen Mohammed began to teach a universalistic, nonexclusive form of Islam. He said that African American Muslims should consider themselves part of the worldwide Islamic community and also an integral part of American society. Not everyone was happy with this change, and around 1978, Minister Louis Farrakhan and his followers left the main body of African-American Muslims. This group professed Elijah Muhammad's separatist beliefs and in time took the name Nation of Islam.

Today the Muslim community in the United States consists of three principal groups. One is an immigrant group comprised of first- and second-generation immigrants from countries such as Egypt, Jordan, India, and Pakistan. Another group consists of African-American Muslims who are followers of W. Deen Mohammed. The third is the Nation of Islam. Muslim immigrant groups have established and support about fifty schools around the country. Almost all of the other sixty or so Muslim schools are connected with communities of African-American Muslims who look to W. Deen Mohammed as their leader.

The first African-American Muslim school was founded in the 1930s by Sister Clara Muhammad. The wife of Elijah Muhammad, she wanted a Muslim education for her children. Sister Clara

Muhammad took them out of the Detroit public schools and began to educate them at home. Soon other parents in the Detroit African-American Muslim community were sending their children to Sister Clara Muhammad to be educated, and thus the first Muslim school came into being. Soon Islamic schools were founded in other cities. By 1975, there were about forty schools in the United States. At first, each Muslim school was called a "University of Islam." Later, many schools changed their name to honor Sister Clara Muhammad. Today most African-American Muslim schools use the name "Sister Clara Muhammad [or Mohammed] School."

There are now about sixty Islamic schools in thirty states as well as in Bermuda.

⌘

There are now about sixty Sister Clara Muhammad schools in thirty states as well as in Bermuda. They range from small, home-based schools with a handful of students to large schools with substantial facilities and three or four hundred students. There is a teacher's training college in Virginia.

Al-Nur Home Education Center
Springfield, Massachusetts

Al-Nur (The Light) Home Education Center is a tiny school affiliated with the Sister Clara Muhammad school movement. It is located in the home of teacher Katara Aleem on a quiet residential street. The school has six students, all of them girls. They range in age from seven to twelve. They are all African-American, though not all are Muslim. The family of one girl is Protestant, that of another belongs to the Jehovah's Witnesses. The school is all girl by chance, not by design. Its two male students moved out of the area.

Aleem is a warm and energetic woman. She

wears a scarf over her hair and a long brown shift with slacks. She founded her school in 1991, responding to local parents who wanted an Islamic education for their children. She describes the school's curriculum:

We have a two-pronged curriculum. Our work is both academic and moral. We aspire to academic excellence. We cover the same subjects as the public schools: reading, writing, spelling, arithmetic, social studies, science, and computers. Sometimes I work with the group as a whole, sometimes with one or two of the children who are at the same skill-needs level—in reading or math, for example.

But we are concerned with moral excellence as well. We start the day by reciting the Fatihah, the first sura of the Qur'an. In the Fatihah we express our appreciation to the Creator for the world and for our own lives, our openness to learning about Him and His world, and our desire to seek His guidance and His protection.

Then we recite the student slogan:

I am a human being and God has made me in the best mold.
He has made me the custodian of the earth.
If I am the most righteous, then I am the most honored.

The children learn to read and write Arabic. The Muslim children and I do the daily prayers at the appointed times. And I am always reminding them that the teachings of the Qur'an are Allah's will for humanity, the basis of our life.

Later on, Aleem drills two of the younger girls on antonyms and synonyms, using a set of flash-cards. She is an engaging teacher. She questions, prods, teases, hugs, and encourages her students into learning. She clearly loves her vocation and her students. The feeling is mutual. At one point, a girl walks over, puts her arms around Aleem, and says simply, "Teacher, I love you."

Later, a girl asks me what I am writing on my notepad. Before I can answer Aleem says to the girl, "Now, dear, it is not polite to ask such a question." Immediately, the girl apologizes to me. At Al-Nur, warmth is not confused with permissiveness.

Each of the girls is dressed neatly in dark blue and white and, like Aleem, is wearing a head covering. Shortly before I leave, one of the girls—the school's "poet laureate"—hands me a newly written poem:

I'm Glad I'm Me

I'm glad I'm me,
And that I'm drug free!
Nobody is going to mess
Up my mind
I'm going to give it
to Allah all the time.

—Sakeenah Fardan, 9

The Sister Clara Mohammed School
Atlanta, Georgia

The history of Islamic education in Atlanta goes back to 1965 when the African-American Muslim community there founded a "University of Islam." This closed in 1977, but reopened in 1980 as the Sister Clara Mohammed School. The Sister Clara Mohammed School and its high-school branch, the W. Deen Mohammed High School, occupy a large, renovated chapel that has eighteen classrooms and is surrounded by six acres of grounds. It has about three hundred students and some forty teachers and staff members. Safiyyah Shahid, principal of the school, sums up its identity and philosophy:

> We are an Islamically based academic institution offering a college preparatory curriculum that is enhanced and focused by extensive Islamic instruction from a universal perspective. The school looks at education as a sacred right and a God-given duty. Therefore every student is entitled to the best instruction and each is obligated to give his best effort. Moral and intellectual enlightenment are combined in every subject. Students who enroll here enter a school of excellence, dedicated to every student developing morally, spiritually, and academically, for self, community, and world leadership.
>
> From kindergarten through grade twelve we have a rigorous academic curriculum with English, math, science, and so on. But we try to integrate an Islamic perspective into all courses. For example, if I were teaching about water in a science course, I might introduce some passages from the Qur'an that deal with water to remind the students that every phenomenon has a religious dimension. One *ayat* or verse in the Qur'an, for example, says, "It is He who has created men from water." This is something we are always working to develop, relating Islam to the academic subject matter.

There are many distinctly Islamic elements in school life. Each morning there is a ten-minute presentation about Muslim etiquette. The students learn about the application of Islam to some aspect of daily life, for example, eating, dressing, or making decisions. From kindergarten the students study Arabic and use it to read the Qur'an. There is a sequential, progressive Islamic studies course that goes through all the grades, which includes Islamic history, culture, philosophy, literature, and stories about the prophet. At the times of the daily prayers, the students gather in the school *musallah* or place for prayer. Every Friday, all students go to the local *masjid* or mosque for the *ju'mah* or congregational prayer. There they are part of a congregation of between twelve hundred and fifteen hundred people.

Shahid emphasizes that the school and the community that supports it practice an inclusive form of Islam and do not isolate themselves from the larger Islamic community or from other religious groups in Atlanta. She recently went to Saudi Arabia to gather materials and advice to improve the Islamic studies and Arabic language parts of the curriculum. The local *masjid* has frequent contact and occasional joint activities with other religious groups in the area.

All students wear uniforms in the school. Elementary-grade girls wear a green jumper and a yellow blouse. Boys wear green pants and yellow shirts. The high-school students dress in blue and white. All girls, and female staff as well, must cover their hair. Teachers are addressed as "Sister ——" or "Brother ——."

Social interactions between boys and girls are discouraged. Courting behavior such as holding hands is prohibited. Shahid comments, "We teach the importance of modesty in dress and behavior, and of sexual abstention until marriage. That is the teaching of Islam."

Currently, about thirty-five students are non-Muslims. Presumably they have come because of the solid academic program, the emphasis on dis-

Girls at the Sister Clara Mohammed School in Atlanta, Georgia. Islamic schools in African-American communities stress self-discipline, academic achievement, and moral and religious values and attract many children from non-Islamic families.

cipline, and the wholesome environment. All students but four (two from Pakistan and two from Africa) are African-American. Although the local Islamic community has Caucasian members, there has never been a Caucasian applicant to the school. "If there were a Caucasian applicant," says Shahid, "we would be happy to accept him or her. The school is committed to serving all children, regardless of race, color, or creed."

In talking with Shahid, one gets a sense of great dignity in her as a person and in the institution she represents. It is the dignity that comes with being devoted to the task of placing a high and inspiring ideal of the human being before the children, and of calling them to the realization of that ideal.

The Sister Clara Muhammad schools in the United States are in the process of establishing a central organization. At a recent Islamic educa-

tional conference, Imam Plemin El-Amin was appointed to convene the committee to establish this organization. El-Amin is the *imam* of the Atlanta *masjid* and the director (Shahid is the principal) of the Sister Clara Mohammed School.

Resources

FOR MORE INFORMATION

Sister Clara Mohammed/W. Deen Mohammed School
735 Fayetteville Road
Atlanta, GA 30316
Tel.: (404) 378-4219
Fax: (404) 378-4600

The school serves as a resource center for information about Islamic education in North America. It will supply on request a list of Islamic schools on the continent.

Islamic Circle of America
166-26 89th Avenue
Jamaica, NY 11432
Tel.: (718) 658-1199
Fax: (718) 658-1255

A resource center for information about Islam. Provides free brochures including one titled "Islam for Americans."

Islamic Publications International
P.O. Box 247
Teaneck, NJ 07666
Tel.: (201) 599-9708; (800) 568-9814
Fax: (201) 599-1169; (800) 466-8111

A source of books, videos, and brochures about Islam.

Muslim Journal
910 West Van Buren, #100
Chicago, IL 60637
Tel.: (312) 243-7600

The *Muslim Journal* is a weekly newspaper published by the African-American Islamic community. The organization also publishes an annual Muslim Resource Directory, which includes a list of Islamic schools in North America.

For Further Reading

Bucaille, Maurice. *The Bible, the Qur'an and Science.* Paris: Seghers, 1987.

The Holy Qur'an, trans. Abdullah Yusuf Ali. Brentwood, N.J.: Amana Corp., 1983.

Lings, Martin. *Muhammad.* Rochester, Vt.: Inner Traditions, 1983.

Maududi, Abu A'la. *Towards Understanding Islam.* Lahore, Pakistan: Idara Tarjuman-ul-Qur'an, 1990.

23

Jewish Day Schools

Jewish education in America dates back to the late 1700s, when there was one Jewish academy in Philadelphia. Because the Jewish population at that time was small, there were few such schools. Between 1880 and 1920, however, about two million Jews came to the United States, most of them from eastern and central Europe. They left a situation in which they were culturally and socially isolated from the dominant culture, were discriminated against, and were frequently persecuted. They brought with them a centuries-old love and respect for study and learning that had been kept alive in Talmudic academies, where the Bible and commentaries on the Bible had been studied by the boys and men of the community.

The Jewish immigrants settled mostly in enclaves in Brooklyn, Manhattan, Philadelphia, and other urban centers. Rabbis and Talmudic scholars set up schools for the study of the Bible and of Jewish law. By this time, however, the public school system was well established and offered a secular education that was free, open to both girls and boys, and that promised the chance for acceptance and advancement in the dominant culture. For the most part, Jews, wishing to gain access to the dominant culture, embraced the public school system. As a result, very few full-

time Jewish day schools were able to attract enough students to survive. In 1940 there were only about twenty Jewish full-time day schools in the entire country.

The task of Jewish education was largely undertaken by the so-called Hebrew school, which was part of the local synagogue. There, for several hours each afternoon after the public school day was over, boys and girls studied the Hebrew language and Jewish history, religion, and culture.

After World War II and the Holocaust, there was great concern in the Jewish community about the survival of Jewish culture. European Jewry had been decimated. In the United States Jewish culture began to be assimilated into American culture. Intermarriage with other faiths was common, and the continued existence of the Jews as a distinct religious, ethnic, and cultural group seemed in question. Jews had been accepted in most areas of American life, and for many the preservation and enlivening of Jewish culture and identity now became a priority. After-school programs in Jewish education were strengthened, and new Jewish day schools began to be founded.

In recent decades this trend has continued and grown stronger. There are now about six hundred Jewish day schools in the country, educating some 190,000 children, or about 17 percent of all school-age Jewish children.

Most of these full-time Jewish schools are run by Orthodox Jews. Orthodox Jews accept the Bible as the revealed and infallible word of God and strictly observe laws about daily prayer, Sabbath observance, and keeping a kosher kitchen. Many schools are connected with the Conservative branch of Judaism. Conservatives accept the divine origin of the Torah and Talmud and observe Jewish customs and laws. They are somewhat less literal and strict than Orthodox Jews. A few schools are run by Reform or liberal groups that see Judaism more as a cultural heritage and racial history than as a religion. There are also community schools in which Jews of the different branches cooperate. While many such schools exist in areas where the Jewish population is small, there are also community Jewish day schools in metropolitan areas with large Jewish populations.

These various types of Jewish schools differ in some respects. In Orthodox Jewish schools, for example, boys wear their hair in the traditional style with long sideburns and girls must dress modestly in long dresses and with head coverings. There are separate classes for boys and girls. In a Conservative school the boys and girls dress like typical American schoolchildren, except that the boys wear *kippot* (yarmulkes). The classes are integrated.

All Jewish schools give a double education. They teach Hebrew, the Torah, and Jewish history, culture, and law. They also offer a general education curriculum similar to that used in public schools and including English, mathematics, American and world history, geography, and science. Children usually spend half their school day engaged in Jewish studies and using Hebrew and half studying the general curriculum and using English. It is a rigorous program. The children have to deal with two sets of teachers, textbooks, homework assignments, and tests.

There is some ambivalence within the Jewish community toward the day schools. Critics see them as isolationist and liable to arouse anti-Semitism in the society. Others believe the dual curriculum requires a compromise in academics. One teacher in a school I visited confided, "We just can't give children in half a day the same education that they would get in a full day at a good public school. Here they may get three classes of Spanish in a week. In a public junior high they have it every day."

Proponents reply that assimilation into the broader culture is no longer a problem for most Jews, and that Jewish day school graduates do well in their further education. Almost all the graduates of the high school I visited are accepted and go to college, many to elite schools. In any case, supporters argue, the benefits of Jewish day education outweigh possible disadvantages.

For one thing, Jewish day schools give their students a sense of cultural and religious identity. One teacher observed: "Today it is harder and harder for every person, including Jews, to have a sense of history, culture, and identity. The Jewish day school gives the child a sense of who they are—a sense of their place as Jews in history and in society—that comes from knowing one's roots and one's inherited culture. Often that is passed on to the parents as well. It is a great gift."

There are other positive features in Jewish day education, features that characterize most religious schooling, including:

Many of the parents who enroll their children in Jewish schools, even Orthodox schools, have had little Jewish education themselves and are not religiously observant.

A common set of ideas, ideals, and practices that bonds the school into a community;

Teachers who have a religious and moral orientation to life;

Explicit teaching of religious and moral principles. For example, the Schechter brochure asserts: "We want (our students) to grow to love and worship God, to be kind to fellow human beings, and to respect and practice *mitzvot* [the Jewish law]."

An emphasis on community service and on acts of charity and kindness. For example, older students at the schools I visited regularly visit the elderly and infirm and engage in other service activities.

Jewish day schools are meant exclusively for Jewish children but not just for children from religious Jewish families. Many of the parents who enroll their children in Jewish schools, even Orthodox schools, have had little Jewish education themselves and are not religiously observant.

The Solomon Schechter School

NEWTON, MASSACHUSETTS

The Solomon Schechter School is a Conservative Jewish day school. It has a Lower School (grades K–4) and a Middle School (grades 5–8) on separate campuses. There are sixty-five Solomon Schechter day schools around the country, each sharing a common educational philosophy.

Lower school director Lucy Tannen talks about the school:

As a full-time Jewish day school we offer two parallel academic programs, Jewish studies and general studies. The children spend about four hours each day with

each. The schedule changes, so for a time they have one program in the morning and then for a time the other. The two are not entirely separate, though. There are many cross-curricular integrated units. For example, when the children study the human body as part of the science curriculum, they are at the same time studying the Hebrew words for the various body parts.

The study of Hebrew is very important. The head of the school, Rabbi Joshua Elkin, says, "We consider Hebrew an essential tool that enables students to engage actively with Jewish texts, participate meaningfully in ritual life, and deepen their connection to Israel. By the time Schechter students complete the eighth grade they are adept at speaking Hebrew and participate in classes in Judaic studies that are conducted in Hebrew. The annual eighth-grade Broadway musical production is entirely in Hebrew. The general education curriculum is very demanding and includes a year each of algebra, biology, and chemistry."

Regarding the makeup of the student body, Lucy Tannen says, "Many of our children come from religious homes, but many do not. Some parents are attracted by the strong academic program and by the Judaic studies which they might have missed themselves. It is not uncommon that parents become more religious and observant through their contact with the school."

Rabbi Elkin adds, "Parental involvement is an important part of the Schechter education. Our goal is to build a community of parents, teachers, and students—a creative partnership dedicated to bringing the values of Jewish life to a new generation. Our family education program allows parents to study the Torah and rabbinic texts just as their children do."

Schechter is committed to making a Jewish education available to all Jewish children, regardless of financial resources. It uses an income-scaled tuition plan. Parents are asked to pay somewhere between 7 and 15 percent of their gross income for tuition, regardless of how many of their children are in the school.

At the time of my visit the Schechter Middle School is located in a large, squarish, red-brick building that belies its former incarnation as a Newton public school. (The school has since moved to a new modern facility close to the Lower School campus.) But inside it is clearly a Jewish school. The lobby is decorated with blue-and-white Israeli flags featuring the Star of David. On the wall is a portrait of the class of 1994, also designated, according to Jewish chronology, as the class of 5754.

The day I visit is not a typical school day. It is Lag b'Omer, a planting season holiday following Passover, and the children are preparing for a schoolwide "color war." Depending on their team allegiance their clothing is mostly red, blue, green, or yellow. Many have their team color daubed on as face paint. There is an expectant and happy frenzy as the children arrive at school.

Gradually the hubbub subsides as the time for morning prayers approaches. In a long, rectangular all-purpose room about forty seventh- and eighth-graders sit in rows of folding chairs. Some of them have striped prayer shawls over their shoulders. A few of the boys wear tefillin, or phylacteries—two tiny wooden boxes with Hebrew lettering on them—that are secured with leather thongs, one on the left forearm and one on the head just above the middle of the forehead. The children recite Hebrew prayers. A girl removes a large Torah scroll from a wooden cabinet at the front of the room and places it on a lectern covered with a purple velvet cloth embroidered with a gold Star of David. She reads a passage in Hebrew. More prayers follow; it is forty-five minutes before the prayer books are collected. Morning prayers are a part of daily life in the school.

After prayers, I see a young woman, obviously a school mother, standing in the lobby. I ask her

Students at the Solomon Schechter School in Newton, Massachusetts, display their artwork.

why she has chosen a Jewish day school for her child. She replies, "I didn't have any education in Hebrew or in the Jewish tradition. When I was a child, our religion was something that we were almost ashamed of, especially outside the home. I want my son to know about his ancestors and his culture, to know who and what he is. When we first brought him here, we didn't observe kosher laws or the Sabbath. But now we do."

The day is filled with *gaga* (Israeli dodgeball), relay races, softball games, and other festive activities. Outside, at the edge of the expansive grass school yard, two sixth-grade boys wearing *kippot* grouse a little about the long days and the double load of homework. But they admit that they are getting a good education. The family of one of the boys has recently immigrated from South Africa.

The Moses Maimonides School
BROOKLINE, MASSACHUSETTS

Not far from the Solomon Schechter School in Newton is the Moses Maimonides School in Brookline. It has about six hundred students in kindergarten through the twelfth grade. It is an Orthodox Jewish school but a "modern Orthodox" one, and its ambiance is quite similar to that of Schechter. In fact many students from Schechter go to high school at Maimonides.

Like Schechter, Maimonides has a two-track academic program with two sets of teachers. Here also some of the teachers in the general studies program are non-Jews. Students have about four hours of instruction daily in each program. "With sports and extracurricular activities, our high-school students typically are at school until five or six o'clock," says Lauriston Cone, assistant principal for the high school.

As at Schechter, the curriculum at Maimonides is obviously content rich, and the main pedagogy is teacher centered. Teachers couldn't cover all the material they need to cover if it were otherwise. Nevertheless here, as at Schechter, some elements of progressive education are used: whole language supplemented by phonics, cooperative learning, and the social curriculum. This is not surprising since, like the humanistic-progressive educational reformers, Judaism by

The study of Hebrew and of Jewish culture and history are central aspects of Jewish day school education. Here, students at the Solomon Schechter School present a dramatic version of a Bible story.

and large has an optimistic view of human nature and human potential. Lucy Tannen expressed the prevailing view: "We believe that the human being is inherently good and through study and training can become a moral and loving person."

When I visited the Maimonides High School I was struck by the similarity in atmosphere to Cathedral High School in Springfield, Massachusetts, a Roman Catholic high school I had visited (see chapter 30). In each there is a quiet, orderly, and purposeful atmosphere. There is a palpable warmth and mutual respect among teachers and students. The students seem bright, well-behaved, highly motivated, and able to relate to adults. That a school has a religious orientation may be more important than the particular religious orientation that it has.

Resources

For More Information

> Jewish Education Service of North America
> (JESNA)
> 730 Broadway, 2nd Floor
> New York, New York 10003-9540
> Tel.: (212) 529-2000
> Fax: (212) 529-2009
> e-mail jesna@ix.netcom.com
> World Wide Web: http://users.aol.com.jesna/
> jesna.htm

JESNA publishes a directory of the central agencies for Jewish education, Jewish educational resource centers, and schools and school systems which provide some central agency services. The directory is available for $10 from JESNA.

Other organizations providing information about Jewish day schools include:

> Solomon Schechter Day Schools
> 155 Fifth Ave.
> New York, NY 10010
> Tel.: (212) 260-8450

> Jewish Community Day School Network
> Dr. Harvey Raben, Chairman
> Jewish Day School of Metropolitan Seattle
> 15749 N.E. 4th Street
> Bellevue, WA 98008
> Tel.: (206) 641-3335

> Torah Umesorah
> The National Society for Hebrew Day Schools
> 160 Broadway
> New York, NY
> Tel.: (212) 249-0100

> Pardes (Reform Day Schools)
> Union of American Hebrew Congregations
> 838 Fifth Ave.
> New York, NY 10021
> Tel.: (212) 249-0100

FOR FURTHER READING

Aron, Isa, Sarah Lee, and Seymour Rossel, eds. *The Congregation of Learners: Transforming the Synagogue into a Learning Community.* New York: UAHC (Union of American Hebrew Congregations) Press, 1995.

Kelman, Stuart L. *What We Know about Jewish Education: A Handbook of Today's Research for Tomorrow's Jewish Education.* Los Angeles: Torah Aura Productions, 1992.

Rauch, Eduardo. "The Jewish Day School in America: A Critical History and Contemporary Dilemmas," in *Religious Schooling in America,* ed. James C. Carper and Thomas C. Hunt. Birmingham, Ala.: Religious Education Press, 1984.

24

Mennonite and Amish Schools

⌦

During the Protestant Reformation of the six-teenth century, the Anabaptists emerged as a radical, dissenting religious sect, primarily in Switzerland, Germany, and the Netherlands. The Anabaptists believed in adult rather than infant baptism, rejected civil authority over religious life, and refused to take oaths and to serve in the military. Severely persecuted in many areas, they withdrew into isolated and largely self-sufficient agricultural communities. When necessary and possible, they emigrated to less hostile domains. In the late sixteenth century many Anabaptists began to call themselves Mennonites, after the Dutch Anabaptist leader Menno Simons (1496–1561).

The first Mennonites arrived in North America in 1683 and settled in Germantown, Pennsylvania. This immigration continued for about a century. In 1727 the first Amish settlers—Mennonites who had broken off from the main body because of differences in belief and practice—arrived in Pennsylvania.

Today there are about four hundred thousand Mennonites in the United States and Canada, with substantial communities in Indiana, Ohio, Maryland, Virginia, and other states as well as in Pennsylvania. There are several different Mennonite groups. Each is distinguished primarily by the particular degree to which it accepts and rejects the trappings of modern American life.

The most strict and separatist are the Old Order Amish. Although there are many minor differences in practice even among the Amish communities, the Amish generally eschew most of modern culture and technology. They do not use electrical appliances, automobiles, telephones, or radios. The horse and buggy is their primary form of transportation. The Amish dress "plain and simple"—the men in black trousers and plain shirts without buttons, the women in dresses of unpatterned material and a head covering. Most Amish are farmers and live in large, multigenerational households. A number of households comprise a "church," which meets for worship in the homes of the church members. Ministers are chosen by lot from among the men of the church. The Amish do not serve in the military and do not buy insurance. If they borrow money, it is usually from family members or other Amish rather than from banks or the government. They travel little and generally keep to themselves, living a life centered on their faith, family, and community.

At the other end of the spectrum are the assimilated Mennonites. While retaining the Mennonite beliefs about adult baptism, pacifism, and the rule of the church by the Bible and the Holy Spirit, these progressive Mennonites have accepted many aspects of modern life, including automobiles, telephones, and television. They do not observe any rules of dress that distinguish them from other members of society. Unlike the Amish, they actively proselytize for new members and have church buildings and a seminary-educated clergy.

Between the Amish and the acculturated Mennonites are several other groups. The Old Order Mennonites are in many respects similar to the Amish, but they use electricity and telephones, dress a bit more flamboyantly—the women's dresses for example, can be of patterned material—and consider the bicycle to be an acceptable means of transportation. The Church of the Brethren and the Brethren in Christ are Mennonite groups that follow an outwardly modern way of life.

Until the late 1940s the Mennonites sent their children to public schools. The small local public schools in their communities were largely under their control and reflected their beliefs and values. Prayer and Bible reading were part of daily school life. The traditional Mennonite values of hard work, honesty, humility, cooperation, and self-discipline were supported by life in the school. The schools taught the children to read, write, and do arithmetic. The major part of the child's upbringing was still in the hands of the family and community.

During the 1950s the movement to consolidate public schools became very strong. Small, rural elementary schools, such as those where most Mennonite children were educated, were closed. Children were bused to larger schools in nearby towns and cities. By the 1970s, prayer and Bible reading were essentially eliminated from

Many of the several hundred Mennonite schools in the country offer a viable educational alternative to families that are not Mennonite.

public school life. For many Mennonites, especially for the conservative Amish and Old Order Mennonites, these changes created an intolerable situation. Mennonite parents did not want their children transported to places and to schools where they would be exposed to alien values, beliefs, and ways of living. Some Mennonite parents simply kept their children at home and taught them basic academic skills. In many areas, Mennonite families banded together to found a school that would reflect their beliefs, values, and way of life. Many Mennonite parents suffered greatly at the hand of zealous public school officials. Some parents were sent to jail, while others were harassed by state authorities until they moved to another state.

Today, all the various Mennonite groups are free to educate their children more or less as they wish, provided they adhere to general state guidelines. There are several hundred Mennonite schools in the country. Each reflects the values and way of life of the community that has founded and maintains it. Some of these schools, such as those of Amish and Old Order Mennonite communities, are interesting to outsiders primarily as a cultural and educational phenomenon. Many, such as those of the assimilated Mennonites, can and do offer a viable educational alternative to families that are not Mennonite.

The schools of the Old Order Amish and Mennonites have a number of features that are, in the context of American education, highly unusual. In many ways they are like the small village schools of pre-industrial, pre–public school America:

The schools are small, both in size and in number of students. Most have one or two rooms and between fifteen and fifty children in grades one through six or grades one through eight.

Parent involvement is very high. Schools are founded, built, and administered by parents. Parents choose, hire, and pay the teacher. Usually the land for the school has been donated by one of the founding families.

Students live close to the school, usually within walking distance.

There is a correlation of beliefs and values between the community, the family, and the school. Each supports the others in the education of the child.

The teacher shares the beliefs, values, and life-style of the families she serves. In virtually all Amish and Old Order Mennonite schools, the teacher is a young, unmarried woman. Her primary qualifications are a strong religious faith, a moral character, and a simple upright style of life. She must be a role model for the children, not just a dispenser of knowledge.

The teacher's relationship to the school and the parents is not a business relationship. The teacher is considered called to a religious "vocation." There is no contract or tenure.

The teacher lives in the community and has frequent contact with the children outside the school.

The school day is framed by religious activities, prayer, and the reading of the Bible.

Moral education is an important part of learning. In many schools, the McGuffey Readers, promoting the virtues of honesty, integrity, hard work, thrift, and self-sacrifice, are used. The verse "Do unto others as you would have them do unto you" is often posted in the room.

The basic academic skills of reading, writing, and arithmetic are emphasized, using teaching methods that are traditional and straightforward.

Material considered important—poems, Bible verses, songs, multiplication tables—is memorized and recited daily in the classroom.

Singing and music are an important part of daily school life. Often the children will go to serenade a shut-in.

Social cohesion based on mutual support, encouragement, and love is taught rather than freedom and individual achievement. Children are not allowed to exclude any child in their play.

Older children help younger children with their lessons.

The schools of the acculturated Mennonites possess some of these features. Parent involvement, the religious and moral orientation of the teachers, and moral and religious instruction are important. But the more acculturated schools are larger and prepare children for higher education and for life in the world. The New Order Mennonite schools are similar to schools of the mainline Protestant denominations and, like those schools, educate many children from outside their particular faith community.

The Diamond Road School
BROWNSTOWN, PENNSYLVANIA

The Diamond Road School is an elementary school founded and supported by a group of Old Order Mennonite and Old Order Amish families. The school building, built in 1954 and remodeled in 1990, is a small, one-story, metal-sided, beige structure separated from the road by a well-worn grass playground and a wooden-post fence. A wooden outhouse stands nearby, as well as a set of swings and a bicycle rack. The school is surrounded by fields and pasture, and across the road is a windmill and a cluster of farm buildings. Not far off, however, tall steel pylons of a high-tension power line march across the rolling farmland, and in the distance a steady stream of cars and trucks on Route 222 moves in and out of the nearby city of Lancaster.

The single, rectangular room of the Diamond Road School is about thirty feet long and twenty feet wide and has a wooden floor. At the front is the teacher's desk and the blackboard; off to one side is a large wood-burning stove. On either side of a large central aisle are two rows of old-fashioned wooden desks fixed to the floor. On the walls are maps of Germany the children have made, placards with different colored stars recording performance on spelling tests, and a large sheet of fluorescent red posterboard with definitions of the parts of speech written on it. The room is illuminated by three pairs of bare fluorescent ceiling lights.

By 8:00 AM on a rainy Monday, teacher Martha Weaver has already parked her bicycle in the bicycle rack and opened the school. Weaver, a pleasant, round-faced, bespectacled woman in her early twenties, is wearing a robin's-egg blue long-sleeved dress, a white lace cap over her neatly bunned hair, and a pair of jogging shoes. The children arrive by scooter, bicycle, horse and buggy, and on foot. They range in age from seven to about fourteen. Almost all the boys are wearing dark-colored trousers, collared shirts, and suspenders. The girls are all wearing dresses. The Amish girls have their hair parted in the middle and then tied in a bun. The Mennonite girls have

their hair parted and then braided. In all there are nineteen children. They talk, work at their desk, or play. The atmosphere is peaceful and subdued. Two of the younger children get a bit noisy over a game they are playing. Weaver says softly, "I think some of our boys and girls need to be a little less loud." The two eight-years-olds immediately quiet down.

At 8:15 AM Weaver pulls on a rope hanging from the ceiling near the school's entryway and rings the school bell, bringing all the children in. In a moment, all nineteen sit quietly at their desks. They stand and recite the Lord's Prayer, and then Weaver reads a passage from the Gospel of John, which had been the gospel reading for the previous day's worship service. She also reads a passage from the Epistle of James, which includes the sentence, "All good things are from God." The children gather at the front of the room and sing several hymns. Then each child "greets" the guest of the day by introducing himself or herself and presenting a brief instructive poem or verse. One third-grader recites, "It is nice to be important, but more important to be nice."

For the balance of the day, Weaver performs a remarkable pedagogical dance—providing instruction and drills for the children in each of the eight grade levels in the basic academic skills. She spends ten minutes with the two members of the second grade going over spelling words, works with the fourth-graders on addition and subtraction, then without skipping a beat, gathers the seventh- and eighth-graders to work on German vocabulary. Meanwhile the children with whom she is not directly involved work quietly at their desks awaiting their turn. Sometimes "Teacher," as the children address her, asks older children to help younger ones, and they show them flashcards with arithmetic or spelling words.

At 10:30 AM there is a break. Despite the wind and light rain the children rush outside to run about, toss a baseball around, or to stand and talk. Then there are two more hours of instruction, drills, recitation, and desk work. By lunchtime, the sun has come out and the air is warm and redolent of spring. All the children, the first-graders as well as the eighth-graders, play a game of tag together. The scene—with the boys with their suspenders and broad-brimmed hats, the girls in their billowing dresses—is at once anachronistic and strangely moving. It is a scene of harmony and tranquillity, one that belongs more to the nineteenth than to the late twentieth century.

Amish and Old Order Mennonite schools, such as the Diamond Road School, try to insulate and protect the children from the outside world and to preserve the distinct and sectarian life of the community. These schools are not meant to educate "outside" children, and it is unlikely that parents from outside the community would want to send a child there.

Still, these secluded schools may have something to offer parents in the outside world, something more than just a nostalgic glimpse at a traditional educational form. In terms of their own goals, these schools are successful. They teach children to read, to write, and to do arithmetic; they educate them about the human and natural world; and they help them develop into moral, conscientious, socially responsible persons who can take a place in their community. The way that these schools are organized and run, their small size, intensive personal pedagogy, and curriculum may provide valuable lessons for parents "in the world" who wish to start their own community-based school or who are looking for an alternative school for their child.

Kraybill Mennonite School
MOUNT JOY, PENNSYLVANIA

About twenty miles west of Lancaster amid rolling farmland and not far from the Susquehanna River is the Kraybill Mennonite School. The school was founded in 1949 by progressive Mennonites and originally occupied the picturesque two-story red-brick Kraybill Meetinghouse.

Although a Mennonite school, Kraybill has much more in common with a typical mainstream Episcopal or Lutheran day school than it has with the Diamond Road School. Today Kraybill occupies a large modern building next to the meetinghouse. It includes three large classroom wings as well as a large, well-equipped gymnasium built in 1993. Parents drive up in station wagons and minivans to deliver their children. The students are dressed like elementary schoolchildren in any part of the country—jeans, shorts, T-shirts, sweatshirts emblazoned with sports team insignia. There are almost four hundred children in classes from kindergarten through the eighth grade. At each grade level there are two classes with between twenty and twenty-five children in each.

In a seventh-grade literature class, Leonore Vargo is leading her twenty or so students through a discussion of plot and character. The students sit in clusters of three and four. They have been reading a contemporary novel for young adults called *Tuck Everlasting* by Natalie Babbitt. They discuss how conflict is necessary to a plot, how there are both primary "round" and secondary "flat" characters in a work of fiction.

In a fourth-grade glass, teacher Mary Jane Smith introduces me as a writer who is going to write something about Mennonite schools. The children immediately and spontaneously begin offering their thoughts about their school's special virtues: "The teachers really care about you!", "We learn about the Bible," "The classes aren't too long!" and similar thoughts are expressed with alacrity. Then Smith directs her energetic and enthusiastic charges through a review of the different parts of speech.

Both in classes and in the school as a whole, the atmosphere is orderly and purposeful. The teachers are competent and dedicated, the children engaged, learning, and well behaved. Early in the morning as I waited for the class change, I walked into the large, impressive gymnasium. A student, a boy perhaps in the fourth grade, was walking out. He looked directly at me and said clearly and with a smile, "Good morning." Such a moment tells much about the ethos and life of a school.

John Weber is the school administrator. Recently, as part of a fund-raising event for the school, he had his beard—of twenty years' standing—shaved off. Sitting behind his large wooden desk and wearing a dark blue button-down shirt and regimental tie, Weber talks about Kraybill:

The school was founded by Mennonite, Brethren in Christ, and Church of the Brethren families. They wanted to have a school that provides a sound education and that supports and nurtures Christian values and a Christian way of living. The school is still governed by past and present patrons and is accountable to the local church congregations.

Both elementary and middle school students have Bible twice a week. We present the Bible from an Anabaptist point of view, but not in a dogmatic way. The children study the Christian life as a journey to God. The Bible curriculum is thematic and requires the active participation of the children. It is not a "memorize and fill in the blank" indoctrination. Each week every student attends a worship session at which a guest speaker relates religious truths to daily life. So religion and worship are an important part of their education. We try to help the children connect their faith with all aspects of life and to develop a personal relationship with Jesus Christ, the

A senior citizen from the Mennonite community shares stories of religious faith with lower grade students at the Kraybill Mennonite School in Lancaster County, Pennsylvania.

Bible, and the leading of the Holy Spirit. Many of our teachers are Mennonites, and all must be committed to the religious and moral as well as the academic development of the children.

In our academic program we generally follow the state curriculum guidelines, use the standard textbooks, and try to provide a very rigorous academic training. In grades one through five the classes are self-contained and the emphasis is on acquiring basic academic skills, habits, and broad knowledge. The children have separate classes in art, music, and physical education. In the middle school the sixth-, seventh-, and eighth-graders rotate among classrooms where they are taught by teachers certified in the particular subject: mathematics, literature, science, and so on. At present, we are raising money for an up-to-date computer center for the school.

About 40 percent of the children come from Mennonite families. Most of the others belong to the Brethren in Christ, the Church of the Brethren, or to other Protestant mainline or nondenominational churches. There are a few Catholic children in the school. All our parents are very concerned that their children get a firm grounding in moral and religious values as well as in academics.

Schools such as Kraybill run by assimilated Mennonites offer a sound academic education as well as religious and Bible instruction in Delaware, Florida, Illinois, Michigan, Oregon, Puerto Rico, Wisconsin, and in Canada.

Resources

FOR MORE INFORMATION

Mennonite Board of Education
500 South Main Street, Box 1142
Elkhart, IN 46515
Tel.: (219) 294-7523

This is the central information resource for Mennonite education in North America and can supply information about Mennonite elementary and secondary schools and colleges.

Lancaster Mennonite Historical Society
2215 Millstream Road
Lancaster, PA 17602
Tel.: (717) 393-9745

This is one of a number of Mennonite historical societies around the country that can supply information about Mennonite history and Mennonite education.

FOR FURTHER READING

Dyck, J.C. *Introduction to Mennonite History*. Scottdale, Pa.: Herald Press, 1993. An excellent introduction to Mennonite beliefs, way of life, and history.

Fisher, Sarah, and Rachel Stahl. *The Amish School*. Intercourse, Pa.: Good Books, 1986.

Horst, Irvin B. (trans.). *The Mennonite Confession of Faith*. Lancaster, Pa.: Lancaster Mennonite Historical Society, 1988. *The Confession of Faith*, originally published in 1633, tells what Mennonites believe about basic topics such as God, the creation, and human destiny. This is the first translation into English directly from the original Dutch.

Hostetler, John. *Amish Society* (4th ed.). Baltimore, Md.: Johns Hopkins University Press, 1993. The classic, comprehensive study of Amish beliefs, practices, and way of life. Written by a university professor who grew up in Amish society.

Hostetler, John, and Gertrude Enders Huntington. *Children in Amish Society*. New York: Holt, Rinehart, and Winston, 1971. This is a fascinating study of Amish culture and life and of the education of Amish children. It points out the basic presuppositions of Amish education, which are very different from those of mainstream public education.

Kauffman, J. H., and Leo Driedger. *Mennonite Mosaic: Identity and Modernization.* Scottdale, Pa.: Herald Press, 1991. A study of Mennonite beliefs, attitudes, and social patterns in today's world.

Kraybill, Donald. *Passing on the Faith. The Story of a Mennonite School.* Intercourse, Pa.: Good Books, 1991.

Shenk, Lois Landis. *The Story of the Ephrata Mennonite School, 1946–1996.* Ephrata, Pa.: Ephrata Mennonite School, 1996.

Wenger, C. J. *Mennonites: What We Believe.* Scottdale, Pa.: Herald Press, 1977. A pamphlet outlining the basic beliefs of Mennonites.

25

Montessori Schools

The Montessori method is one of the best-known and most widespread approaches in the world to early childhood education. Most of the several thousand Montessori schools in the United States are private institutions, but Montessori programs also can be found in public schools. While Montessori schools generally are for preschool- and kindergarten-age children, some Montessori schools go up to the sixth grade, and these are increasing in number.

Montessori education is the legacy of Maria Montessori, who was born August 31, 1870, near Ancona, Italy. At the age of twenty-four, Montessori became the first woman in Italy to receive a medical degree, graduating from the University of Rome. Early in her career as a physician, she became interested in the educational problems of mentally retarded children. She discovered that certain simple materials and objects could arouse interest and mental activity in young children and greatly help their cognitive development. Between 1899 and 1901, Montessori used innovative educational materials and practices with special needs children in a school in Rome. After their schooling with Montessori, the children were able to achieve the same academic level on state exams as other children.

In 1907, Montessori founded the Casa dei Bambini (The Children's House) in Rome, where she applied her educational methods with great success with children from the slums of the city. In her school, these disadvantaged children took a joyful interest in the world around them, worked with great concentration, and learned to read and write by the age of five. Montessori's methods, demonstrated as effective with special needs and disadvantaged children, soon attracted attention in Italy and in other countries as the basis for educating all children. Montessori was in great demand and traveled and lectured throughout Europe, India, and North America.

Montessori's ideas reached the United States before she did. When she first visited in 1911, there was already a Montessori school housed in the Washington, D.C., home of Alexander Graham Bell. Rather than being pleased with the initiative, however, Montessori was enraged by it. She had a strong proprietary attitude toward her ideas and wanted to personally direct and manage their spread. In part because of this attitude, Montessori's methods initially failed to take root in the United States. So while the Montessori movement flourished elsewhere in the world, it did not become firmly established in this country until after Montessori's death in 1952.

Since the 1960s, however, the Montessori

movement in the United States has grown rapidly and steadily. There are now about three thousand schools. These include infant-toddler programs (for children under three), preschools, kindergartens, and some elementary schools. Most of the Montessori schools were founded by trained Montessori teachers or groups of parents. While some of these function as private, for-profit businesses, most are not-for-profit institutions. Montessori programs are also used in Roman Catholic and other religious schools, and about 150 Montessori programs are part of public schools. Proponents of the Montessori method are trying to bring the approach into the federally funded Headstart program for preschoolers from disadvantaged environments. Today the Montessori movement in the United States is large, well organized, and influential. Internationally, Montessori programs are active in over eighty nations.

Montessori based her method on her view that young children possess a divine life force, which she referred to as *horme*. By means of this divine life force the child's physical, mental, and spiritual qualities gradually unfold. According to Montessori, children by nature want to develop their potential and assume an independent identity and role in the world. Crucial to this unfolding are both the surrounding environment and the adults in that environment.

Young children have, Montessori observed, "absorbent minds" that take in and "incarnate" everything from their surroundings. Thus the school environment (and the home) should be beautiful and inviting. Montessori wrote:

> The objects surrounding the child should look attractive to him. The "House of the Child" should be lovely and pleasant in all

Maria Montessori based her method on her view that young children possess a divine life force.

its particulars. It is almost possible to say that there is a mathematical relationship between the beauty of his surrounding and the activity of the child. He will make discoveries rather more voluntarily in a gracious setting than in an ugly one.

Montessori held that cognitive growth occurs in distinct stages. In the early years, there are specific moments when a child is ready to develop certain language abilities, mathematical skills, or patterns of physical movement. This readiness can be expedited by a particular type of sensory experience. It is the teacher's role to sense when the child is ready for that particular enabling experience.

Montessori also maintained that the young child (and the older child as well, to a lesser degree) is largely a being of the sense organs. The child has to experience the world through the senses, must be able to touch, see, hear, and smell in order to grasp a concept, and later must be able to deal with abstractions. Thus in the Montessori classroom, didactic materials or manipulatives—cutout alphabets, strings of beads, map puzzles—play an important role. The use of each manipulative involves physical movement so that the child experiences the concept first in a bodily way.

In the Montessori classroom, the teacher creates and maintains a consistent, orderly, attractive learning environment for the child. The teacher sets limits, establishes a schedule that includes periods of rest, observes the children daily, provides help and direction as needed, makes comments, and deals with conflicts and discipline problems—usually by setting the child to a fresh task at a table by himself or herself. Otherwise, the teacher gives the child freedom to choose a task and carry it through to its successful completion.

The classes in a Montessori preschool and kindergarten are multi-aged. Children of three, four, five, and six years of age learn and play in the same room. Learning is individualized, that is, children are free to learn at their own pace, and much of the contact between student and teacher is one to one. Children are free to move around the classroom. They are not, as Montessori put it, "pinned like butterflies" to a particular seat. The children are free to work alone or in small groups.

While the Montessori approach is known mainly as an educational method for preschool- and kindergarten-age children, Montessori designed a curriculum and educational approach for older children as well. Today many Montessori schools have elementary grade classes and others are planning to establish them. As Carol Fisher, director until 1996 of the Amherst Montessori School, observes, "A child finishing a Montessori preschool at age six has had three years of cognitive work, has been able to read for a year or two, and has had hands-on experience with the four mathematical operations. If these children go to a public school for first grade, they are likely to be asked to learn through rote memorization and drill what they mastered two years ago."

Many of the characteristics of the preschool carry over to the Montessori elementary classroom. Classes are mixed in terms of age, with seven-, eight-, and nine-year-olds grouped together in a "lower class" and ten-, eleven-, and twelve-year-olds grouped together in an "upperclass." Usually a child will have the same teacher for three years.

As in the preschool-kindergarten, it is assumed in the elementary grades that the child wants to and is able to learn. But the type of learning is different. Montessori viewed the preschool child as primarily learning to live in the physical world. Seven- to twelve-year-olds can learn a great deal through their imagination and ability for abstraction. Also, older children are able and in fact are quite anxious to ask basic questions such as "Where do I come from?", "How do I grow?", and "How did the earth get to be the way it is?" So the older child naturally wants to acquire knowledge, to learn about the world, and to deal with the big questions of life.

Hence the Montessori elementary grade teacher presents specific major themes: "The Beginning of Things (God without Hands)," "The World of Plants and Animals," "Man and His Tools," "Language and Communication," "Math and Invention." The students pursue in individual or group work any particular interest that is aroused. They are free to explore human culture, the natural world, the arts, even what may be called philosophy. Montessori asserted that children are capable of dealing with philosophical issues.

Yet even in the elementary grades, knowledge is presented in tangible form through time lines, scientific exhibits, and other objects and displays that are part of the classroom environment. There is no required work, but the teacher helps each child to plan and record his or her learning activities. Art is integrated into the daily curriculum and music plays an important role. In many Montessori elementary schools the students present a play, a musical, or an opera each year.

Because of the large number of Montessori schools and programs and their distribution across the nation, most parents will find that there is at least one Montessori school or program in their area. Visits from prospective school parents and others are easily arranged.

Amherst Montessori School
AMHERST, MASSACHUSETTS

The Amherst Montessori School is an attractive, one-story wooden building set far back from the road and surrounded by a white rail fence. Except for two large playgrounds, one in front and one behind the school, the school could almost pass for a tasteful, suburban residence. It was founded in 1969 by a group of local parents who wanted to make the Montessori method available in their community. In 1995, the school had two pre-school-kindergarten classes with a total of about fifty-five children.

Each classroom has an observation room equipped with a one-way window. Maria Montessori encouraged teachers and parents to observe children in their activities to help them understand what and how children are ready to learn.

Through the one-way mirror one sees a large, airy, sunny room about twenty-five feet square. The room is divided into sections by low wooden cabinets and sets of shelves. A variety of materials is set out on these partitions—colored wooden

blocks in various geometric forms, trays of colored beads, stacks of puzzle maps, trays with tiny glass plates and cups. Materials such as rods of varying lengths and strings of yellow and red glass beads are also stored on the walls. In one corner is a sink with a dishpan and cutting board, each child sized; nearby is a lilliputian ironing board and iron. There is a set of large plastic boxes each with a child's name on it. Potted plants line the window sills; a terrarium that is home to a pair of lizards sits on a table against the wall. The room is clean and well organized. As Fisher, director of the school at the time of my visit, explains, "Each Montessori classroom is a structured and carefully designed 'prepared environment.' All the didactic materials it contains are meant to attract and engage the child and help her develop the skills and abilities for which she is ready."

The room before us is divided into specific areas. Each area is designed to help the child practice and develop skills in a particular type of activity. In the "practical life" area, for example, children learn how to button their shirts, tie their shoes, wash their hands, clean dishes, scrub the

Four- and five-year-olds at the Amherst Montessori School in Amherst, Massachusetts, working with puzzles. In a Montessori school children use a variety of manipulatives in acquiring cognitive and physical skills.

floor, and dust the shelves. They are also shown how to interact socially with the other children and learn when to say "Please," "Thank you," and "May I help you?" Within the practical life curriculum is a group of presentations that Montessori called the "exercises of grace and courtesy."

The "sensorial" area contains materials to be touched, smelled, heard, and tasted, as well as to be looked at. Through experiencing these materials and objects, the children are introduced to concepts and qualities. For example, from touching sandpaper and then rubbing their fingers along smooth wood, children grasp what "roughness" and "smoothness" are.

In the "math" area the "manipulatives" allow children to experience arithmetic first as something concrete and tangible. There are rods in unit lengths from one to ten, strings of beads that can be formed into squares and cubes, and various objects to be counted. Using these, the children can quickly grasp the operations of addition, subtraction, multiplication, and division.

The "reading and writing" area contains cutout or "movable" alphabets, sandpaper letters, labeled pictures, and writing materials. Working alone or in small groups, sometimes with the teacher, sometimes without, the child is immersed in language. Fisher comments, "Many of our students learn to read phonetically simple words, and sometimes more difficult ones, by the time they are four. We are definitely a school, not a day-care center or nursery."

About twenty-five children are in the room, boys and girls ranging from about two years nine months to about six years. A few are walking from one area to another, or talking to one another, or looking dreamily out the window. But the great majority are sitting on the floor or at a low table, quietly and intently involved with some educational material and task. A little girl is arranging brown wooden blocks according to size. Two boys are putting together a puzzle map of the world. Another boy is pouring dried beans from a large jar into small cups. Through the observation-room partition I hear some noise in the room, but for a group of small children they are surprisingly quiet. The concentration and purposefulness that the children exhibit is more usually found in a graduate school library than in a roomful of preschoolers.

At first, as I look through the one-way mirror, it is hard to find the teachers, but there are indeed two of them. An older woman, the head teacher, is sitting alone on a child-sized chair in a far corner looking around at every child in turn, but at no one child for very long. She seems to be taking in both what is happening in the whole room and what is happening with each child. An assistant, a tall woman in jeans, is helping a child who is working with cutout letters. After a moment she walks away, also to sit by herself and to observe the children.

The boy pouring beans finishes his activity and carefully returns the jar, cups, and beans to their place. Then he goes over to observe a frog in a terrarium by the window. After a time he begins to work with a little girl on building a tower of blocks. The other children also move independently and easily from one activity to another. The teachers continue to maintain a low profile, for the most part quietly observing, and only occasionally going over to make a comment or work with a child or group of children.

Fisher explains:

> The children are free to go to any area and to pick a material that they are ready to use. The materials in each area are to be used in a particular order, according to dif-

*A student at work in the Amherst Montessori School.
The Montessori classroom is carefully designed and
equipped to be an inviting learning environment.*

ficulty. The teacher makes sure that the
child has an appropriate material, that
they don't have something which is beyond their stage of development or ability
level. This is important because the child
must have a reasonable chance of success
on a regular basis. The emphasis is on
choice and independence. The teacher observes and directs as necessary and helps
only when she feels it is necessary and useful. Maria Montessori said that any unnecessary help given to a child can be a
hindrance.

A basic idea in Montessori education is
that the child has a natural desire to learn,
to grow and develop. We need mainly to
supply the materials that will make that
development possible and otherwise just
stay out of the way. Montessori believed
that the problems in learning and behavior
that children have are largely due to adult
interference as well as to a deprived environment. If we give the right balance of
direction and freedom to the child she will
acquire a sense of her own independence
and competence, and will be able to live
life "from a position of strength." If you
ask a child here, "Who taught you to
read?" he or she will say, "Nobody taught
me to read. I taught myself."

In midmorning, the head teacher stands in the
middle of the room and rings a tiny hand bell.
The children immediately stop what they are
doing and look at and listen to her as she announces snack time. The children put away their
materials and are soon seated at the tables with
cookies and drinks. Afterward each rinses his or
her cup and plate in a tub of water. Another period of activities in the classroom follows and
then the children go out to the playground. At
noon parents start to arrive to pick up children.
Some of the children remain for an afternoon,
less structured day-care session.

The Montessori movement in the United
States has grown large enough to have a clear
philosophical and political rift, accompanied by
occasionally lively controversy. There are two
main groups: the Association Montessori Internationale (AMI) and the American Montessori
Society (AMS). The AMI was founded by
Montessori in 1929 to oversee the spread of her
methods. Relatively speaking, the AMI is a conservative organization that values Montessori's

ideas and methods very highly and is little inclined to innovate and experiment. Supporters of AMI say that its unique strength is its adherence to the teacher training standards of the international organization. They say too that AMI teaching methods do evolve, albeit slowly and after much consideration. The Amherst Montessori School, for example, is affiliated with and certified by AMI, and as Fisher explains, "We tend to use what is tried and true. AMI Montessori education has very specific methods and materials that give consistent positive results."

The American Montessori Society is a national organization not connected to AMI. Its schools and teacher trainings must adhere to certain standards, but these are not exactly the same as those of AMI. Its members, while loyal to Montessori, emphasize the need to adapt her methods to the particular needs of American culture and of American children at this time. They are more likely to incorporate non-Montessori methods into their classrooms.

Thus in the more traditional classroom of an AMI-affiliated school such as Amherst, there are no toys as such. And there usually is no provision for creative, spontaneous play by the children or for the telling of stories by the teacher. When I asked Fisher about imaginary play, she said that while it is not part of the curriculum, many children enjoy "pretend play," usually during recess. Also, the children may write stories and share any imaginary ideas they have with the class. She added, "There is so much that is imaginary in television and video that what the children need, and what Montessori has provided, are tangible things that they can touch and experience." In contrast, in an AMS-affiliated school, imaginative play, storytelling, and playing with toys are more likely to supplement the standard Montessori curriculum.

Both AMS and AMI have a number of teacher training centers that offer training in Montessori methods, usually as a one-year, full-time program. Recently, several summer programs have been established, typically involving two or three summers of study supplemented by periods of observation and by internships.

Resources

FOR MORE INFORMATION

Association Montessori Internationale–USA
(AMI-USA)
170 West Schofield Road
Rochester, NY 14617
Tel.: (716) 544-6709

This is the American branch of the international Montessori organization that is based in the Netherlands. Its services include accreditation of Montessori teacher training and Montessori schools, school consultations, national conferences and teacher refresher courses, teacher placement assistance, publications, and research assistance. AMI-USA also sells by mail-order books and other materials related to Montessori education.

North American Montessori Teacher's
Association
11424 Bellflower Road, NE
Cleveland, OH 44106
Tel.: (216) 421-1905

An affiliate of AMI-USA (see above) that provides information, books, and educational materials about the Montessori method.

American Montessori Society
281 Park Avenue South, 6th Floor
New York, NY 10010
Tel.: (212) 358-1250
Fax: (212) 727-2254

This is a group of American Montessori teachers and schools that is not connected to Association Montessori Internationale. It accredits teacher trainings and schools, publishes *Montessori Life Magazine* (four times a year), and helps place teachers.

The following companies sell Montessori books and educational materials:

Michael Olaf
P.O. Box 1162
1101 H Street
Arcata, CA 95521
Tel.: (707) 826-1557
Fax: (707) 826-2243

Kaybee Montessori
615-A Lofstrand Lane
Rockville, MD 20850
Tel.: (301) 251-6319; (800) 732-9304

Montessori Services
228 South A Street
Santa Rosa, CA 95401
Tel.: (707) 579-3003
Fax: (707) 579-1604

L.O.R.D. (Lord Our Righteous Development
Co.)
100 Gray Street
Elizabethtown, KY 42701
Tel.: (502) 737-7265
Fax: (502) 737-7265

Neinhuis Montessori–USA
320 Pioneer Way
Mountain View, CA 94041-1576
Tel.: (800) 942-8697
Fax: (415) 964-8162

FOR FURTHER READING

Loeffler, Margaret Howard. *Montessori in Contemporary American Culture.* Portsmouth, N.H.: Heinemann Educational Books, 1992. A collection of papers delivered by experts on Montessori education at a 1990 symposium on issues relevant to Montessori education as it is developing in the United States. It has sections on views inside the Montessori world, views from outside, and Montessori and contemporary social problems.

Montessori, Maria. *The Montessori Method,* trans. Anne E. George. New York: Schocken, 1964. The originator's basic exposition of her theory and practice of education.

———. *The Secret of Childhood,* trans. Joseph Costelloe. Notre Dame, Ind.: Fides, 1989. (Original work published in 1936)

———. *The Absorbent Mind,* Trans. Claude Claremont. New York: Dell, 1966. (Original work published in 1917)

Spietz, Heidi Anne. *Montessori at Home: A Creative Teaching Guide for Parents of Children Ages Six through Nine.* Rossmoor, Calif.: American Montessori Consulting, 1990.

———. *Montessori at Home: A Creative Teaching Guide for Parents of Children Ages Ten through Twelve.* Rossmoor, Calif.: American Montessori Consulting, 1990.

Standing, E. M. *Maria Montessori: Her Life and Work.* New York: New American Library, 1984. (Original work published in 1957)

26

Multiple Intelligences Education

Many educational reformers, including Rousseau, Pestalozzi, and Dewey, have called for the education of "the whole child." Schools, they have urged, should deal not only with the intellectual growth but also with the child's physical, artistic, emotional, social, and spiritual development. Recently, psychologist Howard Gardner has renewed the dialogue concerning multifaceted education.

In 1983, Gardner, a professor at Harvard University's School of Education, published the book *Frames of Mind: The Theory of Multiple Intelligences*. In it, Gardner challenges the definition of intelligence as a single, general capacity manifested in certain linguistic and logical abilities that can be measured and quantified in a number—the Intelligent Quotient or IQ—a definition that has dominated American education.

Gardner suggests that intelligence is the ability to solve problems and difficulties in a particular domain and to create products in that domain that are valued in the culture. According to Gardner, there are at least seven distinct forms of human intelligence, each with its own developmental history in the child, its own way of acquiring information, and its own way of

Gardner suggests that intelligence is the ability to solve problems and difficulties in a particular domain and to create products in that domain that are valued in the culture.

expressing itself and creating products. The seven intelligences are linguistic, logical-mathematical, spatial, bodily-kinesthetic, musical, interpersonal, and intrapersonal.

Linguistic intelligence has to do with language. It involves being able to listen and to read with understanding and to speak and to write clearly and correctly. Grasping the meaning and connotations of words and sentences, mastering vocabulary and spelling, and expressing oneself through the spoken and written word are all indications of linguistic intelligence. Writers and poets are among those especially blessed with it.

Logical-mathematical intelligence has mainly to do with numbers and with patterns. In the child, it involves the ability to count, to do arithmetic calculations, to classify objects, and to recognize causes and patterns. Later this intelligence is manifested in the ability to reason, both inductively (from particulars to generalities) and deductively (from principles to particulars), to deal with abstract concepts, and to see patterns and connections in phenomena. Scientists, mathematicians, accountants, and computer programmers use this intelligence.

Spatial intelligence involves the ability to perceive a form with accuracy; to recognize the form or object when it is seen from a different angle; to conjure up a mental image of the form; to imagine what the form will look like in movement; and to produce a graphic likeness of it. One practical application of spatial intelligence is being able to orient oneself in a physical environment and to navigate one's way through it. It also involves a sensitivity to patterns and to tension and balance in composition. Artists, sculptors, engineers, and wilderness hunters all must have a high degree of spatial intelligence. It is not necessarily linked to the visual system. Blind people often have high spatial intelligence.

Bodily-kinesthetic intelligence involves the use of the physical body in various, skilled ways to express something, to achieve a goal, or to produce a product. It involves both fine motor coordination, as in the manipulation of tools, and gross motor coordination, as in running and jumping. Dancers, mimes, athletes, and craftspersons all must have a developed bodily-kinesthetic intelligence.

Musical intelligence involves being sensitive to sounds, to their distinctive pitch, rhythm, and timbre. The person with musical intelligence can reproduce a tone or rhythm and can sing on key.

Interpersonal intelligence involves the ability to sense the feelings, thoughts, needs, and concerns of others; to look at a situation from the perspective of another person; to communicate both verbally and nonverbally; to get along with other people; and to work well in a group. Therapists, members of the clergy, politicians, and salespersons need a high level of interpersonal intelligence.

Intrapersonal intelligence involves awareness of one's own feelings and thoughts. It is manifested in the ability to concentrate; to look inward; to understand oneself in relation to others; to have a clear and accurate self-image; and to act according to that image.

Gardner points out that intelligence tests focus almost entirely on the linguistic/verbal and logical-mathematical intelligences. They test the child's vocabulary, reading ability, and ability to compute and to perceive relations between concepts, but little else. Hence the usual appraisal of a child's intelligence and learning potential is based on only two of seven types of competency.

Virtually all the learning and assessment that goes on in schools also is based on these two intelligences. Children are expected to listen to and understand what the teacher says, to gather information from books, to remember this information and to produce it on cue on a paper-and-pencil test, to do mathematical computations, and to use logic. A child with a high linguistic and logical-mathematical intelligence probably will do well in school, and IQ test results usually correlate with success in school.

Gardner is not original or radical in pointing out that there are various types of ability and expertise and that human beings are usually blessed more with one of these than with another. Even schoolchildren are aware that one child is "good at sports," another "good at art," and some are "good at school"—that is, at reading, writing, and arithmetic.

But in the context of current educational theory and practice, Gardner's position—that each of the seven forms of intelligence is a bona fide intelligence—is radical. He believes that all seven forms are equally important and that each is essential for the educational process. Each form must be recognized and actively cultivated. Schools have long offered art, music, and physical education classes, but Gardner calls for more than just added specialty classes; he wants to see the use of musical, artistic, kinesthetic, intrapersonal, and interpersonal intelligences integrated into the curriculum and the learning process. Schools should actively cultivate and nurture each intelligence. Gardner also argues that intelligence should be assessed via demonstrations and products of all the intelligences, not just the linguistic and mathematical types.

Unlike some of his interpreters, Gardner does not hold that children should have opportunities to develop their musical, interpersonal, and intrapersonal intelligences every day, or that all parts of the curriculum should be taught using all seven intelligences. But he does call for more balance in what children do in school and for some accommodation of different learning styles.

An article written by Thomas Armstrong and published in *Educational Leadership* provides an excellent description of how multiple intelligences theory can be used in a classroom situation: "Gardner [is] an archaeologist who has discovered the Rosetta Stone of learning. You can use this model to teach almost anything. . . . The master code of this learning style is simple: for whatever you wish to teach, link your instructional objective to words, numbers or logic, music, the body, social interaction, and/or (inner) personal experience."

Armstrong then describes how he teaches "time-telling" to first-graders. He arrives without the usual props for teaching this particular skill—work sheets and a tiny cardboard clock. He begins instead with a story about the land of No Time—where everyone misses their appointments—and the O'Clock family from the land of Time, who come to live there and settle on the highest hill. The O'Clocks have twelve children numbered one through twelve. Armstrong then unveils a five-foot-high handless clock. The students take

turns being the hands of the clock and make up and sing special rhymes for each time. Armstrong then introduces a "clock dance" in which students holding up the numbers one through twelve form a circle and the others dance around it to the music of "Rock around the Clock." He then has the children write their own account of the tale using illustrations of the clock faces showing different times. Afterward, the children gather in a circle and share their pictures and words.

Armstrong lists questions teachers should ask in preparing a lesson so that all the intelligences are called into play:

- How can I use the spoken or written word?
- How can I bring in numbers, calculations, logic, classifications, or critical thinking?
- How can I use visual aids, visualization, color, art, or metaphor?
- How can I bring in music or environmental sounds, or present important points in rhythm or melody?
- How can I involve the whole body or hands-on experiences?
- How can I engage the students in peer or cross-age sharing, cooperative learning, or large-group activities?
- How can I evoke personal feeling or memories and give students choices?

Since Howard Gardner's first presentation of the multiple intelligences theory, it has played an important role in the debate concerning educational reform. Scores of books and articles have been published on it, and many conferences and workshops held. A number of schools, both public and independent, have adopted multiple intelligences theory and practice.

The Milton L. Fuller School

GLOUCESTER, MASSACHUSETTS

The Milton L. Fuller School is a prekindergarten through fifth-grade school on the Massachusetts coast, about thirty-five miles north of Boston. In 1992, the school received a three-year grant from the U.S. Department of Education to further develop a Multiple Intelligences (MI) program that had begun as a grassroots project among teachers the previous year.

The MI program at Fuller is a school within a school. About 325 of the school's 800 children are in MI classrooms. Some of these classes are single grade, and some are multigrade, having children from two grades.

Bill Bruns, the MI project leader, explains, "We try to engage each intelligence as much as possible. There are specialist teachers for art, music, and physical education, and the children get regular instruction in each area. But art, music, and movement are also integrated into their regular studies. The specialists are also involved when other subjects such as history, English, or math are being studied."

In a combined grade-three and grade-four classroom, the children have been working in small groups on a project on the solar system. Each group has researched a particular planet, put together a book of drawings and text, and built a papier-mâché model. The day I visit, the teacher is hanging the models of the sun and the various planets from the ceiling to create a solar system display that is more or less according to scale. She explains, "The project of course involved some reading, and writing, and work with numbers. But it also involved art and crafts work which brings the spatial and bodily intelligences into play. Working together of course develops the interpersonal skills. And having the solar sys-tem actually visually presented in space in the room helps them experience what they have learned in a concrete way."

Cherylann Parker's fifth-grade students have been studying American westward expansion in the 1800s. At the beginning of the project they devised a study plan that would involve all the intelligences. A reference chart still remains on the blackboard. It has seven vertical columns, each with one of the seven intelligences indicated at the top. Under each heading is a list of activities:

Math-Logical: measure distances; work with maps

Musical: study and play Indian music; make instruments

Spatial: make pictures of Indians; make models of wagons and land forms

Linguistic: read Indian tales; have a debate over land seizure; write a story about Indians

Bodily-kinesthetic: do an Indian rain dance; have a wagon race

Intrapersonal: keep a journal of myself as an Indian during this time

Interpersonal: go on a hike together; have a powwow

Today children from another class are in the room. Their teacher has become ill, and Parker discusses a short story with them. Meanwhile, her fifth-graders work quietly and intently on their individual and group projects. Most are using popsicle sticks and glue to build models of the different types of shelters the early settlers used.

Later Parker remarks:

This is a wonderful approach to learning. Each child is stimulated and challenged in a variety of ways. And each has the opportunity to learn and to excel in his or her own way. A child who is not so good at reading or math may shine in the music or in the handwork. It's very good for their self-image and sense of worth. Besides, each child, regardless of their learning style, seems to grasp the material better if they have experienced it in a number of ways.

In the MI program at Fuller, assessment is multifaceted. Students make up portfolios consisting of journals, artwork, photos, audio- and videotapes, and other products that document their work and their progress. They make regular presentations to teachers, classmates, and parents of their completed project work. Students do not receive letter or number grades for their work. Instead, several times a year they take home a narrative report of their "Multiple Intelligences Interest Inventory." For each of several specific aspects of each intelligence the student is given an "S" (strong interest), "I" (interest), or "L" (limited interest). Parents have regular conferences with teachers.

The MI program at Fuller seems to be a success with students, parents, and teachers. Parents report that children seem to enjoy school and that some, for the first time, relish doing their homework. A parent survey indicated that 92 percent felt their child had had a successful year. Eighty percent felt that their child had become a better problem solver. Many parents take an active role in the program and in the school.

As project leader Bruns says, "It is very exciting to teach in this program. The teachers are learners just like the children. We are learning by doing. We are experimenting and discovering, training on the job. We share ideas and projects.

I think most of us would find it hard to go back to teaching in the old way."

While multiple intelligences theory is presented as a new approach in and of itself, in practice, it involves most of the standard elements of progressive education: a whole language approach to reading and writing; in-depth theme projects; cooperative learning; and multifaceted assessment. Thus while multiple intelligences education has a distinct and new vocabulary and conceptual framework, it has a strong connection to the progressive tradition in education.

Resources

FOR MORE INFORMATION

> Project Zero
> Harvard Graduate School of Education
> Longfellow Hall, 2nd Floor
> Appian Way
> Cambridge, MA 02138

This organization directs Howard Gardner's various projects and research initiatives, of which multiple intelligences education is but one. Upon written request it will send a list of public and private schools that are using the multiple intelligences approach (please enclose a self-addressed, stamped envelope).

> Zephyr Press
> 3316 North Chapel Avenue
> P.O. Box 66006
> Tucson, AZ 85728
> Tel.: (602) 322-5090
> Fax: (602) 323-9402

This mail-order company sells books, videos, and educational materials related to multiple intelligences. It also organizes conferences with multiple intelligences as the theme.

*Multiple
Intelligences
Education*

Gardner, Howard. *Frames of Mind: The Theory of Multiple Intelligences.* New York: Basic Books, 1993. This book presents Gardner's basic theory of the seven intelligences. Written for an academic audience, it is accessible, if not light reading.

————. *Multiple Intelligences: The Theory in Practice, A Reader.* New York: Basic Books, 1993. A collection of articles by Gardner and others about the application of multiple intelligences theory in the classroom.

Lazear, David. *Seven Ways of Knowing: Teaching for Multiple Intelligences.* Palatine, Ill.: Skylight Publishing, 1991. While meant for teachers, this book can also be used at home by parents. It contains games, exercises, and brainteasers that will awaken, teach, and expand each of the seven intelligences.

————. *Seven Pathways of Learning: Teaching Students and Parents about Multiple Intelligences.* Tucson, Ariz.: Zephyr Press, 1994. Also meant to help teachers awaken and expand the intelligences of their students, this book can be used by motivated parents working with their own child.

27

Progressive Schools

John Dewey (1859–1952) was one of the most influential figures in modern American thought. A philosopher and a social and educational reformer, Dewey was a major figure in the school of philosophy known as pragmatism, the intellectual and social movement known as secular humanism, and the educational movement commonly called progressive education.

Progressive education has had a substantial though sporadic impact on American education. Starting in the 1920s, many independent schools were founded as progressive schools using Dewey's experiential and child-centered approach to education, and public and already existing private schools also incorporated Dewey's ideas. In the late 1940s and through the 1950s, however, there was a widespread reaction against progressive education. Some private progressive schools closed or changed their approach. Public schools returned to an emphasis on traditional teacher- and textbook-centered pedagogy.

With the ideological, cultural, and political turmoil of the late 1960s, there was a revival of interest in progressive ideas in education. New alternative private schools based on progressive principles were founded. Alternative programs were set up in public schools and, while they usually avoided the word, they were progressive in philosophy and practice. In recent years, many of these schools and programs have disappeared, but some have survived, thrived, and matured.

In progressive schools, students spend most of their time in research and hands-on activities rather than listening to lectures from the teacher.

Progressive schools and programs share a number of distinct characteristics. These include the following:

The curriculum is strongly influenced by what the students are interested in. Students play a large, often determining, role in deciding what they learn and what they study.

Learning is self-motivated, self-directed, and experiential. Students learn by doing real things in real situations. They spend most of their time in research and hands-on activities rather than listening to lectures from the teacher.

The teacher is a guide and facilitator of learning rather than an encyclopedic source of information.

Theme-based projects are a primary approach to learning. Students spend a long time studying a specific, fairly narrow topic very deeply and from a number of perspectives. The approach is interdisciplinary.

The students play a role in making and enforcing the rules of the classroom. The class makes decisions through a democratic or consensual process.

There are few if any written tests, and probably no number or letter grades. Students are assessed by the totality of the work they produce. A noncompetitive atmosphere is nurtured.

Arts, crafts, music, and drama are important. Students are encouraged to express themselves in a variety of ways.

The development in the student of an inquiring, critical, and curious mind is a high priority.

Some or all of the more recently developed addenda to the progressive program are used. These include whole language, cooperative learning, the social curriculum, multicultural education, and developmental education (cf. Part Two, chapters five through nine).

Profiles of an independent progressive school and a progressive program in a public school are presented below.

The Common School

AMHERST, MASSACHUSETTS

The Common School is a small, independent school founded and still run on progressive principles. The school is housed in a cluster of buildings in a beautiful parklike setting. The low, knobby Hampshire mountain range is visible to the south. In one corner of the grounds is a small but challenging ropes course. The main building is a Victorian mansion. One first-floor wall in this building is covered by an immense quilt whose sections, made by alumni, teachers, and friends, commemorate aspects of the first twenty-five years of the school's life.

The Common School was founded in 1967. It initially occupied the parish hall of Grace Episcopal Church in downtown Amherst. The children played on the town common during recess; hence the school's name. The school now has 120 chil-

A child painting on a window picture at the Common School in Amherst, Massachusetts. In Progressive schools, self-expression through art is considered key to the development of the child.

dren between four and twelve years old. It includes a nursery school, a kindergarten class, and three multi-age classes called Primary (ages six to eight), Elementary 1 (ages eight to ten), and Elementary 2 (ages ten to twelve). There are two teachers for each class.

The day begins with "choice time," one hour when each child can choose from a list of activities. This list of options is drawn up by the teacher with various social, academic, artistic, and creative goals in mind and changes periodically during the year. On the day I visit, some older children go to the nursery school and kindergarten to work with the preschoolers. Others memorize lines for their upcoming class play, *The Yeoman of the Guard.* Others are busy sewing cos-

Kindergarten children at the Common School using animal figures and a book to learn about wild animals.

tumes for the production. During choice time, as throughout the day, children are free to get up and move around the room, talk, and go to the rest room without permission. Each classroom contains several tables and small chairs, as well as open areas and alcoves. Books, maps, posters, and other educational materials are abundant. There are no textbooks, workbooks, or duplicated worksheets in evidence.

Each day each child spends a certain amount of time on basic academic skills. But the class as a whole does not necessarily work on these skills at the same time. When I visit the Elementary 2 class, some children are working on reading with one of the teachers, while others are drawing.

Much of the day is arranged in large blocks of time where the children pursue work on theme-based projects. They do individual and group research using books and other resources, engage in related arts and crafts, and prepare for a presentation with which each project culminates. Elementary 2, for example, had spent four months studying China, learning about Chinese history, art, literature, and geography. The culminating event was a schoolwide Chinese fair with Chinese food, clothes, games, and entertainment. Other project themes that are commonly used are "pirates," "classical culture," "birds," "immigration," and "woodland Native Indians."

In this project work, an interdisciplinary approach is used. The class works with the subject in various ways, such as through music, language, stories, ideas, myths, artifacts, and art. In this way each child's primary way of learning, that is, his or her individual learning style, is called into play.

While the academic work seems rigorous and challenging, the school has a relaxed, noncompetitive atmosphere. There are no tests at the Common School and no report cards with grades. Parents receive regular narrative reports on their child and have a conference with the teacher twice a year. Students call teachers by their first name. The "hub of the school" is a cozy, wood-paneled library where students come to read, curled up on oversized pillows strewn on the floor. They are encouraged to read books of their own choosing and to keep a reader's log. There are also reading groups in which students read and discuss the same books.

School director Bud Lichtenstein describes the educational vision of the Common School:

> Our aim is to realize the full human potential in each child, not just intellectually, but also artistically, socially, creatively, and physically. So we present them with a very rich learning environment, with opportunities for discovery, experimentation, and self-directed learning, and opportunities for self-expression in the arts and in craft work. Most of our parents are committed to public school education, but they want to give their child an especially rich and challenging environment in the early years of schooling.
>
> We look on each child as an individual with a unique learning style, and we try to use that. In teaching reading for example, we use the whole language approach, but we also use various phonics methods. Every child is different and we try to address those individual needs.

The Alpha Program, Shelburne Community School

SHELBURNE, VERMONT

Several hundred miles away in Shelburne, Vermont, is the Shelburne Community School. A public school built in the 1960s according to the open school concept, it is a one-story brick structure, with the classrooms as open spaces flanked on each side by a hallway and an exterior wall. Sliding wall panels make it possible for smaller areas to be partitioned off. The roughly five hundred kindergarten through eighth-grade children are divided into "teams."

The "Alpha Team" consists of about seventy-five children in grades six, seven, and eight, three full-time teachers (Carol Smith, Meg Kenny, and Meghan O'Donnell), and several assistants. Its classroom is a large L-shaped area with tables, chairs, overstuffed couches, easy chairs, and even a bathtub lined with thick pillows. The room seems to have everything but a typical school desk. On two sides it opens out onto well-trafficked hallways beyond which are exterior walls with large windows. It seems a combination of living room, classroom, and commuter rail station.

On one of many posters on the walls the students have defined what they feel is "memorable learning." The poster reads, "Memorable learning is—hands-on—happens in and out of school—challenging—fun—provides feedback—is purposeful—goal-oriented—sees all people as teachers—is flexible—is recognized and celebrated—combines learning styles."

At the start of the school day, the students gather in groups of about ten. Each group includes a teacher or school staff member. The members exchange personal news and discuss plans for the day. These "advisories" function like a homeroom class, but provide the children with a small and caring support group that includes an adult.

Next there is the morning team meeting. All members of Alpha Team gather, and one of the teachers goes over the day's schedule and sets the tone and pace for the day. Carol Smith, 1995 Vermont "Teacher of the Year," announces that they will spend the morning finishing up their work on the "Life in the 1990s" project.

Smith explains to me:

> Early in the year we sat down with the students and asked them, "What do you want to learn about? What do you want to study?" Students wrote down the questions they had about themselves and the world. We looked for connections between their self-questioning and the social issues raised by their world questions. After days of discussion and clarification, these questions became the basis for very serious and content-rich themes, such as "Origins," "Adolescence," "Conflict and Resolution," "Cures," and "Mysteries." Working from the students' questions lets us focus on things relevant to them. The students learn skills and acquire knowledge and understanding through work on themes that matter to them. One theme this year was "The Real World: Life in the 1990s." We divided that into three sections: "Business in the 1990s," "Family Life in the 1990s," and "Shelburne in the 1990s," and we looked for connections among the three groups.

For about an hour and a half after the team meeting the children work in small groups. Some groups are simulating setting up a popcorn business. Each group has already decided on a company name, a product line offering different kinds of popcorn, prices, and advertising. The next day the students will actually make and sell popcorn. Other groups are setting up budgets for a hypothetical family, planning nutritious but inexpensive meals, and calculating health insurance and other expenses. A third set of groups is

preparing their exhibits about the town of Shelburne. One student is on the phone trying to get statistics about the town from an official at the town hall. Another student is seated on the floor making a display poster of photographs she has taken of farms in the area. "Next time I plan to make a video," she says. "It's good to work with something you haven't had experience with."

Virtually all of the children are actively engaged during this time. The teachers move from group to group offering encouragement and advice and reminding the occasional malingerer to get back to work. To a girl who has been discovered lounging in the bathtub a second time, a teacher says sharply, "That is not an option, Adrienne."

Smith comments, "Our aim is to create self-motivated, self-directed, responsible students. The children learn to conceive a research project, carry it out using all the available resources, and then to assess their own work. Alpha establishes the basis for lifelong learning. More than they need particular content, children need a love of learning and the skills to answer their own questions. Some of the work is in small groups, while some is individual, so that a student can pursue a personal interest."

All of the project work of the Alpha Team is integrated and interdisciplinary. There are no discrete subjects like American history or biology. Smith says, "If, for example, we were to study adolescence—and we have studied that—we would approach the topic using a variety of lenses. We'd look at the physical, emotional, intellectual, and social needs of adolescents and examine literature that addresses adolescent concerns. We might look at other generations and at the issues they faced as adolescents. We'd use the traditional disciplines and some innovative approaches as well. We would look at the topic from various angles while trying to answer the children's questions."

Describing her students and how they fare later in school, Smith observes, "These students are explorers; they are learners. They are not afraid to try something for the first time. They know how to ask fundamental questions. They do well in high school. They may have had a different set of experiences from students who have been in traditional classrooms, but their strengths and abilities enable them to adapt easily to a typical high-school program."

In addition to their project work, the students on the Alpha Team do ongoing work in basic reading, writing, and mathematical skills. They keep a reading log as a record of the books they have read and of their reactions to them. At all times they must have a piece of writing in process and must be making steady progress through a math textbook. But the children set their own goals, use other students and the teachers as aids, test themselves, and assess their own progress. The students keep a portfolio of their work and three times a year report to their teacher and to their parents on what they have done. There are no tests or grades and no report cards of the usual kind for students on the Alpha Team. As Smith says, "The portfolio and the subsequent conference *is* the test, *is* the report card." She continues:

> This is a purposeful and very meaningful process. Each trimester the students set goals within each of the five areas of essential learning adapted from the state's educational guidelines. Then they organize their work to show evidence of growth in each area. The conference provides an opportunity for students and parents to dis-

cuss the growth and successes and challenges and to set new goals. Our system of assessment is authentic and very rigorous.

Much of the Alpha Team's learning occurs in connection with the outside world. The children use community resources in their research. They go on field trips, to an emergency shelter, for example, or to a home for the elderly. Each year the Alpha Team plans, organizes, and goes on a week-long camping trip. They send representatives to several campgrounds, hear reports on the facilities and costs, and then decide by consensus which to use. Each year they also put on a theatrical production.

Carole Spencer, principal of the school, says of the Alpha Team:

> People who are used to traditional education are uncomfortable with the Alpha Team. They believe school should teach a fixed body of information and certain skills. They believe that learning is going on only when the teacher is standing talking and the children are sitting quietly listening. They believe that children should be with others of the same age. They are concerned that there is not enough structure in the Alpha Team program and that the children will do just enough to squeeze by. The parents who put their children in Alpha tend to have a positive and optimistic view of their child's natural desire to learn. The children in Alpha really develop self-confidence, independence, and responsibility over time. They develop polish and poise. I was not an Alpha fan when I came here, but now I am a strong supporter.

Resources

FOR MORE INFORMATION

Resource Center for Redesigning Education
P.O. Box 298
Brandon, VT 05733–0298
Tel.: (800) 639-4122

This center, founded by educational historian and critic Ronald Miller, offers a wide variety of books and materials on progressive and holistic education. Call for its book review and resource catalog called *Great Ideas in Education*. The Resource Center also sells a video called *Student-Directed Learning—the Alpha Program*, which portrays the Alpha Program at the Shelburne (Vermont) Community School.

Institute for Democracy in Education (IDE)
313 McCracken Hall
College of Education
Ohio University
Athens, OH 45701–2979
Tel.: (614) 593-4475
Fax: (614) 593-4531

IDE promotes educational practices that provide students with experiences through which they can develop democratic values and attitudes. As such, it supports progressive education and the current trends that are related to progressive education—whole language, cooperative learning, the social curriculum, and others.

IDE publishes a quarterly journal, *Democracy and Education*, which includes articles about education, book reviews of new books focusing on "democratic education," and bibliographies. IDE also sponsors regional offices that organize activities on the local level.

FOR FURTHER READING

Dewey, John. *Democracy and Education*. New York: Free Press, 1916. The classic exposition on the relationship between democracy and education.

———. *Experience and Education*. New York: Macmillian, 1938. Dewey's exposition of the importance of experiential education.

Goodlad, John, and Robert Anderson. *The Non-Graded Elementary School*. New York: Basic Books, 1983.

Kohl, Herbert. *Growing Minds*. New York: Harper and Row, 1984. A discussion of the process of education and the role of the teacher, written by a leading and articulate exponent of progressive education.

Lightfoot, Sara Lawrence. *The Good High School*. New York: Basic Books, 1983.

Wood, George. *Schools That Work*. New York: Dutton, 1992. A survey of public schools that have successfully adopted progressive educational principles. Wood is director of the Institute for Democracy in Education at Ohio University (see For More Information, above).

Please consult the resource lists for the following chapters for more books related to progressive education: whole language (chapter 5), cooperative learning (chapter 6), the social curriculum (chapter 7), multicultural education (chapter 8), Comer schools (chapter 13), essential schools (chapter 15), Foxfire (chapter 16), free schools (chapter 17), and holistic schools (chapter 19).

28

Protestant Schools

Several "mainline" Protestant denominations—notably the Lutherans, Presbyterians, and Seventh-Day Adventists—have significant numbers of parish schools around the country. Although they are not as well-known as some other types of alternative schools, they are a significant part of the American educational landscape. Together they educate hundreds of thousands of children.

The statistics concerning these schools are interesting. For example, there are probably more children in Presbyterian schools (80,000) than there are in all independent progressive schools. There are four times as many children in Seventh-Day Adventist schools (52,000) than there are in Waldorf schools. And there are about as many children in parish schools of the Missouri Synod of the Lutheran church (170,000) as in all the Montessori schools in the country.

These mainline Protestant schools offer parents additional alternatives in education. In general they are well-established, stable schools and offer a strong traditional academic education that includes moral and religious instruction. Tuition is often lower than that at comparable independent secular schools. And while the schools are religiously based, church membership and

Protestant schools, in general, are well-established, stable schools and offer a strong traditional academic education that includes moral and religious instruction.

belief are not required of parents or children. All of these schools admit children from families with a religious affiliation other than that of the school; they also admit children with no religious affiliation. In many schools a majority of the children come from outside the church. Also, Protestant denominational schools exist all over the country, in urban, suburban, and rural areas. To parents looking for an alternative to a public school, a Protestant school may be a viable alternative.

LUTHERAN SCHOOLS

The largest mainline Protestant school system is that of the Lutherans. The several Lutheran groups together have about 2,500 schools educating some 250,000 children.

Lutheran education dates back to the colonial period. Many German Lutherans settled in Pennsylvania, Maryland, and Virginia. Believing in the "priesthood of all believers," the Lutherans felt that every person should be able to read the Bible. They valued education highly. By 1820 there were 342 Lutheran schools in 700 parishes.

New groups of German Lutherans

came to the United States in the early 1800s and settled in the Midwest. Very conservative in their religious beliefs and social attitudes, they formed in time their own associations of churches such as the Missouri Lutheran Synod and the Wisconsin Evangelical Lutheran Synod. Dedicated to education, these groups founded many parish schools. By 1872 there were 472 elementary and high schools in 446 Missouri Lutheran Synod parishes. The aim of these schools was to educate devout, theologically knowledgeable, and culturally literate church members. The schools were based on the Gospel and saw the arts and sciences as gifts of God to be used for the service and glorification of God.

The more conservative Lutheran groups believe that the human being is by nature sinful; that the church is the medium of grace; that the mainstream world of politics, popular entertainment, and secular culture is unredeemed; and that education should be based on a religious and moral view of life. Thus, when the public school system gained dominance in the nation, they, unlike some of the more liberal Lutheran groups, fought to retain their parish schools.

They succeeded. The Missouri Synod (2.8 million members), the most conservative Lutheran group, alone maintains over 1,600 parish schools with about 180,000 students. The Wisconsin Synod (400,000 members) has 31,000 children in 374 schools. Other, more liberal, Lutheran groups have but a handful of schools.

Most of these Lutheran schools are in the American heartland—Missouri, Wisconsin, Michigan, Minnesota. But because of the German Lutheran diaspora they are also to be found in most other parts of the country. Lutheran schools, especially in urban areas, educate many non-Lutheran children, including many from minority and disadvantaged backgrounds.

Saint Matthew's Lutheran School
NEW BRITAIN, CONNECTICUT

New Britain, once "The Hardware Capital of the World" and still home of the Stanley Tool Company, has fallen on hard times. In the 1960s its downtown area went through stage one of an urban renewal process—the "knock everything down" stage. The rebuilding phase never occurred, and the center of the city is a curious and depressing patchwork of wide streets, empty lots, and drab, low-roofed retail stores. There are also a number of large, beautiful churches, reminders of a more prosperous past.

One of these downtown churches is Saint Matthew's Lutheran Church of the Missouri Synod. Attached to the spire-dominated church is a flat-roofed two-story brick building, housing Saint Matthew's Lutheran School. The school was founded in 1896 to educate the children of the parishioners, German Lutherans who had come to the area for jobs.

Marty Boettner, an energetic, transplanted midwesterner and the director of the school, talks about Saint Matthew's:

> The school was founded by the congregation to give the children of the church a strong Christian education. In the 1950s and 1960s, the church and school were thriving. There were twenty children in each of the eight grades. Everyone thought that the center of town was about to be rebuilt with high-rise apartment houses and shopping centers. That's when the new school building was built. The urban renaissance didn't happen, though. Many parishioners moved to the suburbs and now the average age of the church members is seventy-one.

Now only one or two of the school's sixty-five children is Lutheran. The school has become part of the ministry of the church. Most of the children are from poor and minority families in the neighborhood. The public schools in New Britain are overcrowded, dangerous, and weak academically. Our parents want their children to get a good education in a safe, orderly school environment, where the basic skills and discipline are emphasized, and where there is the moral element and human warmth that a religious environment can give.

At Saint Matthew's, the children pray together each day and once a week there is chapel where hymns are sung and a brief chapel talk is given. The children have a religion class each day in which they study the Bible, Christian beliefs, and the church. They have to memorize Bible verses as part of their normal schoolwork. Each subject is taught as far as possible from a Christian perspective. Creationism rather than evolution is presented to explain the existence of the world and of humankind.

I spend a day visiting classes at Saint Matthew's, and it seems that to me the school is delivering what it intends. The children are well behaved and enthusiastic. The teachers seem devoted to their work and intent on helping the children academically.

The kindergarten children start the day by saluting the flag and saying the Pledge of Allegiance. Then they do some phonics before engaging in creative play.

The ten or so students in the third-grade class form small groups to work on reading, then gather to drill on phonics. "When some of the children transferred into the school," their teacher proudly tells me, "they could hardly read, and now most of them are above grade level." The teaching methods seem traditional and teacher centered, with textbooks and workbooks much in evidence. The combined seventh- and

Children from St. Matthew's Lutheran School in New Britain, Connecticut, celebrate a holiday with a procession outside the school. Protestant schools, especially those in the inner city, attract children from various religious and ethnic backgrounds.

eighth-grade class is steadily working its way through a science textbook chapter on geology.

At lunch the children file into the huge gymnasium, and smiling matrons from the church congregation serve a lunch of hot dogs, sauerkraut, deep-fried potato nuggets, and green jello from the adjoining kitchen.

Later Boettner, who looks on his teaching and work in the school as a religious vocation, remarks:

> Most Lutheran schools of course are in the Midwest. In my hometown in Wisconsin there are eleven Lutheran churches and most of them have a parish school. But there are Lutheran schools in every state. There's a big one right over in Albany, New York. Many Lutheran schools, especially in New England and in the Midwest, are in an inner-city environment. An old German church down in Bridgeport, Connecticut, runs a school where *all* the students are African-American. Here at Saint Matthew's about 40 percent of the students are not Lutherans and almost 10 percent have no religious affiliation at all. And we have a lot of minority children.

PRESBYTERIAN SCHOOLS

From its birthplace in Geneva, Switzerland, the Calvinist Protestant movement spread to England, Ireland, Scotland, Wales, France, the Netherlands, and thence to America. In the colonial and revolutionary periods a high percentage of Americans were Calvinists. John Calvin taught the absolute sovereignty of God; the utter sinfulness of the human being; the predestination of all human beings to salvation or perdition according to the will of God alone; and the "priest-hood of all believers," that is, the primacy of each individual's relationship to the divine.

When the Dutch state was founded in 1815, Calvinism became the state religion. To accommodate other religious groups, however, a secular, religiously neutral school system was established. Many Pietist groups who believed in religion as a matter of personal piety objected to the institutionalization of the church in the state, and also to the value-neutral and belief-neutral educational system.

Some of these Dutch Calvinist Pietists fled to the United States and settled in western Michigan. They held that every area of life, including business, family life, culture, and education, must conform to the will of God. Thus education must be based on the revelation of God's will in the Bible. It must integrate a religious worldview into the entire curriculum and must prepare the students for living a Christian life. These Presbyterians believed that the family alone has the right and obligation to provide education for its children. Neither the state nor the church, as an institution, should play any role. Therefore, when public schools were founded they refused to enroll their children and founded their own schools. The schools were organized, founded, owned, and run by parents and other laypeople, not by the church.

This system of largely autonomous Presbyterian or Dutch Reformed schools still exists and in recent decades has been growing. A central body called "Christian Schools International" has 382 schools, 3,844 full-time teachers, and over 75,000 students. Presbyterian schools are found all over the country and offer a traditional academic education that is infused with religious and moral values.

The schools are open to children of all faiths and backgrounds. Religious beliefs and practices play a large part in school life but usually in a nonsectarian, nondogmatic way. Many students come from families with another or with no religious affiliation.

SEVENTH-DAY ADVENTIST SCHOOLS

In the 1830s and early 1840s many religious leaders in the United States began to teach that the end of the world was at hand and that Christ would come again to institute the Kingdom of God on earth. When the predicted time for this event (spring of 1844) came and went, these teachings had to be revised. Ellen Harmon White, long active in this Adventist movement, explained that the millennial event was to occur when Jesus finishes his priestly ministry in heaven, and that his followers must purify and ready themselves for it. In 1863, the movement was organized as the Seventh-Day Adventist church and established its headquarters in Battle Creek, Michigan. They opened a sanatorium in the same town. White was one of the founders of the Seventh-Day Adventist church.

Seventh-Day Adventists accept the authority of the Old and New Testaments and the atonement of Christ. They emphasize the free will of the human being to choose to accept and to use the gift of grace. White had a holistic view of the human being and stressed the interrelation between physical, mental, and spiritual life. The body is the temple of the Holy Spirit and should be kept pure. She enjoined her followers to abstain from meat, alcohol, tobacco, and other stimulants and drugs. The Kellogg brothers, developers and advocates of flaked corn as a wholesome breakfast cereal, were followers of White. Dr. Harvey Kellogg was the administrator of the sanitorium of the church at Battle Creek and

used diet, water therapy, exercise, and other natural means to treat illness.

White strongly supported Christian education. In 1874, when the organization founded Battle Creek College, she wrote an essay called "Proper Education," asserting that education is much more than just studying the languages and esoterica of the past. Rather, education involves the development of the physical, mental, and spiritual dimensions of the human being. Education should include physical exercise and manual labor, health education, and the study of the Bible as well as academic work. Its aim is to create a healthy, intelligent, informed Christian who can represent the religion of the Bible and promote the glory of God.

As the public school movement grew in the late 1800s, Seventh-Day Adventists pushed for the establishment of a school for every church. Adventists believe that every child from an Adventist family should go to an Adventist school, and they are willing to make sacrifices to achieve this goal. Although there are only about 838,000 members of the Seventh-Day Adventist Church in the United States, there are 1,106 elementary schools with about 51,000 students, 81 secondary schools with about 16,000 students, and 11 colleges and 3 universities with about 19,000 students. The center of the movement is in Washington, D.C., and there are large communities in California, Michigan, New England, and in 206 countries around the world. For the most part, though, Seventh-Day Adventists are quite scattered geographically and thus the elementary schools are small, most having only between one and three teachers.

The curriculum is based on state educational regulations, but the Bible, as the revealed Word of God, is a basic component. Creationism is taught, but students also learn about the theory of evolution. Bible study and prayer are a part of the daily school activities, and all subjects attempt to integrate faith into learning. In most Adventist schools, cooperation rather than competition is emphasized. As a result, competitive sports and interscholastic athletic competition are not fostered as a part of school life. The schools promote a wholesome, healthful lifestyle, which includes a natural foods diet and regular exercise.

In Adventist schools, as in schools of other religious groups, a substantial and growing percentage of the children are from nonmember families. They are attracted by the small size of the schools, the safe environment, the emphasis on healthful living, the relatively low tuition, and the spiritual and moral dimension of the school life.

Resources

FOR MORE INFORMATION

The Lutheran Church—Missouri Synod
1333 South Kirkwood Road
St. Louis, MO 63122–7295
Tel.: (314) 965-9000
Fax: (314) 965-9917

Wisconsin Evangelical Lutheran Synod
Commission on Parish Schools
2929 North Mayfair Road
Milwaukee, WI 53222
Tel.: (414) 256-3220
Fax: (414) 256-3899

The Commission on Parish Schools has information on schools around the country as well as brochures about Lutheran education.

Christian Schools International (CSI)
3350 East Paris Avenue, SE
Grand Rapids, MI 49512–3054
Tel.: (800) 635-8288; (616) 957-1070
Fax: (616) 957-5022

This is an association of about four hundred Christian day schools, most of them associated with the theologically conservative wing of the Presbyterian church. CSI publishes textbooks, teacher guides, and other resource materials; publishes a magazine for parents called *Christian Home and School*; provides counsel and help in starting a Christian school and in operating and evaluating an existing school; and provides information on how to promote Christian education.

North American Division of the Seventh-Day Adventists
Education Department
12501 Old Columbia Pike
Silver Spring, MD 20904–6600
Tel.: (301) 680-6442

The central source for information about Seventh-Day Adventist schools.

Protestant Schools

Carper, James, and Thomas C. Hunt. *Religious Schooling in America.* Birmingham, Ala.: Religious Education Press, 1984. This book includes chapters on Lutheran, Presbyterian, and Seventh-Day Adventist schools.

From Vision to Action: The Basis and Purpose of Christian Schools. A booklet available from Christian Schools International (see "For More Information, above).

Integrating the Faith: A Teacher's Guide for Curriculum in Lutheran Schools. Helps teachers integrate a moral and religious perspective into the teaching of academic subjects in grades three through eight. Also helpful for prospective parents. It is available from the Concordia Publishing Company, 3558 South Jefferson, St. Louis, MO 63118–3968, or call (800) 325-3040.

Lutheran Schools: Touching Lives Forever, Sharing Christ. This is a booklet published by the Lutheran Church Missouri Synod that describes their approach to education. It is available through the Concordia Publishing Company in St. Louis. See previous entry for address and telephone.

Lutheran Schools: The 21st Century. This series of eight booklets is meant for administrators and teachers in Lutheran schools. It deals with some of the important challenges Lutheran schools face. It is also helpful for parents wanting to understand Lutheran education. It is available from the Concordia Publishing Company in St. Louis (see earlier entry for address and telephone).

McFarland, Ken. *Let's Get Acquainted: Your Friends, the Seventh-Day Adventists.* Boise, Idaho: Pacific Press Publishing Association, 1987. A thirty-page general introduction to Seventh-Day Adventism that briefly treats Seventh-Day Adventist education.

A Quick Look at Seventh-Day Adventism is a pamphlet published by the Communications Department of the General Conference of the Seventh-Day Adventists. This and the previous pamphlet (*Let's Get Acquainted*) are available at Adventist Book Centers, which can be found in most areas of the country. To find out about the nearest center, call the national Adventist Book Center central information number, at (800) 765-6955.

29

The Reggio Emilia Approach

In the United States many preschool kindergarten programs, both public and private, are basically play groups. Many others are copies of an elementary grade class with cartoon alphabets, counting practice, academic curricula, lesson plans, drills, and workbooks, and one teacher in a rectangular room, trying to get all the children to do the same thing at the same time. The search for an effective and inspiring model for working with preschool children recently has led many educators to look to the city of Reggio Emilia in north central Italy, not far from Milan.

Reggio Emilia is an industrial city of about 130,000 people. After World War II, innovative educators there worked with parents to develop new approaches to early childhood education. Until that time, virtually all preschool education was in the hands of the Roman Catholic Church and, according to critics, was strict, unimaginative, and socially segregated. Under the city's socialist government, the newly developed approaches were applied in public preschools beginning in 1963.

Today, there are twenty-two such preschools in Reggio Emilia. These offer free, full-day care to all children between the ages of two and six, regardless of a family's financial resources or a child's level of development. The philosophy and practice of these schools, known as the Reggio Emilia approach, only recently has become well-known to educators in the United States. Beginning in 1987, a traveling exhibition called "The Hundred Languages of Children," featuring artwork of children in Reggio Emilia preschools, has been touring this country. The first book in English on the Reggio Emilia approach, entitled *The Hundred Languages of Children: The Reggio Emilia Approach To Childhood Education*, appeared in 1993. Interest is growing rapidly. In several cities, including St. Louis and Washington, D.C., there are Reggio Emilia pilot programs in public schools. Recently a Reggio Emilia-based school initiative in Williamsburg, Massachusetts, has been approved as a charter school, to be supported by the state. At the University of Massachusetts, the University of New Hampshire, and the University of Kentucky, student teachers are being taught Reggio Emilia theory and practice.

The Reggio Emilia approach is striking in several key areas: school and classroom design; the role of the student; the role of the teacher; the

In a Reggio Emilia school much care is taken to create a beautiful, warm, intimate environment where children, teachers, and parents feel at ease.

197

place of the arts and of self-expression; curriculum; school organization and management; the role of parents; and the role of the community.

In a Reggio Emilia school, the physical environment is very important. It is considered the child's "third teacher," the parent and the teacher being the first two. Much care is taken to create a beautiful, warm, intimate environment where children, teachers, and parents feel at ease. It is an environment that encourages social interaction and stimulates learning. Among the elements common in the Reggio Emilia preschools are:

- A piazza or central meeting place
- A common dining area with an open, visible kitchen
- Much natural light, coming in through large windows, skylights, and exterior glass walls
- Many potted plants, sometimes including vines that traverse the ceilings of the piazza or classrooms
- Walls painted in pleasant subtle colors rather than primary colors
- Interior glass walls, particularly between the classroom and the atelier or workshop– art room
- Classrooms with alcoves and other separate, private places for the child who wants to be alone
- Carpeted floors and comfortable furniture, such as easy chairs and couches
- Partial or full walls of mirrors
- "Real art" on the walls in the form of prints, paintings, and drawings, and of aerial sculptures on the ceiling
- A studio or atelier for small group-project work
- A music room and an "archive room," in which the students' artwork is stored

The children are assumed to be curious, creative, and willing and able to explore the world around them and to express themselves in many ways. They are provided with many different types of activities: spontaneous play with blocks, role playing, outdoor play, listening to stories, acting out plays, housekeeping and dress-up, as well as long-term projects involving clay, painting, and collage.

Teachers do not present a predetermined, fixed curriculum. Rather, they offer a "negotiated curriculum" based on the interests of the children and developed through the interaction among children, teachers, and parents. Teachers carefully observe and listen to the children to discover what they are interested in and what they would like to learn about. It might be trains, or what goes on in a supermarket, or dogs, or as was the case in a class some years ago in Reggio Emilia, how a city is transformed by a rainstorm. Then an in-depth, long-term project is initiated to pursue that interest. The children are the protagonists in the development as well as the origin of the project. The research is carried out by small groups of children working together. Focusing on a particular subject or theme, the children collect objects, make observations and predictions, and test their theories. The children represent their observations, ideas, memories, and feelings in speech, movement, sculpture, drawings, paintings, shadow play, dramatic plays, collage, and music. The young children typically demonstrate great creativity and skill in their artistic and symbolic representations. In the Reggio Emilia context, the use of the various expressive, communicative, and cognitive "languages" is understood to enhance later intellectual development.

The projects are open-ended. Once they begin, no one, including the teacher, knows how long they will continue or what they will encompass. The teachers have regular staff meetings to discuss the development of the project and the various ways it may continue. The project and further steps in curriculum development depend primarily on the interest, imagination, and activity of the children. Group problem solving and group learning are emphasized, and with the help of the teachers, the children often meet together to "negotiate" the project.

In a Reggio Emilia classroom the teacher is a facilitator, guide, helper, and documentarian. She or he interacts with the children as a co-worker on "our project," empowering the children to help shape the curriculum and engaging in the research and artistic activity along with the children. As documentarian, the teacher tape-records and transcribes students' conversations and interviews; takes photographs, slides, and videos of the children's research activity and artistic products; and constructs display panels to publicly show the children's work. In a Reggio Emilia classroom, the child is not seen as an uninformed, needy being, into whom information has to be poured. Rather the child is assumed to be a competent, gifted, curious researcher, with substantial artistic and intellectual capacities, who already possesses much knowledge and insight about the world, and who can find out what else he or she wants to know.

Since the young child needs security, the teacher-child relationship is long-term. Two teachers stay with a group of about twenty-four children from the time the children enter the preschool at age three until they are six. This rather high child-to-teacher ratio is believed to result in better social development among the children. There is also an *atelierista* or art specialist in the school who works with the children on the various art and construction projects.

The teachers and *atelieristas* meet frequently and for substantial periods of time to discuss developments and problems in the class and the school. It is assumed that all staff members also are learning and developing their skills and that they are therefore liable to make errors. Free and frank discussion is encouraged. Regular staff meetings are also held with pedagogical specialists, educational administrators, and city officials.

Parents play an important role in the life of the school. The schools in Reggio Emilia are parent-teacher cooperative ventures with parents and teachers working together as equals. Parents are involved in all planning and decision-making processes in the school. They are welcome to visit anytime and are encouraged to participate in the life of the class. The school is meant to be an intimate community, even an extended family, comprised of teachers, children, and parents. Relations are informal and long-term and involve shared responsibility. Each child's character, interests, aptitudes, and needs are documented and frequently and regularly discussed by teachers and parents.

The Reggio Emilia approach to early childhood education requires several factors:

Generous funding: The aesthetically rich, homelike environment, the art supplies, the technical equipment, and the funding of a full-time art specialist are expensive.

Flexible and dedicated teachers: Teachers must be willing and able to let preschoolers "follow their noses" and largely set the agenda for classroom life; they must also be willing to discuss their work frankly and openly and to stay with one group of children and parents for three years.

Parental involvement: Parents must be willing to invest time and energy in the school and its operation.

Many of the important features of Reggio Emilia are also basic elements in classic Deweyan progressive education. These include the central role of the child in creating the curriculum, project-based studies, group research and discovery, the facilitator role of the teacher, an emphasis on the arts, and the active involvement of the community. What is striking about the Reggio Emilia approach is that these are applied to the education of preschool children as young as two or three.

The Early Childhood Laboratory School
University of Massachusetts at Amherst

The University of Massachusetts at Amherst offers training in early childhood education that features the Reggio Emilia approach. The Early Childhood Laboratory School functions as a Reggio Emilia school and allows teacher trainees to experience and to work with the approach in a real school environment. About thirty children between three and five years old come to the school three days a week. The school is located in Skinner Hall, a modest red-brick building dwarfed by the many concrete monoliths that dominate the sprawling campus. In the hallway outside the rooms used by the school are large panels with photographs of colorful tropical birds, a collage of hawks and other raptors, snapshots of children holding papier-mâché models of dinosaurs and volcanoes, and excerpts of children's conversations.

The school itself occupies two large rooms that are on ground level and that open out to a large fenced-in playground. The indoor space obviously was not designed to house a Reggio Emilia school. There are no interior glass walls, no panels of mirrors. Nevertheless, it is a pleasant, comfortable space—carpeted, open, containing potted plants, stuffed animals, lots of nooks and crannies where children can hide, and a nature area. In the course of the morning, a number of parents, both fathers and mothers, visit the class and spend time playing and working with their own and with other children. Some spend time just observing. For each room there is a viewing booth where, through a one-way mirror, one can look into the classroom and remain unobserved.

It is late in the school year and several major projects have been concluded. One project focused on birds and dinosaurs. The children read books on birds, went bird watching, listened to a naturalist talk about birds, made papier-mâché birds, and drew and painted birds and dinosaurs. The project culminated with a class presentation for parents and teachers. Four- and five-year-olds stood up before a large group of adults and children and told what they had learned about raptors, tropical birds, and dinosaurs.

Another project, still in progress, has to do with masks and theater. Some children expressed an interest in masks and made papier-mâché masks in the Discovery Room or atelier. They then decided that the masks could be used in a play. Some children got involved in making props for the play. The older children began to make up characters, little stories, and dialogue, which the teachers tape-recorded and transcribed. At the end of the year the class will put on the play for the parents.

On the morning of my visit an undergraduate art student who has offered to decorate the school door is meeting with the class. The children sit in a circle and give their suggestions about how the door should be painted. A teacher sits just outside the circle recording their ideas on a large easel pad.

Later I speak with Dotty Meyer, School of Education faculty member and director of the Laboratory School. She explains the panels hanging in the halls: "The panels are a means of communicating what has been important to the children. They describe what children and teachers have been studying together. They are also a means for us to revisit experiences with the children, so that further thinking and learning are stimulated. The children and parents enjoy seeing the class projects on the walls because the panels not only provide helpful information, they also validate the children's work, show how truly important it is."

Meyer describes how a recent class project developed:

> We always listen carefully to the children's comments and ideas and write them down. The class had done studies of wind and of natural disasters, and the children were expressing an interest in volcanoes. We asked them what they already knew about volcanoes and what they wanted to learn about them. We found the children had some misconceptions, but we didn't rush to correct them. We let the children discover things themselves. For example, the children thought that chemicals are the cause of a volcano erupting. We did some simple experiments that showed that pressure causes eruptions.
>
> During these experiments the children were encouraged to express what they were seeing and thinking in drawings. Drawing makes knowledge visible, and it helps develop the children's understanding of what they are studying. Drawing and other art and craft work also represent the development of the child's knowledge and understanding. The culmination of the project was the construction of a model of a volcano. Throughout, the emphasis was on the active role of the children in learning about something in which they were truly interested.

The understanding of the young child on which Reggio Emilia is based is that, even at three or four, the curious child is a curious learner who wants to find out about the world, who wants to relate to the world, and who is able to express himself or herself about the world in many different languages—in speech, painting, clay modeling, collage, and the like. The children are called to be the protagonists in the learning and creative process. The teacher serves as a guide, helper, and documentarian.

FOR MORE INFORMATION

The Merrill-Palmer Institute
71-A East Ferry Avenue
Detroit, MI 48202
Tel.: (313) 872-1790
Fax: (313) 577-0995

This organization serves as a clearinghouse for information about the Reggio Emilia approach. It publishes a newsletter four times a year called *Innovations*, which lists upcoming workshops and conferences; books, book chapters, articles, and videos about the Reggio Emilia method; and information about Reggio Emilia networks around the country. It also tells where the traveling exhibit "The Hundred Languages of Children" is located at the time.

FOR FURTHER READING

Edwards, Carolyn, Lella Gandini, and George Forman (eds.). *The Hundred Languages of Children: The Reggio Emilia Approach to Early Childhood Education.* Norwood, N.J.: Ablex Publishing Corporation, 1994. This is the principal book in English on the Reggio Emilia approach. It contains a variety of articles on the history, theory, and practice of Reggio Emilia educational methods and their implementation in the American context. It lists other published materials about the Reggio Emilia approach and also lists video resources. This book is essential for anyone wanting to learn about this method of early childhood education.

30

Roman Catholic Schools

Thirty years ago, the Roman Catholic school system in the United States was at its height. About 5.5 million children attended some 13,000 Catholic elementary and high schools. Since then enrollment has declined and many schools have closed. But the Roman Catholic educational system is still the largest alternative to the public school system, with almost 2 million children attending close to 7,000 schools. Forty percent of all children not in public schools are in Catholic schools. Recently the Catholic schools have begun to gain new strength. In the suburbs and in the inner city, increasing numbers of Catholic and non-Catholic families, many of them minority families, are sending their children to Catholic schools.

The first Roman Catholic school in the United States was founded in 1784 in Philadelphia. At that time, there were only four hundred Catholics in the city out of a total population of eighteen thousand. In the mid-nineteenth century the first massive immigrations of Catholics—mainly from Germany and Ireland—took place. This coincided with the industrialization and urbanization of the nation and with the birth and development of the public schools.

While the public schools were meant to be nonsectarian and hence appropriate for children

of all faiths, they posed major problems for Catholics. Horace Mann and other leaders of the common school movement held that a moral and religious element was necessary and made Bible reading and moral instruction part of the public school curriculum. But Catholics objected to the particular biblical translation used and to the textbooks on religion and morality. The public schools taught Pan-Protestantism, they complained, and were in effect "Unitarian parochial schools."

Thus, Catholic clergy and Catholic parents saw the public school as a place where Catholic children would be acculturated into the dominant Anglo-Saxon Protestant culture and deprived of their religious and ethnic identity. It was also a place where Catholic children might encounter prejudice. During this period, want ads reading "No Thieves or Irish Need Apply" appeared in the newspapers of Boston and other cities.

In 1875, the Roman Curia, pointing out that morality is the overriding aim of education, called for the establishment of Roman Catholic schools. In 1884, the American Catholic bishops decreed that every parish should establish a school, that Catholic parents should take responsibility for educating their children to be moral and pious human beings, and that they should give their child a Catholic education. For the Catholic parent sending a child to Catholic school became a religious obligation.

About this time, the second great wave of Catholic immigration began. More Irish and more Germans arrived, as did millions of Poles, Italians, and Portuguese. Between 1880 and 1918 the Catholic population grew from 6.1 million to 17.1 million. The Catholic school system grew with the increased Catholic population. Almost every local parish founded an elementary school. Tuition fees were minimal or nonexistent, and many schools taught classes in the language of the old country. After World War I, when the public secondary school system burgeoned, Catholic high schools also increased in number. Many were established by dioceses, many by independent religious orders.

The system grew steadily. In 1930, there were 10,000 schools and 2.5 million students; in 1950, there were 11,000 schools and 3.5 million children. By 1965, about half of all Catholic children and one in eight of all children in the United States were in Catholic schools.

Until the mid-1960s, the Roman Catholic schools reflected the reality of a hierarchical, authoritarian, and dogmatic Church. Almost all the teachers were priests, nuns, or brothers. The schools' chief goal was to produce obedient believers. Roman Catholic belief and practice were presented as things to be accepted without question. Children were taught that "there is no salvation" outside the Roman Catholic Church. Discipline was stricter, punishments were harsher, and academic standards were lower than in the public schools, or at least such was the reputation of the Catholic schools. As a child, I looked with pity on my Catholic peers

Many of the charac-
teristics researchers
find important for a
successful school are
commonly found in
Catholic schools
today.

who attended Saint Thomas Aquinas, the local parish school. They had to wear drab brown uniforms and were liable, we believed, to have their knuckles rapped bloody for little or no reason by stern-faced nuns.

The Second Vatican Council was held between 1962 and 1965. It transformed the Church from a conservative, medieval, inward-looking institution to a modern one, engaged with the world. From the Council came word that the Church was now to be guided by new principles. It must consider itself a community of the people of God, not a hierarchical organization; it must promote religious freedom, ecumenism, and religious dialogue; it must focus on Jesus and on the teachings of the Bible rather than on dogma; it must strive for the realization of social justice; and it must adapt to the conditions of modern life.

Around the same time, throughout American culture, the authority of most existing institutions was being questioned. The directives of the Second Vatican Council and the simultaneous turmoil in American culture had a devastating effect on the Catholic school system. Catholic parents looked critically at their parish schools and saw them as outdated relics of a medieval Church. Many withdrew their children. Enrollment dropped precipitously and schools began to close. In the early 1970s, it seemed that this once large and vital school system was going to wither and die.

This did not happen. Catholic schools adapted to the changing times. They became less dogmatic, less strict, and less intent on indoctrinating their students. They raised academic standards. At the same time they retained the positive aspects of traditional Catholic education. Consequently many of the characteristics researchers find important for a successful school (and that advocates for public school reform and restructuring seek to create) are commonly found in Catholic schools today. These include:

- Small size. Most Catholic elementary schools have under two hundred students. Most Catholic high schools have fewer than eight hundred students.
- Decentralized, nonbureaucratic organization and control. Each Catholic school is largely independent; decisions about the life of the school are made by the principal and teachers.
- High academic expectations for all children. Tracking and ability grouping at the elementary level is much less common than in public schools. In most Catholic high schools, all students have to take a common core curriculum. There are no business or vocational courses.
- Strong emphasis on basic academic skills.
- Teacher commitment. Today there are few priests, nuns, and brothers teaching in Catholic schools. Most of the lay teachers, however, are Catholics devoted to Catholic education, to the moral and spiritual development of their students, and to their academic success.
- Teachers who are able and willing to be role models for social interactions and lifestyle.
- An inspirational ideology of values, beliefs, and goals held in common by teachers, administrators, students, and parents.
- An orderly classroom environment where the energy of teachers and students can be focused on the learning process. Teachers and administrators can exercise the pre-

rogative of a nonpublic school and tell students who have behavior problems that they must "shape up or ship out."
- An active and committed parent body.
- Community support and involvement.

Generally speaking, Catholic schools use the traditional teacher-centered pedagogy. In Catholic elementary schools classroom activity is focused on the teacher. Children sit in rows, listen to the teacher, answer questions, read textbooks, and fill out workbooks. The open classroom, whole language, cooperative learning, child-centered or "emergent" curriculum, and other innovations of progressive education are not widely used in Catholic schools.

Each Catholic school is virtually autonomous, however, and many Catholic schools are increasingly open to innovative ideas and practices, especially for the lower grades. Some Catholic preschools and kindergartens use the Montessori approach. Grace Pilon, a nun and teacher in New Orleans, has developed a method of classroom management and teaching called the "Workshop Way" that incorporates various progressive elements and is starting to spread to other Catholic schools. In most Catholic high schools, the teacher lecture is the focus of classroom life, supplemented by question/answer and discussion.

In most Catholic schools the combination of small school and class size, local control, dedicated teachers, a disciplined, hard-working student population, and a demanding curriculum presented by traditional methods seems to work. Catholic school children, including those from disadvantaged homes, do significantly better on standardized tests than public school children. Catholic schools have gained a positive reputation in the public mind. They are seen as safe, well-managed schools where basic academic skills are taught well and where religious and moral values are presented but not in a dogmatic or oppressive way. In the inner city, once all-Caucasian Catholic schools now have substantial percentages of African-American and Hispanic children. And many of these minority children (often 50 percent or more) are non-Catholics. In the suburbs, even in areas with reputable public schools, many parents, Catholic and non-Catholic alike, choose a Catholic school. Overall enrollment has stabilized and school closings have slowed if not stopped. Many schools are flourishing.

Catholic schools are accessible to families in many parts of the country. There are high concentrations in New England, down the East Coast, and in the urban areas of the Midwest and Far West. There are few Catholic schools in the South and in the Rocky Mountain states. There are, however, a number of Catholic boarding high schools.

Tuition at Catholic schools is relatively low. At elementary schools it can be as low as $1,500 per year, and at a typical high school it may be $2,400 a year. This is more than the $207 average annual tuition at a Catholic school in 1967, but it is much less than the $6,000 to $10,000 one is likely to pay at a typical private high school.

Cathedral High School

SPRINGFIELD, MASSACHUSETTS

Cathedral High School is typical of many suburban Catholic schools today. Cathedral was founded in 1883 to educate the children of the Irish laborers who had come to work in the armories and factories of Springfield. The present building dates from 1959. It is a large structure with long, wide immaculate halls and high banks of windows that flood classrooms and other areas with natural light. Built for 2,400 students and

currently serving 1,350, the school seems at times strangely quiet, especially for a high school.

Denise Granger, a member of the Sisters of Saint Joseph, the order that founded the school, is principal of Cathedral. A bright-eyed, good-humored woman in her early forties, dressed in a skirt and blouse rather than a clerical habit, Sister Denise talks about her school:

We try to give our students a strong, well-rounded education so that they have basic skills, know about the world and how it works, and so that they know how to think. We also try to nurture a strong moral and spiritual awareness, a respect for all people, and a sense of social justice.

The day starts with a prayer that goes out over the PA system. Each week there is a certain theme—this week it is forgiveness. I do the opening prayer on Monday and teachers and students do it on the other days.

Most of the students come from Springfield, but many commute from towns quite a distance away. About 10 percent are African-American or Hispanic, and that percentage is growing as the demographics of the city are changing. Most of the children come from stable families and the parents are very committed to the school and to their children's education.

Of course, we are a reflection of society. We have students from broken homes, with alcoholic parents, and with serious problems themselves. We work with them, but the students know that here there are rules to be followed, norms to be upheld, and consequences to deal with. Recently a boy was referred to us by Juvenile Services. After a couple of days, he said pleadingly to me "But Sister Denise, there are *so many* rules." And I said, "That's right, Carlos, and if you follow them you will get along here just fine."

Discipline is a minor problem at Cathedral. Virtually all detentions students serve are for being late to class. At lunch a teacher, who had turned down an offer of a $12,000 salary increase to teach in a public school, remarks, "The students here really come to learn. The biggest discipline issue I have in class is kids sticking chewing gum under the desk. Here I can teach. In a lot of public schools I would spend most of my time keeping the peace. This is a great place; there is a real sense of community, of common belief and shared purpose."

A dress code at Cathedral specifies the style and color of the skirts, blouses, pants, shirts, and sweaters that students can wear. The typical male student is wearing a white shirt, dark pants, and plain tie. The typical female student is wearing a white or pale blue blouse, a gray plaid skirt, and a maroon sweater. All students must wear dress shoes; sneakers are allowed only in the gym. The typical student tries not to look too neat by tucking in only the very bottom of his or her shirt or blouse and letting the rest hang down as a kind of attenuated teenage paunch. Still the generally uniform and attractive dress adds to the atmosphere of decorum. Although the code stipulates nothing about hair style, most of the boys have short hair and the girls long hair. There are no shaved heads here, no purple mohawks, no metal rings in ears, noses, or lips. I asked a girl how she felt about wearing a uniform and she said with a laugh, "Oh, it's great. It gives me one less thing to worry about in the morning. And it's economical."

The academic program at Cathedral is rigorous and focused, emphasizing basic skills and featuring fundamental courses in English, history, mathematics, science, and religion. "We use the old-fashioned approach," says Sister Denise. "We present the students with what we consider are the skills and the information that they need to master. We work with them until they have a command of both the skills and the information. Then we move on. There is basically one academic program which everyone takes. This Core Curriculum is for every student. We have very little ability grouping. The students have a limited choice in the courses they take."

"Also," she continues, "we don't have the range of electives that a public high school does, or all the shop and vocational courses, or the special education teachers. But it seems to work; 93 percent of the seniors go to college."

Each classroom in Cathedral contains a crucifix and an American flag. Each forty-minute class begins with a prayer or a recitation of the Hail Mary. All students have one religion class a day. Religion teacher Sandra Gelinas explains, "Each year there is a different focus in the religion curriculum. The freshmen study the Bible and the life of Jesus. Juniors study world religions. Seniors study the history of the Church and worship. We encourage them to go to church and to read the Bible, but we don't indoctrinate. We try to introduce moral and religious issues and to make the students think about them. One important aim of Catholic education is the development of a social conscience. We hope the students realize that they have to work for social justice in the world."

Sister Denise sees the study and practice of religion as a major benefit for students at Cathedral:

> Students study in a systematic way an important, even central dimension of human

life. They are called to look at the issues of life from a religious perspective. They are presented with a vision of human life and destiny that goes beyond the ambition of becoming rich and successful. They learn that belief, ritual, and symbols can give meaning to life. They learn the importance of being aware of social injustice and of responding actively to it. The life of the school is founded upon an inspirational ideology that gives meaning and value to human life. The students are free to share that vision, with the teachers, the staff, and with each other.

The value of this part of the curriculum is appreciated by the students. Later, when I am lost in a maze of corridors, Mara Allen, a junior, offers to guide me back to the school office. "Do you like going to school here?" I ask. "Oh yes," she says, smiling. "The academics are very strong and you get a chance to develop yourself spiritually—which I don't think is the case in the public schools."

All students take a course in sex education. It is taught separately to boys and girls and approaches sex both as a biological phenomenon and as a religious and moral issue.

Sports and extracurricular programs are important in life at Cathedral. A high percentage of students take part in intermural and intramural athletics, and attendance at games is very high. Various other schoolwide events also seem to generate a lot of community spirit. The evening prior to my visit there had been a father-daughter dinner and dance, attended by a sizable percentage of the school's girls accompanied by their fathers. In some ways the school ethos seems closer to 1959 than to 1996.

Resources

FOR MORE INFORMATION

National Catholic Education Association
(NCEA)
Suite 100
1077 30th Street, NW
Washington, DC 20007–3852
Tel.: (202) 337-6232
Fax: (202) 333-6706

This is the national association of teachers in Roman Catholic schools. Its main mission is to promote Catholic education. It publishes a journal called *Momentum* and a newsletter for Catholic schools; it also publishes and sells books and audiotapes. Call for a catalogue.

Workshop Way, Inc.
P.O. Box 850170
New Orleans, LA 70185
Tel.: (504) 486-4871

All Roman Catholic schools in a given diocese, whether run by the diocese, a parish, or a religious order, are controlled by the diocese. Each diocese has an office of education. To find out about Roman Catholic schools in a particular area, call the local diocesan office of education.

FOR FURTHER READING

Bryk, Anthony S., Valerie Lee, and Peter B. Holland. *Catholic Schools and the Common Good.* Cambridge, Mass.: Harvard University Press, 1993. This book deals with the history and current situation of Roman Catholic education in the United States and argues that Catholic schools should receive public support for the work they are now doing among our society's poor and disadvantaged children.

Carper, James C., and Thomas C. Hunt. *Religious Schooling in America.* Birmingham, Ala.: Religious Education Press, 1984. Chapter 1, "Catholic Schools: The Nation's Largest Alternative School

System," provides a survey of the history of Catholic education and of the present place of Catholic education in the United States, particularly in the inner city.

Kealey, Robert J. *Curriculum in the Catholic School.* Booklet available from the NCEA (see For More Information, above).

McDermott, Father Edward J. *Distinctive Qualities of the Catholic School.* Booklet available from the NCEA (see For More Information, above).

Traviss, Sister Mary Peter. *Student Moral Development.* Booklet available from the NCEA (see For More Information, above).

Welch, Sister Mary Leanne. *Methods of Teaching in the Catholic School.* Booklet available from the NCEA (see For More Information, above).

31

Teenage Liberation

Self-Schooling for the Adolescent

❧

Work on your own.

Learn by doing.

Seek out worthwhile people and make
them your friends.

Read books.

Take advantage of every opportunity to
learn something.

Remember that mature people enjoy
helping young people who are trying to
realize their potential.

Have a sense of wonder and be interested
in everything that goes on.

—Vincent Schaeffer, quoted in
The Teenage Liberation Handbook

The great majority of homeschoolers are children
between seven and twelve who ordinarily would
be in elementary or middle school. There are relatively few high-school-age homeschoolers. Adolescents, even those who have never been to
school before, usually have a strong desire to be
with their peers, to have a varied social life, and
to be tested in a broader environment. Many parents don't feel confident about teaching at a
high-school level. Parents and the young person
probably are thinking about college entrance and
the grades, credits, and recommendations that
that usually entails. Besides, there are few prece-

dents that show how an adolescent can get an
education outside of high school.

The number of teenagers who do not go to
school but who are continuing their education at
home is increasing, however. This trend has been
greatly helped in recent years by the publication
of *Homeschooling for Excellence* (1989) and *Hard
Times in Paradise* (1992) by David and Micki
Colfax. The Colfaxes, both college professors,
left teaching, bought a farm in a remote area of
California, and raised and homeschooled four
sons. During their teenage years the boys largely
planned, directed, and carried out their own education. They never went to high school. Three
of them were admitted to and attended Harvard
University.

The work of Grace Llewellyn also has promoted adolescent self-schooling. A former middle school teacher, Llewellyn has written and
edited two books—*The Teenage Liberation Handbook: How to Quit School and Get a Real Education* and *Real Lives: Eleven Teenagers Who Don't
Go to School*. These books are addressed largely
to the teenager in high school who wants to get
out, but they are also relevant for the homeschooler who does not want to go to high school.

Llewellyn praises the "de-schooling" or "un-
schooling" tradition founded by John Holt and

carried forward by critics of education such as John Taylor Gatto, author of *Dumbing Us Down*. Llewellyn attacks high schools as being for the most part useless and destructive; affirms the ability of teenagers to educate themselves; and gives practical advice on how they can do this. Her book is a step-by-step guide for the teenager who has had enough of formal education, wants to drop out of school and, as Llewellyn puts it, "to drop in to life." It is also a handbook for the parent whose child announces at the dinner table that he or she would rather go to prison than continue in high school and for the parent whose child, on turning sixteen, simply refuses to go to school anymore.

Advocates of teenage self-schooling believe traditional education can destroy a young person's self respect, democratic instincts, and natural love of learning.

Llewellyn's approach is based on a categorical rejection of schools and formal education. For her, school is a kind of part-time prison characterized by forced attendance; rigid schedules; enforced learning; dictatorial teachers who do little more than keep children under control; dull textbooks; tests that assess rote, short-term memory and little else; and sterile buildings. Schools turn out passive, nonthinking cogs for the vast societal machine, individuals who are self-seeking, competitive, and dependent upon grades for self-validation. Schools make learning boring and unpleasant. They stress and humiliate students and force them to learn by rote memorization. As a result they destroy the young person's self-respect, democratic instincts, and natural love of learning. Schools denigrate and stamp out minority cultures. They create people who obey authority, don't think much, and work hard for little.

Llewellyn's approach is also based on an optimistic view of the inborn curiosity, desire to learn, initiative, and potential for self-discipline of the young person, even of the young person who, in school at least, seems to have lost all interest in learning. Adolescence is a time of magic and discovery. Llewellyn asserts that it is a time "to go flashing from one end of the world to the other in body and in mind." Traditional cultures initiate adolescents into adulthood, with real, exciting challenges, with myth and magic. Our culture makes them sit at desks for six hours a day staring at a blackboard. The healthy adolescent is a person wanting to find out about the world and about his or her place in it.

Given freedom and a little encouragement and direction, adolescents out of school can learn all they desire or need to know and get into a good college in the bargain.

Llewellyn allows that high school does provide students with an opportunity to study certain academic disciplines, such as English, mathematics, and history, and to learn to express themselves in writing and speech. It gives them a social world in which to live and opportunities to participate in athletics. It exposes them to educated, experienced adults, and occasionally to wise ones. It prepares them for college. Llewellyn asserts, however, that the teenager outside of school can have these same opportunities and benefits without the hassles, limitations, and general unpleasantness of high school. She then clearly and systematically describes how to go about finding those opportunities.

To the adolescent who wants to leave school, Llewellyn advises:

> Write a statement to be presented to your parents. This statement should contain the reasons you want to leave school, and your plans for alternate activities. When you have convinced your parents of your

sincerity and motivation and have actually dropped out, take a little vacation. You need a period of decompression and relaxation after the pressures and frustrations of school life. Dream, dream, dream! Get used to a natural rhythm of life, one not determined by school; give yourself time; don't feel guilty; don't be afraid of the loss of structure; don't be afraid of going slow. You have a natural curiosity which will enable you to educate yourself and to make your way in the world.

To parents, Llewellyn says:

Relax and let go of your anxieties about status—your own and your child's—and about your child's academic and vocational future. The list of famous and successful people who did not complete a regular high-school program is long and impressive. It includes Margaret Meade, Frank Lloyd Wright, Mark Twain, Thomas Edison, and Pearl Buck. And the list of accomplished and famous people who went to school but wish they hadn't also is long and impressive, and includes Winston Churchill, Woody Allen, and Claude Monet. It is not the end of the world if your child does not go to high school.

Llewellyn goes on: "Relax, also, because your child is not asking you to be an all-purpose high school teacher, to tutor them every day in all the academic subjects at a high school level. That's probably the last thing a schoolphobic adolescent wants. Your child will want and need your approval, support, direction, advice, and occasionally perhaps some instruction. You will need to be a friend and guide, not a leader."

Llewellyn's advice on how a teenager can get everything high school offers and more includes the following:

Seek out an adult guide or mentor, someone you like and respect who will pay attention to you and give you advice, guidance, and support.

Spend about two hours a day on academics. Few adults read two hours a day, and if you read the right books you can get a comprehensive education in literature, history, geography, the sciences, and mathematics. If you plan to go to college, read those books usually required for admittance and further study. (Llewellyn provides a list of such books.)

Take private lessons in things you want to learn, such as playing a musical instrument or weaving or auto mechanics.

Take courses at local adult education centers, community colleges, schools, and craft schools.

Use the resources of the community—museums, art museums and galleries, science and technology centers, libraries, bulletin boards, small, specialized retail stores, local and city governments—as educational resources.

Use school resources as you need them. In a large and growing number of school districts, homeschoolers have access to the library, to art, shop, and other classes, and to athletic programs, even if they aren't enrolled full-time.

Seek out internships and voluntary or low-level paid work at businesses and organizations that deal with areas in which you are interested. For example, if you are interested in writing, work on a neighborhood newspaper. Better yet, start your own.

Seek out an apprenticeship, a long-term work-study arrangement with a craftsperson or expert in a field you're interested in. You can learn pottery, for example, by becoming an apprentice to a local potter.

Make field trips to historical places, factories, businesses, institutions, banks, and other places where you can learn something about your area and local community.

Maintain an active social life by having regular, scheduled contact with friends, joining clubs and organizations, getting involved in a regular work situation, taking a class in the community, or starting a weekly study circle.

Do volunteer work with the aged, the poor, or other persons in need.

Spend time hiking, camping, and bicycle touring.

Travel to other countries or take part in international volunteer work camps.

Consider taking the high-school equivalency exam to get a General Education Diploma that shows you have the skills and knowledge of a high-school graduate.

If you want to go to college, prepare for and take the Scholastic Aptitude Test.

Design your own graduation or rite of passage into adulthood.

The main point of *The Teenage Liberation Handbook* is that, without going to high school, teenagers can get an education and learn what they need to learn both for college and to become happy, mature adults. Llewellyn tells the stories of numerous teenagers who have designed and carried out a varied and challenging program of self-education and self-development. These young people keep up their academic studies and pursue special interests such as music, art, or butterfly collecting. Llewellyn quotes deans of admission at colleges and universities who affirm that self-schooled applicants get admitted to and do well at college. Some hint that the successful self-schooler often receives preferred treatment since he or she is clearly a motivated self-learner.

Parents play an important role in the education of their liberated teenage son or daughter. At the outset, they must decide whether to let an underage child leave school. Parents must judge if their child is mature enough and has the basic academic skills, self-discipline, curiosity, and motivation to carry out a self-education program.

If the child does leave school, the parents are crucial to the success or failure of the self-schooling process. While parents probably will do little or no direct instruction, they supply support (emotional and psychological, as well as material), give advice, make suggestions, and provide encouragement and external motivation to the young person. Parents need to support their adolescent children in setting goals, arranging activities, staying involved in these activities, and in getting through difficult periods. The accounts of the successful non-schoolers make it clear that parents must invest time, energy, and interest in their self-schooling teenager, that they need to play an active but nonintrusive role.

Llewellyn makes self-schooling for the adolescent sound easy, fun, and rewarding. For some teenagers and families it is doubtless so. But it obviously requires a particular type of student (motivated, curious, independent) and a particular type of parent or other adult mentor (supportive, compassionate, willing to commit time and energy, but, if necessary, able to exercise discipline) to make it work. As Llewellyn points out, however, many successful (i.e., motivated, curious, independent) non-schoolers were apathetic and unmotivated in school. Thus the attitude and the performance of a student in school is not always a good predictor of that student's success as an autodidact.

The list of the famous and accomplished who did not graduate from high school is indeed long. But a list of high-school dropouts who have led financially, socially, and culturally impoverished lives would probably be much longer. Llewellyn cites examples of successful "liberated" teens, but there are certainly other adolescents whose experience of self-education is not a success. A student who consciously and intentionally pursues a program of self-education is more likely to have a rewarding life than an adolescent who simply drops out of school.

There are many options open to a family with a teenager who is discontent with formal public schooling. Self-schooling is certainly one of them. But there are also alternative schools in both the public and private sector. Parents unsure of their child's or their own ability to follow the road of teenage liberation would do well to look into them. These schools offer a wide variety of approaches, from the extreme libertarian to the highly disciplined. There probably is somewhere an appropriate school for the adolescent discontent with mainstream high-school education but also perhaps unsuited to self-schooling.

Resources

FOR MORE INFORMATION

> John Holt's Bookstore
> 2269 Massachusetts Avenue
> Cambridge, MA 02140
> Tel.: (617) 864-3100
> Fax: (617) 864-9235

The store and the bimonthly magazine _Growing without Schooling_ are an important source of information about home education for the adolescent as well as for the younger child. It offers an "Older Homeschooling Set" to help adolescent homeschoolers get started. It also offers books and educational materials for learning music, art, science, history, math, social studies, writing, and other subjects. (See also the entries at the end of chapter 20, "Homeschooling.")

FOR FURTHER READING

Farrenga, Patrick. _Teenage Homeschoolers: College or Not?_, 1995. A booklet dealing with the common questions homeschoolers have about college. Published by and available from John Holt's Bookstore (see For More Information, above).

Gelner, Judy. _College Admissions: A Guide for Homeschoolers._ Sadalia, Colo.: Poppyseed Press, 1988. Available from John Holt's Bookstore.

Gibbons, Maurice. _The Walkabout Papers: Challenging Students to Challenge Themselves._ Vancouver, B.C.: EduServ, 1990. The walkabout is the rite of passage by which an Australian Aboriginal boy becomes a man. Gibbons describes how young people in Canada have designed their own rites of passage, including adventure (adaptation to new environments), creative expression, community skills, development of practical skills, and intensive inquiry into areas of special interest. A testimony to the relevance and power of experiential challenge in education for today's teenagers.

Llewellyn, Grace. _The Teenage Liberation Handbook: How to Quit School and Get a Real Life and Education._ Eugene, Oreg.: Lowry House Publishers,

1991. Indispensable for its rationale for the self-education of adolescents, its inspiring examples, and its resource information. To obtain a copy, write to the publisher, P.O. Box 1014, Eugene, OR 97440-1014.

———. *Real Lives: Eleven Teenagers Who Don't Go to School.* Eugene, Oreg.: Lowry House Publishers, 1991.

Peterson's Independent Study Catalog. Princeton: Peterson's Guides, 1995. A guide to the hundreds of academic courses-by-mail that are available at the high-school, college, and graduate level.

32

Waldorf Education

It was the spring of 1919, a few months after the end of World War I. Emil Molt, director of the Waldorf-Astoria cigarette factory in Stuttgart, Germany, approached Austrian philosopher Rudolf Steiner with a request. Concerned about the moral, social, and economic disorder of the time, Molt asked Steiner to design a school that would educate children to become free, responsible, and active human beings, able to create a just and peaceful society.

Steiner was an important figure in European cultural life. For many years he was head of the Theosophical Society in Germany, and in 1913 he founded a spiritual and cultural movement called Anthroposophy—"knowledge of the true nature of the human being." Lecturing and writing on such topics as philosophy, religion, psychology, art, history, economics, and politics, Steiner had attracted a large, sophisticated, and international following. He urged that modern humanity awaken to the reality of the spirit, both in the individual human being and in the universe as a whole, and that individual and social life be based on this reality.

Steiner accepted Molt's invitation. He recruited teachers from among his followers and gave them an intensive training in his educational philosophy and its application. In autumn 1919, the Free Waldorf School opened in Stuttgart with 175 students, most of them children of workers in Molt's factory, and with eight teachers. It was a radical school for that time. Free of government control, it educated all children in the same way, whether they were destined for university or for the factory workshop. The school emphasized art, music, and handcrafts as much as reading, writing, and arithmetic. Its explicit purpose was to create free, creative, independent, moral, and happy human beings. Steiner summarized the school's task: "Accept the children in reverence; educate them with love; send them forth in freedom."

Waldorf education spread rapidly. Soon there were schools in other parts of Germany and in England, Holland, and Switzerland. The first Waldorf school in North America was founded in New York City in 1928. Today there are over 600 schools in over eight countries. There are now about 140 Waldorf schools in the United States. Virtually all are independent schools, but a number of public school Waldorf programs have been established. The movement continues to grow rapidly in the U.S. and around the world.

In the context of American education, Waldorf education is an anomaly. Unlike almost all of the other approaches to education presented in this book, it does not belong clearly to the traditional-religious or progressive-humanistic stream of educational theory and practice. It has elements characteristic of both, and many elements unique to itself. To understand Waldorf education as it is practiced at the kindergarten, elementary, and high-school level, one must understand Steiner's view of the nature and development of the human being.

According to Steiner, there are three major human functions—willing, feeling, and thinking. Willing is manifested in physical movement and activity and is centered in the human limbs—in the arms and legs. Feeling is manifested in imagination, in sympathy and antipathy, and in the range of human emotions. It is connected to the organs that function in a rhythmical way—the heart and lungs. Thinking involves the use and manipulation of concepts and abstractions. Its locus is the brain and nervous system.

Steiner held that from birth the human being develops these functions in a predictable, universal pattern. During the first seven years of life, children are largely beings of will and movement. They are completely open to their immediate environment and constantly in motion as they explore the world through their senses and experiment with their own body as an object in the world. Preschool children are imitators, who internalize and then manifest as their own, the speech, movements, and even moods of those around them.

With the loss of the baby teeth at the age of six or seven, children enter the next stage of life. Between the ages of seven and fourteen, they are primarily beings of feeling, aesthetic sensitivity, imagination, and artistic creativity. During these years, children will develop and learn at their best if

At each stage of a child's development, the approach to education must appeal to and nurture the special capacities that are emerging and developing.

they engage their aesthetic and affective capacities.

With puberty children enter yet another distinct stage. New faculties emerge. In the next seven years the thinking function develops and dominates. The adolescent becomes able to think abstractly, analyze, conceptualize, and be highly critical. At this stage of development, too, education must appeal to and nurture the special capacities that are emerging and developing.

The Waldorf Kindergarten

Although the original Waldorf school did not have a kindergarten, today virtually all Waldorf schools have one or more kindergarten classes, and there are many Waldorf kindergartens unattached to schools. Waldorf educators generally are not enthusiastic about having children younger than five or six in a school setting. They feel that until that age a child is best served by being at home primarily in the care of its parents. Nevertheless, the realities and pressures of life today have caused many Waldorf kindergartens to include younger children.

A Waldorf kindergarten prepares preschoolers for the move into first grade. The typical Waldorf kindergarten is a beautiful place. Its wooden floor is polished and shining. Its little tables, when arranged for snack time, are adorned with a tablecloth, fresh flowers, colored cloth napkins, and fresh-baked bread. On the windowsills are pinecones, colored stones, crystals, seashells, and potted plants. In one corner, on a nature table draped with silk cloth, are the special gifts of nature for the time of year. The five- or six-year-old child, open and innocent, internalizes the external environment. That environment then must be clean, beautiful, orderly, and harmonious.

The Waldorf kindergarten curriculum is based on the importance of movement, play, and fantasy for the young child. The children play circle games involving clapping and skipping and do other full-body activities every day. Around the room are large baskets containing wooden blocks, cut logs, cloths of various sizes and colors, simple dolls, plain wooden toys, and child-sized pots, pans, and dishes. The children are left free each day to use these simple props to create situations, stories, and dramas, which for them are entertaining and real. There is also a daily story time when the children gather, a candle is lit, and the teacher tells (rather than reads) a fairy tale or folktale or puts on a simple puppet play. Waldorf kindergarten teachers hold that the full exercise of the child's gift of fantasy is necessary to the later development of intellectual and academic capacities and skills. Since the children need a stable and predictable environment, the activities of each day—play, story time, nap, snack— take place in a definite sequence.

Five- and six-year-olds internalize and replicate what others, particularly adults, do, say, feel, and think. Thus the kindergarten teacher is very important. The teacher's dress, speech, manner, and behavior all profoundly affect the children. The teacher seeks to embody the grace, poise, warmth, equanimity, and enthusiasm that will be a proper nourishment and guide for the children. Each day the teacher does a simple task. He or she bakes cookies, sews a doll, carves a wooden toy, makes a decorative display of flowers, works in the garden, cares for the potted plants. The children are free to watch the teacher, to work alongside and "help," or to imitate the activity in their play. Waldorf kindergarten teachers, like

Waldorf elementary and high-school teachers, generally complete a special two-year full-time training. The first year consists largely of artistic and craft work to help the trainee's personal development, plus the study of Anthroposophy. The second year includes studying the theory and practice of Waldorf education and internships in Waldorf schools.

In a Waldorf kindergarten there is no effort to teach reading or arithmetic. There are no workbooks or flashcards. And you are as likely to find a television or computer in a Waldorf kindergarten as you are to find a nuclear warhead. Television is seen as a negative influence, making children physically passive and weakening their power of imagination.

From the Waldorf perspective, keeping the preschool years as years of fantasy and play is not a frivolous luxury. It is a wise, critically important educational technique. Children who through the age of six have been allowed to remain children are ready for the next stage of life. The years of fantasy, play, exploration, and imitation have made the child ready to learn to read, write, compute, and begin to think in a totally different way.

The Waldorf Elementary School

Steiner held that between the ages of seven and fourteen, children want and need a single, primary teacher, a symbol of authority to be respected, loved, and obeyed. Thus, each first-grade class has a "class teacher" who will accompany it through the next eight years and take primary responsibility for its education. Hence also, the Waldorf pedagogy is generally teacher centered.

Between the ages of seven and thirteen, the child's capacity for intellectual work is growing very slowly. Intellectual work is important but it must be balanced by activities that engage the will and the feeling life. Thus art, music, handwork, and crafts are seen as essential to education, helping children develop in a balanced way. Steiner believed that these activities lay the groundwork in the nervous system and brain for the later development of the full intellectual capacities. This assertion, made seventy-five years ago, is being corroborated by current brain research. It has been found, for example, that the brain centers involved in manual dexterity are interconnected with those involved in higher-order thinking (analysis, synthesis, etc.).

Waldorf elementary schools do not pressure children to learn to read or to master other academic skills in the early grades. Children learn to form letters and write words first, then to sound out words. Numbers and arithmetic are introduced in games and through objects, such as small stones used as counters. In the early grades, imaginative activity and stories form the context in which learning goes on.

As stated earlier, from the first grade, art, music, and handwork play an important role. Each child learns to play the recorder or a similar flute and learns to sing. Every day the children draw, paint, and model with beeswax or clay. In the third grade each child begins to study a stringed instrument. Children learn knitting in the first grade, crocheting in the second, sewing later on, as well as other handcrafts. Beginning in the fifth grade, they learn to carve and work with wood and metal. The children practice tongue twisters to develop diction and clarity in speech. They memorize and recite poems and dramatic passages and sing songs, incorporating gesture and movement. This work culminates each year in a class play that is related to a theme in the year's curriculum.

The Waldorf school day has a definite rhythm. It begins with some physical activity (a clapping game, for example), the recitation of a morning verse, singing, and playing music—all activities that wake up the children (and teacher) in body and mind.

Then there is a ninety-minute main lesson taught by the class teacher. The main lesson is the pivotal academic period of the day and deals with a specific topic in English, mathematics, science, or history. The schools follow a prescribed comprehensive curriculum that was largely developed at the first Waldorf school. In the eight elementary years students study human history, literature, and culture from pre-biblical and biblical times to the Middle Ages to the modern period. They also study grammar, mathematics, and science.

Each main lesson and each study block involves not only the intellect but also the artistic sensibility and physical activity of the children. In learning to count, first-graders will do clapping and stepping exercises, sing a song about numbers, and then draw pictures showing one of this, two of that. Sixth-graders who study ancient Rome may write a play about the career of Caesar, make the costumes and sets, and perform the play for the school community. Main lessons are taught in three- or four-week blocks. For example, in the fourth grade, there might be, in succession, blocks about local geography, fractions, the Norse myths, and human beings and animals.

After the main lesson, there is usually a recess and snack followed by a class such as music, chorus, or foreign language. In almost all Waldorf schools children study a foreign language (such as German or French), and in many schools they study two. In the early grades, foreign languages are taught largely through songs, poems, and games. Handwork and crafts are usually taught in the afternoon. These special classes usually are taught by "subject teachers," rather than by the class teachers. Waldorf students also learn eurythmy, an art of movement developed by Steiner in which specific gestures express the various vowels and consonants of speech as well as the elements of music. They have physical education, playing games and learning sports. Many schools teach a form of gymnastics called Bothmer gymnastics (developed by a teacher at the first Waldorf school), which develops balance, coordination, and ease of movement. Many Waldorf teachers start each class with a few minutes of Bothmer exercises. Competitive sports are not emphasized. Even the physical education activities are integrated into the curriculum. In the fifth grade, for example, when they are studying ancient Greece, the students engage in the events of the pentathlon—running, jumping, wrestling, and throwing the javelin and discus.

For the elementary school student, especially in the early grades, the main medium for learning is the spoken word of the class teacher. Teachers tell stories, recount myths, and re-create in narrative the events and epochs of history. No textbooks are used. For each main lesson topic, students create personal textbooks with handwritten text and colored drawings, maps, and diagrams. Electronic teaching aids, television, audio- and videotapes, and films are not used. These are thought to interfere with the direct relationship between teacher and child and to undermine the imagination and creativity of both.

Homework usually begins in the third or fourth grade. Written tests on main lesson blocks usually begin in the fifth or sixth grade. Student assessment is based on the child's total activity in the school—for example, academic work, artistic and craft work, and social interactions with adults and other students. Students do not receive letter or number grades. Twice a year teachers write a detailed narrative report about each child. These narratives plus regular parent-teacher conferences keep parents informed of their children's progress.

In a Waldorf elementary school, the important role of the arts, music, and crafts and the usual absence of workbooks, textbooks, ability groups in reading and math, computers, and most of the other common accoutrements of public school education can give the impression that the children are not acquiring the academic skills or knowledge that they will need for high school. Waldorf educators believe, however, that the curriculum is designed so that the child does acquire all the necessary skills and content. The students learn to read and to comprehend and analyze what they read. They learn to write, to express themselves clearly, artistically, and in accordance with the rules of grammar and usage. They learn arithmetic, algebra, and geometry. They are also exposed to a full range of knowledge, studying world, American, and local history and literature, as well as chemistry, physics, botany, geology, and zoology. An experienced Waldorf class teacher will attest that the Waldorf curriculum, addressing all aspects of the child's being, promotes rather than limits the intellectual and academic development of the child.

The Waldorf High School

Only a small minority of the Waldorf schools in this country have a high school (about 12 out of some 140 schools). There is one Waldorf boarding high school in New Hampshire. Yet many Waldorf schools are planning to establish a high school.

According to Steiner, the adolescent is ready

for rigorous intellectual and conceptual learning and needs contact with teachers who are experts in particular fields. Thus in a Waldorf high school the class teacher has given way to the special subject teacher and students study English and English literature with an English teacher, geometry, algebra, and trigonometry with a mathematics teacher, and so on. In this and in other ways, the life of Waldorf high-school students resembles that of other high-school students. They analyze poems and short stories, write research papers, and perform and document laboratory experiments. They take tests, engage in competitive sports with other schools, take the college boards, worry about getting into college, and do get in. A Waldorf high school might easily be mistaken for another good, small, independent high school. But there are differences.

Waldorf high-school teachers are acutely aware of certain nonacademic needs of their students. Steiner saw adolescents above all as searching for ideals by which they can shape and give meaning to their lives. David Sloan, a high-school teacher in the Green Meadow Waldorf School in Chestnut Ridge, New York, observes, "Adolescents want to believe that the world has meaning, that their own life has meaning, and that they can have a positive impact on the world. These aspirations have to be supported and met. They are necessary to the development of a mature, healthy adult. But modern education and modern life do little to support these aspirations which are necessary to the development of a mature, healthy adult."

The Waldorf high school, while providing students with academic skills and broad knowledge, also seeks to foster this budding idealism and hunger for meaning. Important themes in the curriculum include the unity and harmony of na-

ture; the dignity of the human being; the accomplishments and interrelatedness of human culture; and the potential of the human being to make a difference in the world.

In studying science, Waldorf high-school students are trained to carefully observe the natural world and to perceive its beauty and harmony. In anatomy they study the human body as the wonder of form and structure that it is. When they study music theory, they learn about the profound relationship between music and mathematics. Biographies of great persons such as Socrates, Elizabeth Cady Stanton, Booker T. Washington, and Albert Schweitzer provide inspiring role models, depicting persons whose lives embody high ideals and who had a positive impact on human history.

The arts and crafts continue to play an important role in the Waldorf high school. All students, gifted or not, study a musical instrument, play in the orchestra, sing in the choir. They paint, draw, compose and memorize poetry, write and put on plays. They learn how to bind a book, make a chair, craft a candlestick out of copper, weave a shawl, and rewire a broken lamp. In high school, as in elementary school, Waldorf education develops the whole person—head, hands, and heart.

The Waldorf School

LEXINGTON, MASSACHUSETTS

The Waldorf School of Lexington, Massachusetts, is fairly typical of Waldorf schools in this country. It is located in an affluent suburb, occupying a squarish, red-brick, former public school building. It has almost two hundred children in two kindergartens and eight grades. The school is planning to found a high school in the near future.

Mary Ann Wells's seventh-grade class slowly assembles for the start of the school day. Some of the girls exchange affectionate good morning hugs. The fifteen boys and girls, many of them with the braces, jeans, and untied high-top sneakers that bespeak this age group, stand in a semicircle, each behind a desk. They recite a verse, sing a song about the coming of spring, and play a tune together on their soprano recorders.

Then the class recites from memory a poem about parallel lines "meeting at infinity" and act out the poem in the center of the classroom. Each student receives a wooden stave about a yard long. They form a circle, holding the staves vertically. As they walk in step, causing the circle to revolve, the students recite another poem. Several times during the recitation, apparently on cue, they set the tips of their staves on the floor and release them backwards to the student behind, and simultaneously grasp the stave coming from the student in front.

A few students are handed alto recorders and the class practices a new two-part piece. Wells, working with an intern, moves the class effortlessly from one activity to another. The class seems like a large family which, in a sense, it is. Most of the students and their teacher have been together since the fifth grade.

Downstairs, the first-grade class is sitting in rows and reviewing a fairy tale that teacher Anita-Christina Calcaterra has told the previous day. "Why did the princess have to leave home?" "What things did she have to do to get home?" Calcaterra asks. The children squirm, confer, shoot up their hands, and offer answers. Later they act out the story and draw pictures based on it.

Toward the end of main lesson time, Marc Bruehl's fourth grade is midway through a lesson in New England geography. On the board Bruehl has drawn a colored-chalk map of the state of Maine, its long coastline and large northern areas stretching in green toward the upper right corner of the board. He talks about some of the area's rivers, which are depicted as serpentine lines of blue on the map, and then asks students to replicate the map in color in their main lesson book. The students pull out their personal textbooks containing other colored maps and pages of handwritten information and begin to draw an outline of New England. They work quietly and

A student at The Waldorf School in Lexington, Massachusetts, practices the violin. Seeking a balance of heart, hand, and head, Waldorf schools stress arts and crafts in addition to academics. From the third grade every child learns to play a stringed instrument.

carefully, creating maps of that part of the world in which they live. One boy stops work, raises his hand to ask a question, and while waiting thumbs through the *Book of Runes* with the other.

One corner of the room is filled with viola and cello cases, one for each student. The walls of the room are painted a pale lemon yellow, and large yellow muslin curtains tie-dyed with blue accents cover the windows.

Students at The Waldorf School of Lexington come from all over the greater Boston area, some commuting an hour each way. Like most Waldorf schools it is run by the teachers. Steiner felt that the people most intimately connected with the education of the children should make the decisions that affect the children and school life. The school has an administrator, but the administrator facilitates rather than controls the decision making.

The Waldorf movement is growing quickly. Each year new school initiatives organized by parents and Waldorf teachers spring up. These usually start with a nursery school and kindergarten program and then begin a first grade, if possible adding a grade and a teacher with each successive year.

Very few of the Waldorf schools have an endowment or substantial outside assistance. Kindergarten tuitions range from about $2,200 to $4,000, elementary school tuitions from $3,800 to $7,000, and high-school tuitions from $6,000 to $10,000. Fund-raising through fairs, raffles, and other means are an important part of school life. Strong communities often grow up around Waldorf schools, consisting of teachers, school staff, families (sometimes including grandparents), and friends of the school.

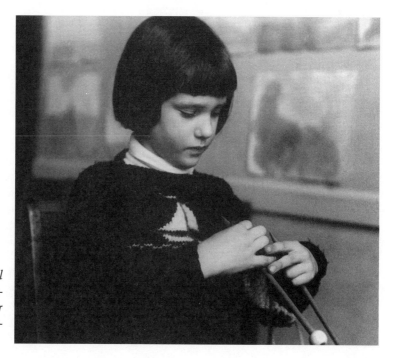

A first-grader at The Waldorf School in Lexington, Massachusetts, learning knitting. Waldorf schools consider crafts an integral part of the developing child's education.

FOR MORE INFORMATION

Waldorf Kindergarten Association
1359 Alderton Lane
Silver Spring, MD 20906
Tel.: (301) 460-6287

This organization has a list of the Waldorf kindergartens operating in North America.

The Association of Waldorf Schools of North
America (AWSNA)
3911 Bannister Road
Fair Oaks, CA 95628
Tel.: (916) 961-0927
Fax: (916) 961-0715

This association provides information about Waldorf education, Waldorf schools in the United States, Canada, and Mexico, and teacher training programs. It helps initiatives hoping to start a Waldorf school, and also acts as a consultant to public schools and public school systems that want to incorporate Waldorf elements into the curriculum. AWSNA publishes a twice-yearly magazine called *Renewal: A Journal for Waldorf Education.*

Rudolf Steiner College Press
9200 Fair Oaks Boulevard
Fair Oaks, CA 95628
Tel.: (916) 961-8727
Fax: (916) 961-8731

This small press, affiliated with an anthroposophical educational center that trains Waldorf teachers, publishes and carries a large number of books about Waldorf education and related topics. Free catalogue on request.

Anthroposophic Press
3390 Route 9
Hudson, NY 12534
Tel.: (518) 851-2054
Fax: (800) 925-1795

This press publishes and carries many books on Waldorf education and related topics. Call for free catalogue.

FOR FURTHER READING

Baldwin, Rahima. *You Are Your Child's First Teacher.* Berkeley: Celestial Arts, 1989. A rich resource for parents of young children; contains sections on receiving and caring for the newborn, helping your toddler's development, and parenting issues of the first three years. Contains excellent bibliographies.

Edmunds, Francis L. *Rudolf Steiner Education.* Hudson, N.Y.: Anthroposophic Press, 1987. An excellent general introduction.

Fenner, Pamela Johnson., and Karen Rivers (eds.). *Waldorf Education: A Family Guide.* Amesbury, Mass.: Michaelmas Press, 1995. A collection of articles dealing with child-rearing, family and home life, and education from the Waldorf perspective.

Finser, Torin M. *School as a Journey: The Eight-Year Odyssey of a Waldorf Teacher and His Class.* Hudson, N.Y.: Anthroposophic Press, 1994. An engrossing, personal narrative about a Waldorf teacher and his class at the Rudolf Steiner School in Great Barrington, Massachusetts.

Harwood, A. C. *The Way of the Child.* Hudson, N.Y.: Anthroposophic Press, 1979. A clearly written introduction to Waldorf education, giving the Waldorf understanding of the development of the child and of how children at each age should be educated.

Spock, Marjorie. *Teaching as a Lively Art.* Hudson, N.Y.: Anthroposophic Press, 1978. A description of the underlying philosophy and practice of Waldorf education for the elementary school years.

Thomson, John. *Natural Childhood: The First Practical and Holistic Guide for Parents of the Developing Child.* New York: Simon and Schuster, 1994. Based largely on Waldorf principles, this is a helpful guide to caring for infants and bringing up the young child.

IV

PRACTICAL MATTERS

33

Choosing a School

Forty years ago, most American parents had few options in choosing a school for their child. If the family was Catholic or belonged to a conservative Protestant denomination, the parents might send their child to the parish or parochial school. If the family was wealthy, it might opt for an expensive private school. But most families didn't have a choice. Little Sally and Jimmy went to the neighborhood public elementary school, and later to the nearest junior and senior public high school. Most people didn't mind. The public schools were generally considered a good place to be educated.

Today the neighborhood public school still exists. It has changed, though, and parents—for any number of reasons—may not want to send their children there. But today they have a variety of alternatives. A magnet public school nearby may have a Montessori kindergarten and a child-centered "discovery" program in the first four grades. There might be a Waldorf school just starting up in the next town, and a Core Knowledge academy and two Christian schools also within commuting distance. Some parents and teachers may have just had their initiative for a Reggio Emilia school approved as a state-supported charter school.

The educational options are now many. Mak-

ing a choice among them can be complex and difficult. The following step-by-step process may be helpful. It is meant primarily for choosing a school for children who are just starting school or who are in the early grades. But it also applies, with obvious adaptations, to choosing a school for older children and adolescents.

Please remember that you are not looking for the perfect school. You are looking for a school that will meet the needs of your child and your family. There is no such thing as a perfect or absolutely "good" school, just as there is no such thing as a "bad" school. Schools are appropriate for certain children and families or they are inappropriate. A school will be right for one child and not right for another child—even a child from the same family. For example, children who are motivated self-learners probably will be well served by a child-centered program where they get to direct and carry out their own learning. A child who is a poor reader and needs structure, direction, and drill in basics may be better off in a more structured educational environment.

The steps of the process are as follows:

1. Find out about the whole range of alternatives in education today. If you have read this book through to this point, you have pretty much fulfilled this step of the process.

227

2. Get more information about the educational approaches and types of schools that appeal to you. Read books listed in the resource bibliographies. Send away to the organizations listed in the resource lists.

3. Construct a portrait of the ideal school for your child. Take into consideration your own preferences, the child's individual personality, and his or her own preferences—especially if the child is older and has had experience in school. Let your imagination be free. Design your ideal school with the assumption that your financial and other resources are great, even limitless. Be specific about ambiance, class size, pedagogy, curriculum, the role of art and music, homework, where parents fit in the running of the school, and so on. Be aware that you are not constructing an absolute educational ideal. You are only designing a school that is appropriate for a particular child and a particular family at a certain time.

4. Make a list of all the candidate schools in your area, including the neighborhood public schools, other public schools to which you have access, and independent schools. Seek out and include smaller and less well-known private schools. Check the telephone book under schools and education. Consult a copy of *The Almanac of Educational Choice*, which lists about six thousand schools (see Resources at the end of this chapter). You probably will be surprised at the number and variety of schools in your area. If your work is not place-specific and you are free to relocate, spread your net wider. Many families move to another state or to another part of the country so that their children can attend a particular school.

5. Arrange to visit as many schools as possible. Keep an open mind. Visit schools that seem a

Making a choice among the many educational options there are today can be complex and difficult.

———— ❧ ————

long shot (e.g., a Lutheran school if you are agnostic, an arts-based school if your child is a computer buff). Each school is a type of school, but it is also an individual and unique institution. There is tremendous variety even among schools that share a common educational philosophy and practice. The school you expected to love may disappoint you, and you may find a gem where you didn't expect one.

6. Visit the schools. Sit in on classes and talk with teachers and students. Keep a written record of every visit. Note the obvious facts—size, distance from home, class size, ambiance of the school as a whole and of individual classrooms, absence or presence of a dress code, general demeanor of students and teachers. Note also your visceral reactions. In the school, did you feel comfortable, relaxed, and peaceful, or did you feel restless and anxious?

7. Interview the school principal or school director. Ask a series of specific questions about the school. These might include:

Are the classes single age or multi-age groups?

When and how is reading taught?

What kinds of books do the children read in school? Who chooses them?

When and how is writing and composition taught?

Is there an established curriculum or does the curriculum emerge from students' interests?

What role do textbooks play? Workbooks? Duplicated worksheets?

What role does independent research play?

What is the main role of the teacher?

When do children start getting homework?

How are children assessed?

If the children take tests and receive grades, when does this start?

Is there computer education and, if so, when does it start?

How much time is spent on art, on music, and on crafts?

Is there cooperative learning? A social curriculum? Multicultural education?

Is there sex education? If so, when, and what kind?

Is the day broken up into periods for each subject or are there blocks of time for interdisciplinary projects?

How are disciplinary problems handled?

How do teachers qualify to teach in the school?

Who actually owns the school?

Who makes the decisions about school life?

What role do parents play in the life and governance of the school? What level of participation is allowed? What is required?

Is there any effort to teach moral principles? If so, how?

Is there a religious or spiritual dimension in the curriculum or in school life?

Do not be shy about asking these and other questions. The answers will give you a sense of the philosophy—the view of the world and human nature and education—behind the school and how that philosophy manifests in the life of the school. They will help you see to what degree that philosophy and practice coincide with those of your ideal school. If the school is an independent school, the director should be interested in your business and should be happy to answer these and other queries. If the school is public, the principal is your employee. If a school director or principal tries to stick a parent handbook

in your hand and steer you toward the door, resist. If he or she persists, leave and don't go back.

8. Talk to a teacher, preferably the teacher who would have your child in class. Ask how he or she got into teaching and what he or she likes and doesn't like about the work. Don't be concerned that you sound as if you are interviewing the teacher for a job. That's exactly what you are doing! And it's an important job—educating your child. Look the teacher in the eye and ask yourself, "Is this someone I would entrust my child to for six hours a day for a year?" In the end, education is something that happens primarily between an individual child and their teacher, so it's important you like and trust your child's teacher.

9. Get the names of several school parents who would be willing to talk to you about the school. Ask them what they like about the school and what they dislike. Also, get the names of parents whose child did not stay at the school. All schools have wonderful success stories, but no school works for every child. Find out about a child who did not thrive at the school.

10. Make a list of four or five schools that appeal strongly and, in terms of cost and commuting distance, are viable alternatives for your family. Don't let cost count too heavily. Many independent schools offer liberal financial aid. And don't feel you have to save money for the child's college tuition. By that time the dies are already long cast. Money spent on quality elementary, middle, and even high-school education is a good investment.

11. Visit these schools with your child. Have your child meet the teacher, and if possible spend time alone with the teacher or in the teacher's class.

12. Take your own intellectual preferences, your visceral feelings and intuition, and your

child's preferences and make a decision. It almost certainly will involve compromise. You probably will not get your ideal school. But you may get something very close to it.

The process of choosing a school for your child can be time-consuming, tiring, and complex. But it is an important and necessary process that should be carried out with care, energy, and attention to detail. Your child's immediate and future happiness and well-being may rest on the outcome. You should choose a school for your children with at least the same care as you choose a new car or house.

If you don't find a school that you really like, please reread the chapter on homeschooling and consider that possibility. Or if you are adventurous, determined, and enjoy a challenge, read with special care the following chapter on starting your own school.

Resources

FOR MORE INFORMATION

Mintz, Jerry. *The Almanac of Educational Choice: Public and Private Learning Alternatives and Homeschooling.* New York: Macmillan, 1995. Lists state by state, according to zip code, over six thousand alternative schools.

Peterson's Guide to Private Secondary Schools. Princeton: Peterson's Guides, 1995–1996. A comprehensive guide that includes a family guide to choosing and affording the right school. Available at most public and school libraries.

The Handbook of Private Schools. Boston: Porter Sargent Publishers. This is an annual descriptive survey of all independent schools in the United States. It includes a classified section that, for example, lists all single-sex schools, schools with an ungraded curriculum, and schools offering an elementary boarding division. Available at most public and school libraries.

34

The Ultimate School—Your Own

As a parent looking for a school for your child, you may find in your area a school that

- reflects your thinking about education;
- is within a reasonable commuting distance;
- you can afford; and
- your child is happy with.

If you find such a school, count yourself among the lucky and blessed.

You may not find a school that suits your child or you. You may find it but it is too far away—and you can't relocate—or it is too expensive—and you can't remortgage the house.

Homeschooling is one option, but there is another. You can start or help to start a new school. Many schools offering alternatives to mainstream education in the United States were founded by a parent or group of parents who had a vision of the education they wanted to give their children and brought that vision into the world as a school. Some of the schools founded in this way have served generations of parents and children. Many have come into being in recent decades. There are many compelling and inspiring examples, each showing one of the many ways in which this can be accomplished.

You may not find a school that suits your child or you. Homeschooling is one option, but there is another. You can start or help to start a new school.

As a concerned parent, Anna May Jeffs campaigned against the adoption of the Carden, phonics-based reading program in the public schools of Salt Lake City. When she heard Miss Carden explain her approach in a lecture, though, she changed her mind. A few years later, Jeffs started a school in a basement in Logan, Utah, for her own and for other children. Soon The Carden School (later the Carden Memorial School; see pages 69–72) was occupying a large, former public school building in Salt Lake City. Today it has an enrollment of almost four hundred students. Jeffs and her husband, Donald, have run the school as a regular business, not as a tax-exempt institution. They pay property and sales and income tax as a school, but are spared much bureaucratic meddling from the state and city.

The School Around Us in Maine (see chapter 17) was founded in 1970 by a group of parents who wanted to design and control their children's education. They acquired the land, built the building, taught the children, and through the years have guided the school's development.

In the early 1980s several families living in the

Pioneer Valley of western Massachusetts were interested in starting a Waldorf school. They invited a speaker and were surprised to find a large audience of interested parents. Soon a Waldorf kindergarten was established in the basement of a private home, with a trained Waldorf teacher. In a couple of years a first-grade class was started, and each year thereafter another class was added. A school building was purchased and then a new, second building was built. In 1993, the Hartsbrook Waldorf School graduated its first eighth-grade class of eight students. Today the school has almost two hundred students and about twenty full- and part-time teachers. Throughout the history of the school, leadership and direction have been shared by parents and faculty.

In Hanover, New Hampshire, former history professor Mary Beth Klee started a kindergarten on the basis of the Core Knowledge approach because she felt the public schools would not provide a challenging environment for her son (see chapter 14). After one year in the basement of Saint Dennis's Roman Catholic Church, the school added a first grade. It continued to grow. An articulate and outgoing person, Klee wrote articles for the local newspaper and gave talks about what she was doing. At the end of one public lecture, a local real estate developer walked up to her and said, "How can I help?" Klee replied, "How about a school building?" Today Crossroads Academy has about one hundred children and a beautiful, two-story brick building. Klee is still the dominant force in the school, both as its director and as a teacher.

When educational historian Ronald Miller moved to Burlington, Vermont, he couldn't find a kindergarten or school that would satisfy his high ideals regarding education. Working with preschool teacher Beth Stadtlander, he designed a holistic school. Using independent financial resources, Miller built a $400,000 state-of-the-art school building in suburban Burlington and advertised for students. In September 1995, the Bellwether school opened with about thirty-five children, Miller's child among them, and with two teachers (see chapter 19).

In Williamsburg, Massachusetts, a few parents became interested in the Reggio Emilia approach to early childhood education. They got help from Lella Gandini, a teacher from Italy and an expert on the approach. Their application for charter school status was approved, and the school opened with thirty-five children in September 1995.

These are not isolated instances. As they always have been, parents today are major creative and innovative forces in American education. Whether or not they are professional educators, parents can still help to start a school that will meet the needs of their own and of other children. Phyllis Conway of the Shady Hill School in Cambridge, Massachusetts, says:

> We are a small school and our waiting list is long. When a parent wants to send a child here and is disappointed, I often encourage them to start their own little school. Shady Hill was started by a small group of parents who used the back porch of one of their homes as classroom. If you are strongly motivated and have a clear idea of what you want, you can certainly start a school. There will be difficulties, financial and otherwise, but they are surmountable. There is much capital in the community and many resources that can be used to support small-scale appropriate education that meets the needs of children and families. Small is beautiful.

There are no handbooks for starting a school. The following suggestions come from several individuals who have experience in the process:

- Involve a number of like-minded people in the planning and decision-making process early on. Most of the successful schools have been started by a group of committed parents. There is a lot of work to be done, much more than one person or two can manage easily, even as a full-time activity.
- Use democratic or consensus decision-making and problem-solving procedures. These encourage people to become involved and committed. If you plan a democratically run school, include future students in the planning process. Be aware, though, that some efficiency is lost in a democratic or consensual arrangement.
- Be patient and persistent in seeing through the decision-making processes. There are many important decisions to make about governance, principles, curriculum, pedagogy, finances, and other matters. The process may be slow and difficult. People today are busy, and they may feel they don't have time for meetings and long discussions about large principles or little details. Don't be discouraged, especially in the early stages.
- Have a clear idea of the type of education you want to bring into being. Prepare a statement about the goals and educational principles and practices of the projected school. You must answer for yourself and for others the basic questions: What is education? What will we teach? How will we teach it? What kind of human beings do we want our students to become?
- Define the approach to be neither too narrow nor too broad. If it is too specific it will exclude almost everyone and not attract support. If it is too broad, ill-defined, or wishy-washy, it will offer nothing concrete and specific enough to interest people.

- Visit other schools, particularly schools similar to the one you envision. But visit schools that are different from what you intend. They too may give you some good ideas.
- Talk to people who have had the experience of starting a school. Get as much advice as you can.
- If you wish to adopt an existing approach such as that of Waldorf education, or multiple intelligences, contact the parent organization to get advice and support. It may be worthwhile to engage a consultant from the group.
- Invite speakers to give public talks that present the type of education you would like to apply. Publicize the talk through local media.
- If your approach is a well-known and proven one that could be established in your local public school system—for example, Montessori, Core Knowledge, Foxfire—lobby for it in your area. Go to the local school board and to the administrators of your neighborhood schools and say, "This program has been a success in a lot of places. It meets the needs of the children. Why can't we have it here?" School officials may take your suggestion seriously and look into it. Many public school administrators and teachers are desperate for new ideas and new approaches and are open to something that is innovative but that has a track record. They may ignore you. If they do, be persistent. Come back with other parents as reinforcements. Parents can and should play a major role in forming public educational policy. After all, as taxpayers, parents are paying for the whole show.
- Look into having your school be a charter

school. The first charter school legislation was enacted in Minnesota in 1990. Already close to half the states have such a law, and many others are now considering one. A charter school law allows a parent or group of parents, or an educator or group of educators, to make a proposal for a new school based on an alternative approach and, if the proposal is approved, to receive public funding for that school. There are already a variety of charter schools for arts-based education, for foreign language education, and for the education of gifted children having difficulty in school. Because the charter school program is new, no one knows exactly how it will work out over time. Specifics of the law vary from state to state. There is always the danger that the state, as holder of the purse strings, will try to control the school or perhaps change the intended program. In any case, charter school laws mean that if you have a viable and coherent educational approach and can convince the state officials of it, you can get funding.

- If it looks as if your school will wind up being an independent school, inform yourself about the laws in your state about independent schools. There will be statutes concerning incorporation and governance of schools (as tax-exempt entities), teacher qualifications, facilities, curriculum, liability, accessibility, diversity, and other issues. Conforming to all these laws probably will seem very challenging, and it is. But it is clearly in the realm of the possible.
- Hire a lawyer or find volunteer legal assistance to help with the issues of founding and operating a school and also to meet outside legal challenges that may come

up—from concerned neighbors, for example. Especially in its early stages a school is vulnerable to such challenges.

- If you don't get public support, establish a firm economic base in another way. This is important for young and small schools. Meeting capital and operating expenditures through tuition alone is very difficult. One approach is to found a small business run cooperatively by parents and friends of the school to help support the school. The founders of one urban free school bought and renovated several old houses and have used the rental income to help support the school. The Clonclara School in Michigan is partially supported by money earned giving advice about homeschooling. In any case, gird yourself for fund-raising fairs and campaigns. Find a volunteer who is an expert fund-raiser or find out about fund-raising yourself.
- Have a clear idea of the image you want to have in the community. Work to cultivate that image. If you do not define yourself, the community will do it for you, but not necessarily as you would like. Have open houses and public educational programs at the school. Make it a place of learning for all in the community.
- Hire teachers strongly committed to your approach to education. Do not be discouraged if this is not easy. Ronald Miller received several hundred applications for the first-grade teaching position at the Bellwether School but found that only a few really shared his vision of the school.
- Don't underestimate expenses. Expenses include school furniture, playground equipment, books, office supplies, art supplies, library materials, building maintenance,

advertising, and copying costs, as well as teachers' salaries. Hire a good accountant.

- Start small with a few students in a modest space and grow to meet demand. Ten or twelve children between the ages of six and eight in a mixed-age classroom with one qualified, dedicated teacher is a good start for a school. Schools can be located in a home, a church basement, or in a rented storefront. You can do a lot with second-hand furniture, used books, and a lot of commitment. In the early stages at least, the facilities and the space are less important than the individuals involved—the teachers, children, and parents—and the guiding vision behind the school. Making a big initial investment requires prior assets and involves risk.

- Stay small. Forty to sixty children in three or four mixed-age classrooms covering kindergarten through grade six can comprise a healthy, ongoing school. Quality, not quantity, is key. Social organisms in which each individual knows every other individual, at least by name, seem to be the most healthy ones.

The monopoly of mainstream public education no longer exists. Today viable and successful schools, both public and private, represent a wide range of educational approaches and philosophical, religious, and political points of view. The school that is appropriate for your child and your family probably does exist. But it may be far away or beyond your means. Being involved in starting a school can be a worthwhile way to use your time, energy, and resources.

FOR MORE INFORMATION

Christian Schools International
3350 East Paris Avenue, SE
Grand Rapids, MI 49512–3054
Tel.: (800) 635-8288

An association of mostly conservative Presbyterian schools that has a booklet on starting your own school. See Resources, chapter 18, for complete listing.

Sudbury Valley School
2 Winch Street
Framingham, MA 01701
Tel.: (508) 877-3030

A free school that has a school starter kit. It also holds a "new schools conference." See Resources for chapter 17 for complete listing.

National Coalition for Alternative Community Schools
P.O. Box 15036
Santa Fe, NM 87506
Tel.: (505) 474-4312

Offers help in starting schools. Its affiliate, the Home School Legal Defense Association, gives legal advice to people wanting to start schools.

FOR FURTHER READING

Blumenfeld, Samuel L. *How to Start Your Own Private School—And Why You Need One.* New York: Arlington House, 1972. A guide to starting your own school, written by a leading conservative critic of public education.

Dennison, George. *The Lives of Children: The Story of the First Street School.* New York: Random House, 1969. The account of the starting of an alternative school during the heyday of community schools.

Bibliography

<hr>

Arons, Stephen. *Compelling Belief: The Culture of American Schooling*. New York: McGraw Hill, 1983. A study that charges that compulsory public education is designed to program children to accept the values and lifestyle of the mainstream society.

Blumenfeld, Samuel L. *Is Public Education Necessary?* Boise, Idaho: Paradigm Company, 1981, 1995. A highly critical assessment of American public education.

——. *The National Education Association: Trojan Horse in American Education*. Boise, Idaho: Paradigm Company, 1984. A probing critique of the aims and methods of the major teachers' union in the United States.

——. *The New Illiterates: And How to Keep Your Child from Becoming One*. Boise, Idaho: Paradigm Company, 1988. A critical review of current methods of teaching reading and writing, written by a leading conservative historian of education.

——. *The New American* (August 1994). In this issue of a very conservative journal, Blumenfeld and others strongly criticize the public school system and the education policy of the federal government as outlined in Goals 2000.

Carper, James, C., and Thomas C. Hunt. *Religious Education in America*. Birmingham, Ala.: Religious Education Press, 1984. Excellent short treatments of the various major religious school systems in the United States, including Roman Catholic, Lutheran, and Jewish schools.

Dewey, John. *Democracy and Education*. New York: Free Press, 1916. Published eighty years ago, this is perhaps the most important work on the philosophical foundations of American education. It contrasts traditional education with a progressive education that seeks to develop persons able to participate in a democratic society.

——. *Experience and Education*. New York: Macmillan, 1938. Dewey's classic and still relevant exposition of the importance of experience—active involvement with learning—in education.

Downs, Robert. *Heinrich Pestalozzi: Father of Modern Pedagogy*. Boston: Twayne/G. K. Hall, 1975. A biography of the Swiss educational reformer whose ideas greatly influenced progressive education in the United States.

——. *Friedrich Froebel*. Boston: Twayne/G. K. Hall, 1978. A biography of the German educational reformer who originated the kindergarten.

Duffy, Cathy. *Government Nannies*. Gresham, Oreg.: Noble Publishing Associates, 1995. A conservative critique of government programs for preschool and kindergarten children.

Eakman, B. K. *Educating for the New World Order*. Portland, Oreg.: National Book, 1991. An interpretation of what is happening in American education that sees sinister motives behind state and federal policies.

Elkind, David. *The Hurried Child*. New York: Alfred A. Knopf, 1984. An insightful critique of our tendency to rush children into adulthood, written by an expert on child development at Tufts University.

———. *Miseducation: Preschoolers at Risk.* New York: Alfred A. Knopf, 1987. An examination of the academically oriented and accelerated early learning programs now in use.

Fiske, Edward B. *Smart Schools, Smart Kids.* New York: Simon and Schuster, 1991. A survey of the various reform and restructuring programs that have been initiated in schools and school systems in the United States. A thoroughgoing critique of the existing mainstream educational system with recommendations for change. Its suggestions are in line with the Coalition of Essential Schools, Foxfire, and other progressively oriented approaches.

Froebel, Friedrich. *The Education of Man.* New York: Appleton, 1893. First published in 1826, this book outlines the educational philosophy and practice of the originator of the kindergarten.

Gatto, John. *Dumbing Us Down: The Hidden Curriculum of Compulsory Schooling.* Philadelphia: New Society Publishers, 1992. A searing indictment of public education and what it does to children, written by a former Teacher of the Year in New York State.

Gutek, Gerald Lee. *Joseph Neef: The Americanization of Pestalozzianism.* Tuscaloosa: University of Alabama Press, 1978. The life and thought of the educational missionary who helped to introduce humanistic and progressive education in the United States.

Healey, Jane. *Why Our Children Can't Think and What We Can Do About It.* New York: Simon and Schuster, 1992. A sobering analysis of the educational, social, and environmental factors that have led to the decline of the thinking and learning ability of today's children.

Hegener, Mark, and Helen Hegener. *Alternatives in Education.* Tonasket, Wash.: Home Education Press, 1992. A collection of articles and essays on alternative education focusing on different types of humanistic/progressive education. There are sections on the politics of education, homeschooling, Waldorf and Montessori schools, alternative high schools, and options in higher education.

Holland, Robert. *Not with My Child, You Don't.* Richmond, VA.: Chesapeake Capital Services, 1992. A conservative's critique of what is going on in public schools today.

Holt, John. *How Children Fail.* New York: Pitman, 1964. The classic indictment of traditional education and of public education. The book that helped launch the modern progressive homeschooling movement.

Illich, Ivan. *Deschooling Society.* New York: Harper and Row, 1983. A profound critique of public schools and of the social attitudes and patterns that produce them.

Iserbyt, Charlotte. *Back-to-Basics Reform . . . Skinnerian International Curriculum?* Bath, Maine: published by the author, 1993. A critical consideration of the back-to-basics movement by a former official in the U.S. Department of Education. Write to the author at 1062 Washington Street, Bath, ME 04530 to obtain a copy.

Karier, Clarence, J., Paul C. Violas, and Joel Spring. *Roots of Crisis: American Education in the Twentieth Century.* Chicago: Rand McNally, 1973. The standard history of twentieth-century American education.

Klicka, Christopher. *The Right Choice: The Incredible Failure of Public Education and the Rising Hope of Homeschooling.* Gresham, Oreg.: Noble Publishing Associates, 1992. A conservative's appraisal of public education and of homeschooling as a necessary response to the current crisis.

Kohl, Herbert. *The Open Classroom: A Practical Guide to a New Way of Teaching.* New York: New York Review, 1969. A book that helped to spread progressive ideas and practices. Written by an important and articulate advocate of reform in education.

Miller, Ronald. *What Are Schools for? A History of Holistic Education in America.* Brandon, Vt.: Holistic Education Press, 1990. An excellent account of the historical and philosophical development of humanistic/progressive/holistic education in the United States. Contains interesting material on the development of public school education and an excellent bibliography.

Mintz, Jerry, et al. (eds.). *The Almanac of Education Choices: Public and Private Learning Alternatives and Homeschooling.* New York: Macmillan, 1995. A comprehensive directory that lists, state by state, over six thousand alternative schools, programs, and learning resources across the United States.

Neill, A. S. *Summerhill.* New York: Hart Publishing, 1960. Neill's account of the school at which troubled children learned without imposed rules and regulations. This book helped start the resurgence of progressive and liberal education in the United States.

Pearce, Joseph Chilton. *Magical Child.* New York: Dutton, 1976. Pearce brings together brain research, education, and his own spiritually informed understanding of the nature and destiny of the human being. He argues strongly not to rush children into adulthood. His *Magical Child Matures* (New York: Dutton, 1984) is a sequel.

Rafferty, Max. *Suffer, Little Children.* New York: Signet Books, 1963. An attack on the aims and methods of public education and of the progressive movement by the former California State Superintendent of Public Instruction.

Richman, Sheldon. *Separating School and State: How to Liberate America's Families.* Fairfax, Va.: Future of Freedom Foundation, 1994. A critique of state control of education by a conservative writer.

Rousseau, Jean-Jacques. *Emile: On Education,* trans. Allen Bloom. New York: Basic Books, 1979. First published in the late eighteenth century, this book is the original expression of the ideas and educational practices that have informed progressive and humanistic education to the present day.

Schlafly, Phyllis. *Child Abuse in the Classroom.* Alton, Ill.: Pere Marquette Press, 1984. A compendium of court hearings in which parents challenged public school curricula and teaching practices.

Sowell, Thomas. *Inside American Education: The Decline, the Deceptions, the Dogmas.* New York: Free Press, 1992. A conservative review of the recent history of American education and the forces shaping that history.

Spring, Joel. *The Sorting Machine: National Education Policy since 1945.* New York: Mackay, 1976. A critical view of American education as a means of separating children according to ability rather than as a means of educating all children to their full potential.

———. *The American School: 1645–1985.* New York: Longman, 1986. A historical survey of education in the United States from colonial times. It is considered the standard work on this topic.

Toch, Thomas. *In the Name of Excellence.* New York: Oxford University Press, 1991. Contains an excellent account of the development of public school education in the United States, of the current state of American public school education, and of the various important reform initiatives.

Wells, Amy Stuart. *Time to Choose: America at the Crossroads of School Choice Policy.* New York: Hill and Wang, 1993. Primarily an analysis of the present state of American education, this book also discusses the origin and development of public education in the United States. It also surveys alternative (progressive) programs that have developed both within and outside the public school system. Wells holds that we need to clarify the goals of education. We need to decide what kind of adults we want our children to be and what kind of society we wish to have.

Wood, George H. *Schools That Work: America's Most Innovative Public Education Programs.* New York: Dutton, 1992. A survey of schools that have been successfully reformed and restructured. Wood points out that it is helpful to look at healthy schools to see what they are doing, rather than just at troubled schools. Most of the schools he treats are operating according to the guidelines of the Coalition of Essential Schools, Foxfire, and other progressively oriented approaches.

Index